# ENTREPRENEURS AND PARASITES

AFRICAN STUDIES SERIES   57

GENERAL EDITOR
J. M. Lonsdale, *Lecturer in History and Fellow of Trinity College, Cambridge.*

ADVISORY EDITORS
J. D. Y. Peel, *Charles Booth Professor of Sociology, University of Liverpool.*
John Sender, *Faculty of Economics and Fellow of Wolfson College, Cambridge.*

Published in collaboration with
THE AFRICAN STUDIES CENTRE, CAMBRIDGE

# OTHER BOOKS IN THE SERIES

# ENTREPRENEURS AND PARASITES

The struggle for indigenous capitalism in Zaire

JANET MACGAFFEY

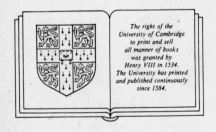

The right of the
University of Cambridge
to print and sell
all manner of books
was granted by
Henry VIII in 1534.
The University has printed
and published continuously
since 1584.

CAMBRIDGE UNIVERSITY PRESS

CAMBRIDGE
NEW YORK   NEW ROCHELLE   MELBOURNE   SYDNEY

Published by the Press Syndicate of the University of Cambridge
The Pitt Building, Trumpington Street, Cambridge CB2 1RP
32 East 57th Street, New York, NY 10022, USA
10 Stamford Road, Oakleigh, Melbourne 3166, Australia

First published 1987

Printed in Great Britain at the University Press, Cambridge

*British Library cataloguing in publication data*

MacGaffey, Janet
Entrepreneurs and parasites: the struggle
for indigenous capitalism in Zaire. –
(African studies series; 57).
1. Zaire – Economic conditions –
1960 –
I. Title   II. Series
330.9675'103  HC955


*Library of Congress cataloguing in publication data*

MacGaffey, Janet.
Entrepreneurs and parasites.
(African studies series; 57)
Bibliography.
Includes index.
1. Capitalism – Zaire – Kisangani. 2. Capitalism –
Zaire – Haut – Zaire. 3. Capitalism – Zaire – Kivu.
4. Capitalists and financiers – Zaire – Case studies.
5. New business enterprises – Zaire – Case studies.
6. Entrepreneur. I. Title. II. Series.
HC955.Z7K49956 1987  338.09675' 1 87–13160

ISBN 0 521 33533 7

# Contents

*Contents*

vi

# Tables

# Illustrations

All photographs by Wyatt MacGaffey

# Maps

# Figures

# Acknowledgements

Many people have helped immeasurably in the production of this book. I first want to thank all those in Zaire who patiently answered my questions and supplied their own insights and comments, offered most generous hospitality and friendship, and enhanced life with their wit and humour. Circumstances in Zaire are such that it is better not to name individuals, so I can only express my gratitude and appreciation generally.

My fieldwork was helped by my affiliation as Research Associate of CRIDE (Centre de Recherches Interdisciplinaires pour le Développement de l'Education), Kisangani, and by a Grant-in-Aid of Research from Sigma Xi, the Scientific Research Society. For library research, I am much indebted to the unfailing helpfulness of the staff of Haverford College Library.

I am grateful to many people for their encouragement and suggestions, and for helpful discussion or comment on the manuscript or on earlier working out of my material, and particularly to Michael Schatzberg, Sandra Barnes, Keith Hart, V.Y. Mudimbe, E. Mudimbe Boyi, Gavin Kitching, and Benoît Verhaegen. I owe an especial debt to Tom Callaghy, for reading the manuscript and for his most valuable and helpful comments. Above all, I want to thank my husband, Wyatt MacGaffey, for all his help, support, encouragement and solutions to irritating problems, at all stages of this enterprise, and for many long and fruitful discussions of anthropology often far too early in the day. None of these people are responsible for the opinions expressed here; the errors are mine.

The substance of Chapters 5 and 7 have already been published in four articles. I acknowledge permission to reprint from the editors of *African Affairs* for parts of 'How to Survive and Get Rich Amidst Devastation: the Second Economy in Zaire' (1983, 82: 351–66); to Holmes and Meier Publishers for parts of 'Women and Class Formation in a Dependent Economy: Kisangani Entrepreneurs', in *Women and Class in Africa*, edited by Claire Robertson and Iris Berger (1986); to Africa World Press for parts of 'Fending for Yourself: the Organization of the Second Economy in Zaire', in *The Crisis in Zaire: Myths and Realities*, edited by

*Acknowledgements*

Nzongola-Ntalaja (1986); to Westview Press for parts of 'Economic Disengagement and Class Formation in Zaire', in *The Precarious Balance: State and Society in Africa*, edited by Donald Rothchild and Naomi Chazan. Copyright © 1986 by Westview Press, Boulder, Colorado.

# Abbreviations

| | |
|---|---|
| ABAKO | Alliance des Bakongo |
| AFCO | Association des Femmes Commerçantes |
| ANEZA | Association Nationale des Entreprises Zairoises |
| CEC | Centre Extra-Coutumier |
| CECOPANE | Centre de Commercialisation des Produits Agricoles du Nord-Est |
| CEDAF | Centre d'Etude et de Documentation Africaine |
| CND | Centre National de Documentation |
| CRISP | Centre de Recherche et l'Information Socio-politiques |
| GECAMINES | Général de Carrières et des Mines du Zaire |
| INSS | Institut National de Sécurité Sociale |
| IRES | Institut de Recherches Economiques et Sociales |
| JMPR | Jeunesse du Mouvement Populaire de la Révolution |
| MIBA | Société Minière de Bakwanga |
| MPR | Mouvement Populaire de la Révolution |
| ONAFITEX | Office National des Fibres Textiles |
| ONATRA | Office National des Transports du Zaire |
| ONC | Office National du Café |
| OZACAF | Office Zairois du Café |
| SDID | Société de Développement International Desjardins |
| SNCZ | Société National des Chemins de Fer du Zaire |
| SOFIDE | Société Financière de Développement |
| SOGEMIN | Société Générale des Minerais |
| SOMINKI | Société Minière et Industrielle du Kivu |
| SOTEXKI | Société Textile de Kisangani |
| SOSIDER | Société d'Exploitation Sidérurgique |
| SIDERNA | Société Nationale de Sidérurgie |
| UNAZA | Université National du Zaire |
| UNTZA | Union National des Travailleurs Zairois |

1 Hectare = 2.47 acres
All translations from French are by the author.

For Neil, Andrew and Margret

# Introduction

In 1979 reports on the drastic decline of Zaire's economy and the situation of appalling hardship for ordinary people made the prospect of ten months in Kisangani a grim one. But the reality turned out to be that in an apparently impossible situation not only were people surviving but some were doing very well for themselves. The city, previously known as Stanleyville, is a thriving business centre; all sorts of people are running successful and substantial enterprises, despite the shortages of goods, the deterioration of infrastructure and the rampant bribery and corruption so amply documented in the social science literature and the local press. In the midst of irrationality and unpredictability some things work in an organized and efficient way and some individuals engage in rational enterprise. Zaire's failures are amply documented; its successful elements are less well known.

Previous writers have generally dismissed the possibility of the development of any local productive capitalism and the rise of a true indigenous bourgeoisie in Zaire. They have stressed the country's economic dependence on the developed West, its exploitation by metropolitan capitalism, and the ruin of its economy by the predatory, pillaging activities of its state-based class. However, a close look at Kisangani, one of Zaire's principal cities, shows the emergence of some local capitalists without position in the state. These entrepreneurs, both men and women, are investing in productive enterprise for the local market, managing and expanding their businesses in rational capitalist fashion, and reproducing themselves as a class. The aim of this study is to show how it has been possible for this nascent bourgeosie to form despite conditions that appear so inimical for its development.

Arguments surge back and forth to explain the root causes of the underdevelopment of countries such as Zaire. One view explains underdevelopment in terms of the global capitalist system, in which the developed countries further their own industrial growth by creating and maintaining the underdevelopment of the rest; this process is carried out in collaboration with the state-based class of the underdeveloped countries. The

1

opposing view holds that the global approach cannot account for observed variation in the economies of underdeveloped countries, and explains differences in terms of internal class structures. Recent discussion has centred on the question of the emergence of indigenous capitalism in Africa, with lively debates on whether it exists in Kenya and the Ivory Coast. The emphasis has shifted from the significance of the state and of foreign domination to that of internal class struggle and the part played by the development of local indigenous capitalism in the process of class formation.

In keeping with this shift, this book focuses on struggle between Africans in post-independence Zaire. Foreign domination and Zaire's place in the world economy are significant factors in this struggle, but the data from Kisangani predominantly reveals the effects of historical, political and socio-economic factors within Zaire. Analysis of this situation raises several issues currently hotly debated in African studies: the nature of African capitalism, the effect of the persistence of non-capitalist systems of production and the political and economic consequences of the weakening of the post-independence state.

A striking feature of Zaire is the extent of the second, or parallel, economy, consisting of unmeasured and unrecorded economic activity that evades taxation or in other ways deprives the state of revenue. Its implications for class formation in Zaire and elsewhere are profound but have as yet received little attention. The enormous expansion of this sector of the economy in the 1970s and 1980s, and the failure of state control of the economy that this reflects, indicate that the state is no longer the principal means of class formation that it has been held to be since independence.

The major themes of this book are the emergence of a true capitalist class, investing in production for local consumption not just in distribution; the role of capital accumulation from second economy activities in this process; and the effects of the weakening of the post-independence state and the incomplete penetration of capitalism. Historical factors, particularly Zaire's colonial experience, affected the development of the economy and the nature of the dominant class that emerged after independence. Other factors to be examined include the role of individual initiative, innovation and skill, and the significance of gender and ethnicity, in class formation.

Because the Belgian colonists controlled economic surplus to a greater extent than most African colonists, it is not possible in Zaire to trace social differentiation resulting from surplus accumulation and investment by Africans over an extended period of time, as in Kenya and Nigeria (Kitching 1980; Cowen 1981; Berry 1985). The most intriguing feature of Zaire is that an indigenous capitalist class could emerge at all.

Chapter 1 reviews theories of underdevelopment; it assesses different approaches to peripheral economies and to the articulation of capitalist

2

and non-capitalist modes of production. In Africa, the difficulty of extending capitalist relations of production and the weakness of the administrative apparatus permit workers and petty producers to challenge both the state and capital, as the expansion of the second economy testifies. Scholars dispute the degree of autonomy of petty producers, however; argument centres on mechanisms for their control by capital. Nevertheless, in Zaire the accumulation possible outside the state for individuals in a wide range of class positions has affected the process of class formation: this situation confounds the reasoning that foreign domination and the interests of Western capital are a monolithic cause of underdevelopment, and leads to a focus on the struggles among Africans. The background necessary for understanding the historical and socio-political factors influencing the nature of Zaire's post-independent state, its dominant class and the kind of economy that has developed is briefly outlined in Chapter 2.

Chapter 3 documents the emergence of the small local capitalist class outside the state that is the focus of the study, and gives an account of the lifestyle and culture of the entrepreneurs making up this class. Details of the kinds of business engaged in by other class sectors provide the context for the emergence of this new sector; they show that members of the state-based class have acquired vast holdings that they pillage, instead of expanding and managing them in rationalist capitalist fashion, and that the size of multinational firms and the cooperative networks of the foreign commercial class pose formidable competition for local capitalists. The interests of foreign and indigenous capital both converge and conflict. The chapter concludes with a look at the effect of ethnicity and patron-clientage on class formation.

A number of personal histories of men and women who have achieved success in business and accumulated capital are given in Chapter 4. Opportunities to acquire business arose from the indigenization of foreign assets abandoned in the violence of the sixties or handed over in Zairianization; some individuals were able to accumulate capital through trade between rural and urban areas. These histories include the social background of the entrepreneurs, their sources of venture capital and details of their relations with family and kin. They reveal the process of class formation as it takes place in the actual experiences of individuals.

Another source of capital accumulation for these entrepreneurs is the second economy. Its scale and extensiveness, organization, and significance for class formation are explored in Chapter 5. Since it is unrepresented in official figures it is left out of assessments of economic development; the chapter ends with a discussion of the implications of this misrepresentation.

The next two chapters deal with two categories in the population who have particularly benefited from accumulation in the second economy. Nande traders from North Kivu, Zaire's easternmost region, described in

3

Chapter 6, furnish a particularly striking instance of social mobility outside the state and of the role of the second economy in this process. A number of Nande are prominent in commerce in Kisangani, shipping vegetables from Kivu to Kisangani and thence down river to Kinshasa. They lack political influence and connections but have participated extensively in the illegal gold trade and coffee smuggling to East Africa. Making use of ethnic ties, investing their wealth in productive enterprise and in trade, some of them have moved up into the new class of local capitalists.

The various means of upward mobility are gender specific: Chapter 7 shows that women in Kisangani have made their way into the new capitalist class in different ways from men. Zaire is a male dominated society, imposing social and legal disadvantages on women and making it difficult for them to enter politics or the professions. Some women, however, have found opportunities to become wealthy and successful in business, establishing themselves as members in their own right of the emergent commercial class. In particular they have developed profitable trade in the second economy, taking advantage of diminishing male control to the weakening of the administrative apparatus.

Chapter 8 follows up the significance of the weakening of the state apparatus for class formation. State policies and regulations to organize labour and structure production cannot be implemented because of declining administrative efficiency. This situation, combined with the existence of alternatives to wage labour in non-capitalist modes of production and in the second economy, allows resistance to the state and provides opportunities for capital accumulation. Examples of this process from other parts of Zaire put the emergence of the new class in Kisangani into the wider context of class formation and class struggle throughout the nation.

Before proceeding, it is appropriate to give some details on methodology, given the difficulty, in Zaire's political climate, of research on activities that may be clandestine. The introduction concludes with a brief sketch of the physical setting of the study: the city of Kisangani and its hinterland.

RESEARCH METHODS, RESEARCH CONTEXT AND
THE NATURE OF INFORMATION

This is an anthropological study, an attempt at an ethnography of class formation, but it draws on economics, history, sociology and political science as well. Its particularly anthropological contribution lies in its holistic approach and its method of intensive fieldwork, using the techniques of direct observation, participation and personal contact. The particular advantage anthropology brings to development studies is its empirical and personal base; in this it contrasts with studies relying heavily on quantitative data, which often tell us little about what is really going on.

Sample surveys and other quantitative techniques are not possible for a study of businesses in a situation such as Kisangani's where, as one Asian wholesaler put it, '90 per cent of wholesalers operate by means of personal connections and business is unofficial from the top to the bottom levels'. Evasion of government regulations and taxes is widespread and makes people wary and unwilling to talk. In this situation, informal interviewing, direct participation and observation, and personal rapport make it possible to acquire information denied to researchers relying on formal question-naires and official figures.

The business owners who were the principal subject of my study were dispersed throughout the city: they lived in one area and worked in another; there was no 'community' in which to participate and belong. I participated, nevertheless, in the general life of the town, September 1979 to June 1980, attending public and private events, taking part in daily existence and leisure activities and gathering information through observa-tion and casual conversation. I conducted informal interviews, often on repeated visits, and compiled personal histories. In addition to participant observation and interviewing. I made use of published sources, especially the newspapers and government archives.

The paucity of quantifiable data and the need to rely on personal contacts and observation made the research more like the classical anthropological village study than is usual in urban research. The struggle to resolve discrepancies between different official lists of businesses seemed very similar to the classic anthropological task of resolving conflicting genealogies.

The context in which research is carried out powerfully affects the nature of the information collected and merits discussion. Marc Abélès empha-sizes the importance of analysing the 'ethnological relationship', the sociological dimension of the anthropologist's presence, to find out 'who is participating and in what?' The nature of the interference of the anthropologist's presence is an important component of the context in which research is carried out; Abélès calls for an account of the local conflicts into which the anthropologist is drawn and of informants' motives, social standing and relationship to the researcher (Abélès 1976:192–208).

My research in Kisangani was not focused on a community so I did not find myself drawn into local conflicts. In my relations with informants, my position conspicuously lacked any authoritative backing. I had no car, one of the most important local prestige symbols, but rode a bicycle; I was a woman in a society in which men dominate; and I was white, a foreigner and new to the town. From the point of view of business entrepreneurs I was a non-threatening figure, unlikely to represent the interference from the government they feared. As a result I felt that some of them talked more freely than they might otherwise have done. University affiliation, a necessary official authorization for research, gave me the social status of the educated and the respect that went with it. One busy government official, reluctant to grant an interview, relented at once when I mentioned this connection: 'Ah! Moi, je suis aussi intellectuel.' Althabe has pointed out that in ways such as these the structures of the wider society operate between the researcher and the people who are the subject of research (Althabe 1977: 71). They are essentially class structures: the researcher is given a class position and accorded appropriate behaviour.

Like Abélès I found that informants tended to be either dominant or marginal in society (Abélès 1976: 207). High officials, protected by their status, were willing to talk, as were those well established in business; those whose success was more precarious tended to be reluctant and would often give me only the most obvious and public information. The informants who talked the most freely were the disaffected, who saw themselves as oppressed, or were fed up with the country and wished they could leave. Some were marginal, not making it, people who had little to lose; some hoped I could influence the authorities on their behalf for their businesses, others that I could channel some of America's abundant wealth to them (in the form, for example, of a second-hand truck) or put pressure through the embassy on the American government to do something about situations that made their daily lives so difficult.

The political and economic situation in Zaire makes it a stressful place for research. The political climate is one of extreme uncertainty and insecurity; the suspicion, accusations and disillusionment prevailing among the population, as well as the economic hardships with which they struggle, made Kisangani a painful place to observe. It also made systematic data gathering very difficult. This political and economic situation affected the nature of information in various ways.

President Mobutu prevents the build-up of local political power bases by appointing administrators to regions other than their own and by rotating them frequently to different areas. The government is thus always perceived as alien, repression as coming from other regions. Who 'they' (the oppressors) are depends on the level in question at a specific moment, but this policy successfully divides the population against itself. The broadest division is between east and west Zaire, with regions grouped roughly on the basis of language, the dividing line varying according to the particular situation: at one level Lingala speakers constitute a western block, consisting of people from Lower Zaire, Equateur, Bandundu and Kinshasa; Swahili speakers plus the Tshiluba speakers of Kasai make up the east, consisting of Upper Zaire, Kivu, Kasai (East and West) and Shaba. Within these blocks people divide on regional, and within them on ethnic, lines. Relations between people take place in an atmosphere of mutual suspicion, hostility and even outright violence. In the general atmosphere of fear and uncertainty people suspect one another of being informers for the secret police on very flimsy grounds; no one gets credit for being honest whether he or she deserves it or not. In such circumstances people's statements about one another proved to be highly unreliable. They assumed that all officials were irresponsible and corrupt, traders dishonest, women in business sexually promiscuous and foreigners exploitative. After several apparently well-substantiated accusations against particular individuals proved to be completely false, it was clear that such allegations reflected the political climate rather than fact.

This general situation also affected the nature of documentary sources. In a city such as Kisangani, an administrative centre with a university, one would expect to have an important source of research material in government archives and university research reports and publications. To an extent this was true but the nature of these resources was somewhat unexpected.

In 1977 a conference held at Lubumbashi issued a report deploring the systematic depletion of the national archives which were simply being looted by those who came to consult them. The author of this report quotes one culprit as saying: 'I took them to read the history of my ancestors which I did not know very well' (Ndaywel 1978: 209). In Kisangani, reports that one would normally expect to be part of the archives no longer existed. The annual economic reports for the region of Upper Zaire for 1972, 1973 and 1975 had disappeared from each of the government offices that were supposed to have copies. Several of my sources are secondary ones because primary sources used in student theses written only a few years before no longer existed.

Not only are government records fugitive but their production is dwindling. In 1970 the annual economic report for the region was a substantial paper-bound volume of 122 pages, of which 32 pages consisted of tables of statistics. The same report for 1976 consisted of only thirty-six pages in all, of mimeographed sheets stapled together. No report at all appeared in 1978. In successive reports complaints appear regularly that firms and departments have not turned in their figures for the year; in some, pages of tables appear but have blank spaces instead of figures. Statistics that do appear are not always consistent or reliable; the population figures provided by the Town Hall disagree in several instances with those given in annual reports. One report states flatly that 'statistics on employment are fantasies and do not reflect reality' (*Rapport Annuel des Affaires Politiques, Région de Haut Zaire* 1971).

The difficulties of carrying out systematic documentary research, however, were in themselves data. The inadequacies of government reports and archives reinforced the statement that most business was unofficial. When business transactions are unofficial or illegal no formal records are given to the authorities and no reports turned in. The archival situation supports the conclusion that in Zaire it is the second economy, which lacks official records, rather than the official economy, that flourishes. The confusion engendered by the breakdown of record keeping and report writing is a smokescreen deliberately put out to cover the other activities in the very offices in question, carried out by the personnel of those offices themselves. In this situation, one can place very little reliance on official figures and statistics; they can be used only to indicate trends and give rough approximations.

Given the shortcomings of archives and libraries, one of the best sources of written data is Kisangani's daily newspaper, *Boyoma*, a local name for the city. Written in French, this local paper continues to appear, in the face of great difficulties, not every day but several times a week. It accurately portrays a wide range of the details of life in Kisangani and in general is more informative about what really goes on than are reports and statistics.

The businessmen and women who are the principal focus of this study own substantial businesses in Kisangani; we will turn now to some details of the city and rural areas in which these entrepreneurs conduct their affairs.

THE CITY OF KISANGANI AND ITS HINTERLAND

Directions in downtown Kisangani are always given with reference to business establishments rather than to the revolutionary and authentically Zairian names of streets and boulevards: 'Turn right by Magasin Kajilos, then left at Etablissements Kana and there it is, opposite the Renault garage.' This mapping of the town in terms of its business enterprises reflects their importance in its life. Kisangani, one of Zaire's three principal cities, is a major commercial as well as an administrative and transportation centre. Strategically situated at the head of navigation up from Kinshasa on the Zaire River, it distributes imported manufactured goods to a hinterland rich in natural resources, and affords extraordinary opportunities for making money, now as in the past. Such opportunities to accumulate wealth make the city a particularly suitable place in which to look for the emergence of local capitalism and to study class relations and class formation.

Kisangani is the major city of northeast Zaire. It is the seat of government of Upper Zaire, one of the country's nine regions (see Map 1), and it is itself an urban sub-region. A road network and railway connect the city to its hinterland and it also has one of Zaire's major airports. Agricultural products from the fertile regions of Upper Zaire and Kivu are exported down river through Kisangani. Manufactured goods, foodstuffs, fuel and construction materials are imported in turn for the city and interior from Kinshasa, about 1,000 miles down river. The city has some light industry, forty wholesale firms, a large central market and many retail stores.

The climate shows little seasonal variation, since Kisangani is half a degree north of the equator in the forest zone and less than 500 metres above sea level. The average annual rainfall varies between 1400 and 1800 mm (55–70 inches) and it is always hot and humid. Darkness falls by 7 p.m. year round, often after spectacularly beautiful sunsets.

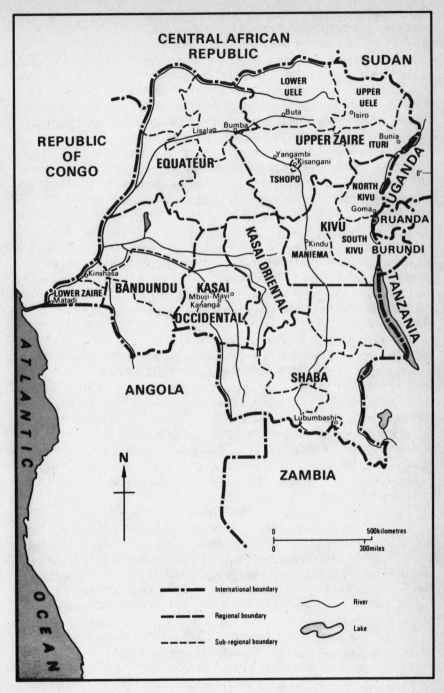

Map 1. Republic of Zaire: administrative divisions

9

The city is built on both banks of the Zaire River. A ferry for cars and trucks and several fifty-foot motorized canoes make the half-mile crossing against a formidable current. The six zones, units of local government within the urban sub-region, are Makiso (the commercial, administrative and upper class residential area), Tshopo, Kabondo, Kisangani and Mangobo on the right bank; Lubunga, the poorest zone, on the left bank.

Kisangani is remarkable for its ethnic diversity and unusual among African cities because its population is not dominated by any one ethnic group. Figures specifying ethnic origin do not exist but the records of the mental hospital alone show that eighty-six different languages are spoken in the city. Two linguae francae are spoken, Swahili and Lingala, in addition to French, Zaire's official language. The majority of the population of 280,000 originates among the surrounding forest peoples but also includes people from other regions of Zaire and a variety of foreigners, many of whom come because they perceive Kisangani as a place in which to make money quickly. Relations with the Belgian colonizers affected the incorporation of the different groups into the city and are reflected today in the different class positions of the members of these groups. The population has increased two and a half times since independence, according to the approximate figures supplied by the Town Hall (see Appendix).

The buildings and layout of the city reflect the social and historical forces that have shaped its growth: 'Le plan urbain est donc un langage qu'il faut décoder' (Verhaegen 1975: 20). The zone of Makiso was formerly the Belgian colonial town, separated by a greenbelt from the African residential areas. It is the centre of town and extends back from the port facilities and the imposing Catholic cathedral on the river bank. The oldest buildings, along the river, are built in pseudo-Arab style with elaborate arched façades. Some of the administration buildings are old colonial showpieces, with dark, wood-panelled walls and high rooms cooled by ceiling fans. Many of these buildings are crumbling with age and the tropical climate; ferns and other plants sprout not only from trees but from old rooftops. Besides these monuments to the colonial past, downtown Kisangani has multi-storied buildings of air-conditioned offices or of large stores with apartments above them, and luxurious villas with ornamental gardens of exotic flowers and shrubs. The wide streets are paved and lined with trees. Out towards the big market, the warehouses of the wholesalers take up whole blocks and shops are small and crowded together. Out here the intense tropical sunlight reflects in a blinding glare from pastel buildings and ochre-yellow dirt roads, whose surfaces alternate between thick dust and the mud and puddles left by the frequent heavy rains. Further out still, the residential zones, formerly the 'African quarters' of the city, extend in three directions. Houses are concrete block and tin-roofed or mud brick and thatch, and are interspersed with tress and patches of cultivation. Some areas are neatly swept, some overgrown and

10

unkempt, with drains clogged by litter and filth. Colourful flowers, birds and butterflies abound.

Upper Zaire is one of Zaire's principal agricultural regions. Its principal products are coffee, rice, timber, rubber, cotton, gold and ivory. The four sub-regions making up Kisangani's hinterland (see Map 1) are Tshopo, producing primarily rice, palm oil, manioc and bananas; Lower and Upper Uele to the north, rich in coffee and rubber; and Ituri to the northeast, with higher cooler land suitable for beans and beef cattle, and with an abundance of fish from Lake Mobutu. Northern Lower Uele, Upper Uele and almost all Ituri are savanna; the rest of the region consists of equatorial forest. North Kivu counts as part of Kisangani's hinterland because of its extensive trade in beans and other vegetables to Kisangani and thence down river to Kinshasa. In 1950 Upper Zaire and Equateur produced 66 per cent of the nations's agricultural exports; in 1975, these two regions and Kivu together produced 70 per cent (Bézy *et al.*, 1981: 154).

Over much of this hinterland the population is sparse. For the whole of Upper Zaire, including Kisangani, it totals about 4 million. The northern part of the region is mostly unoccupied, with an average population density of only 1–6 per square kilometres, except around urban areas and in the zones of Wamba, Isiro and Niangara (see Map 3, p. 83). This area coincides with the ancient Mangbetu kingdom and with later development connected to cotton cultivation and construction of the railway to Aketi. The south is likewise sparsely populated in general, with only 6 per square kilometre, but with denser islands around Lokutu, Isangi and Yangambi which reach as much as 100 per square kilometre because of the activities of the big plantation companies and the railway from Kisangani to Ubundu. The east has a higher density, averaging around 50, with almost 100 per square kilometre in the zones of Bunia, Kilo, Djugu and Mahagi, linked to the development of agriculture and the road network associated with the Kilo Moto gold mines (Obatela Rashidi 1976: 60–1).

These details of Kisangani and its hinterland set the scene for an account of Zaire's developing capitalism and the class formation associated with it. John Clammer finds the most pressing conceptual issues of economic anthropology to lie in the study of development (Clammer 1978:18). This study takes up a question he poses: 'How do we in concrete terms *account for* the emergence of classes at particular junctures in the history of certain societies? (*ibid.*: 14).

# 1

## Indigenous capitalism in peripheral economies: some theoretical considerations

> It is not enough to construct an abstract model and provide an explanation of how it operates; it is just as important to demonstrate the explanatory effectiveness of such a model as applied to historic realities. (Furtado 1964:1)

Zaire's abundance of natural resources and hydro-electric power give it great potential for economic development. Yet its spectacular decline into debt, the impoverishment of the mass of its people, and the huge scale of corruption and of wealth accumulation by a few of its most powerful citizens make it one of Africa's most intractable development problems. The purpose of this chapter is to explore the theories on the causes of underdevelopment and the debates concerning the state and the economy to provide a conceptual framework for this study, with which to explain why the situation in Zaire is so calamitous and how, in spite of it, some positive change is taking place.

Dependency theory radically changed the earlier idea of underdevelopment as a local historical phase, conceptualizing it instead as an integral part of the development of capitalism on a world scale. But this global approach could not explain the observed variations in degree and kind of development in different countries. Class analysis within a specific historical context remedied this deficiency. The kind of capitalism that develops in the peripheral underdeveloped countries of the world is different from that now existing in the developed core countries of the West; it generates a different process of class formation in Africa. The nature of post-independence African states and their new dominant classes, and the success of various forms of resistance to their control, has called into question the role ascribed to the state. Recent theories on these topics have very interesting implications for the development of new class structures and illuminate what is happening in Zaire.

### DEPENDENCY THEORY AND CLASS ANALYSIS: EXTERNAL OR INTERNAL EXPLANATIONS?

Dependency theory, which originated with André Gundar Frank (1967), introduced a global perspective into development studies. Comprehensive discussions of it and of its critics abound (for example Laclau 1971; O'Brien 1975; Brenner 1977; Portes and Walton 1981; Goodman and Redclift 1982; Ollawa 1983), so it needs only brief mention here. This theory views development and underdevelopment as a structural situation in the global economy created by capitalist expansion, not as different stages in history as did the previous paradigm of modernization. The metropolitan countries of the developed West are held to have appropriated for their own development the economic surplus of the colonized countries. Deprived of their own surplus and suffering from the exploitative relations introduced into their domestic structure by the metropole, the satellites remain underdeveloped, while providing raw materials and markets for the industrialization of the West. The evolution of satellite and metropole is thus combined and unequal and its patterns self-perpetuating.

In this perspective, the dominant state-based class of underdeveloped, dependent countries derives political power from partnership with multinational corporations and other agents of Western capitalism. This class does not control the state from a base in the economy, as does its counterpart in Western capitalist systems, but forms a 'comprador' bourgeoisie, whose members are mere clients of international capital. This system of peripheral capitalism and its associated class structure has a limited capacity for capital accumulation and cannot generate the development of its own productive forces. Several analyses of Zaire explain its disastrous political and economic situation in these terms.

Critics of Frank argue that, in fact, capitalist development does take place in dependent countries (Cardoso 1972: 90; Warren 1973). The figures offered as evidence of this development are disputed (Emmanuel 1974 and see Ollawa 1983: 134), but recent writers agree that the differences in degree and kind of capitalist development that manifestly exist between countries and between regions within them are not accounted for by the global perspective of dependency theory. They criticize the lack of an empirical data base in the discussion both for and against this theory, which relies too much on official statistics, and they deplore the lack of detailed information on what is actually going on at the local level (Portes 1976: 75–9; O'Brien 1975: 19; Hopkins 1976:44).

Others point out that Frank misses the unique characteristic of capitalist exploitation:

> Plunder and appropriation of surplus product by one country at the expense of another derives from domination, and while it continues under imperialism (the monopoly stage of capitalism), it is no more characteristic of capitalism in its imperialist stage than it was characteristic of competitive capitalism or of ancient Rome. What is unique to capitalism is the appropriation of the surplus product of labor through the exploitation of labor in the social form of labor power (free wage labor). (Weeks and Dore 1979: 65)

Frank's theory is based on analysis of exchange relations; his critics insist that capitalism should be conceptualized at the level of productive relations, as a system in which labour power and the means of production circulate as commodities. They make clear that the specifically capitalist form of exploitation is the appropriation of surplus labour as surplus value.[1] This conceptualization leads to analysis in terms of class relations and class struggle and to an emphasis on the salience of domestic class structures in determining the development or underdevelopment of particular countries (see Portes 1976; Brenner 1977; Petras 1978; Leys 1978, 1980; Portes and Walton 1981; Goodman and Redclift 1982).

In a Marxist model, class is used to refer to positions in the system of relations of production; it is the relationship between classes that is important, rather than the classes themselves or the siting of individuals in particular classes. It is assumed that the workers are deprived of ownership of the means of production and control of land; their only source of livelihood is to sell their labour to capitalists. Divisions and conflict exist within as well as between these two classes of the bourgeoisie and the proletariat. Particular situations need to be analysed in an historical framework, however, according to 'concrete constellations of class forces and not to some abstract explanatory class schema' (Vercruijsse 1984: 107).

Michael Schatzberg has analysed Zaire in class terms, in his study of Lisala, a town downriver from Kisangani in the region of Equateur (Schatzberg 1980a; forthcoming). He employs a situational, contextual approach to class in which class positions of individuals change, depending on the particular situation, and are allocated by the perceptions of others. In this perceptual, subjective view, class is defined as 'the manifestation of a process by which allied actors obtain or lose, open up or close off, become increasingly or decreasingly conscious of access to life and mobility chances' (Schatzberg 1980a:28). Before there is a social class 'there will have to be both differential access to, and unequal distribution of, life and mobility chances as well as social consciousness of these patterns' (*ibid.*: 30).

This approach seeks to allocate individuals to particular classes. 'Classes' in this sense are closer to Weberian 'status groups' than to the Marxist concept of classes as agents or supports of relations of production in the process of social reproduction and change, an approach concerned primarily with the relations *between* classes. From the Marxist perspective the separation of producers and those who appropriate surplus production entails specific relations of domination and subordination (Therborn 1976:5, 7); they are thus political relations. Class structure, then, is defined here as 'the social relations by which an unpaid for surplus is extracted by the ruling class from the direct producers' (Brenner 1977: 64) and the reproduction of these relations over time.

THE NATURE OF CAPITALISM IN PERIPHERAL AFRICAN ECONOMIES

Modern industrial capitalism, as found in the West, is little developed in Africa, although Thomas Callaghy has pointed out that the forms of capitalism that have developed are not all that different from early European capitalism (Callaghy 1987 (forthcoming)). The penetration of capitalism in African countries is incomplete and it coexists with other non-capitalist modes of production.

From a Marxist perspective, capitalism refers to that organization of production involving the wage labour relationship, and its reproduction over time; it is that organization of production in which the labourer is separated from the means of production and subsists by selling his labour for wages, so that labour power exists as if it were a commodity. Labour, labour power, labour value and class conflict are central in this concept of capitalism.

In contrast, in Weber's view, class conflict is not important. For him rational calculability in both the production process and the legal and administrative system are crucial for the development of capitalism. Industrial capitalism for Weber entails market exchange with the calculating pursuit of self-interest; exact and unambiguous monetary accounting; a strictly disciplined workforce, separated from the means of production; the precise control of the means of production through reliable technical knowledge; and a predictable legal and administrative context, involving the application of general legal norms, with a bureaucracy governed by formal rules, procedures and technical efficiency (Brubaker 1984: 9–22; and see Callay 1987).

Another view is that of Schumpeter, who emphasizes the importance of the individual entrepreneur in revolutionizing the pattern of production, by exercising leadership through personal talent, forcefulness and success (Schumpeter 1976: 132–3).

This study draws on all these approaches. It shows the effect of the weakening of the state on class formation and class struggle; it reveals the detrimental effect on the development of capitalism of the absence of calculability and rationality in the social and economic environment; and it points to the part played by entrepreneurial talent, innovation and hard work in overcoming this difficulty.

The kind of capitalism found in Africa is generally referred to as peripheral capitalism. Industrial capital saw the continent as a source of raw materials and new markets, but not as a place in which to invest in order to expand the local economy. Colonial economies were oriented primarily to production of primary materials for export with only minimal necessary processing, not to manufacturing; manufactured goods were imported. Zaire constitutes a typical example: its economy is oriented towards production of primary commodities for export; it is dependent on the developed countries of the West for capital, technology and manufac-

15

tured goods; it is susceptible to the fluctuations of the prices of primary commodities on the world market; and its underdeveloped productive and manufacturing sectors are dominated by foreign companies.

African capitalism, then, developed as peripheral capitalism; the late stage at which it emerged in the history of world capitalism also affected its nature. African societies were subject to the impact of a capitalism that arrived from a late stage of development elsewhere rather than developing locally (Iliffe 1982: 3). The imported products of large-scale, technologically complex and capital-intensive enterprise provided formidable competition for local firms, which have been slow to develop, leaving the field open to merchant capital trading in imports. In contrast to Latin America where early industry was started by local businessmen and only later dominated by foreigners, Africa's first modern manufacturing firms were often started by foreigners; only in richer countries after independence could local businessmen obtain a growing share in the development of urban enterprise (*ibid.*: 65).

John Iliffe defines three forms of African capitalism according to differences in the part played by the state in the economy. In the first, the state seeks to prevent the emergence of private capitalism by nationals, as for example in Ghana and socialist countries such as Tanzania, Guinea and Mali. In the second, state power is used to acquire private property and businesses so that surplus is channeled into the 'pockets of a parasitic bourgeoisie whose wealth and business interests derive from their political and administrative positions', creating a 'parasitic capitalism'. This form of capitalism is particularly evident in Zaire but also appears in Zambia and the Ivory Coast. The third form is the 'nurture capitalism', described by Sayre Schatz for Nigeria[2] and also found in Kenya. In this form of capitalism the state deliberately attempts to create an economy run substantially by private capitalists and nurtures the growth of the private sector (Iliffe 1982: 81).

'Parasitic' aptly describes Zaire's form of capitalism. The virtually unlimited power of those at the top has allowed them to pillage and plunder the natural riches of their country and to amass vast fortunes. They have been in truth, parasites, sucking the lifeblood of the economy for their own benefit.[3] The rise of the entrepreneurs described in this study is a recent phenomenon. They are investing in productive, rationally managed enterprises and moving into manufacturing, thus initiating a form of capitalism which expands the local economy.

THE POST-INDEPENDENCE STATE AND ECONOMY

The colonial powers in Africa handed over political control at independence but retained economic control through the large companies that continued to run the agro-industrial and mining sectors of African economies. The capitalism developed in the colonial period, oriented towards export of primary commodities, resulted in economies that were by their nature unstable because dependent on the price fluctuations of the world market. This in turn tended to destabilize the post-colonial state and to undermine its ability to exercise control and reproduce legitimacy for itself, for the ruling class and for its foreign allies. The state became an arena for factional infighting and the control of patronage; the subordinated classes grew increasingly impoverished and disillusioned as the purchasing power of real wages declined and imports became scarce (Beckman 1980: 106).

In Zaire this situation has developed in association with a patrimonial form of the state, in which President Mobutu and a ruling clique maintain their power and influence through their access to state resources, disbursed as rewards for political support through a network of patron-client relations:

> The fundamental distinction between a patrimonial and a rational-legal (or what is ethnocentrically called a 'modern') state is whether or not offices may be appropriated for personal wealth. In a patrimonial state there is no sharp distinction between the public and private domains. (Kasfir 1984:14)

The use of patronage by state officials to further their personal and class interests in this way, however, produces problems:

> Since patronage depends on material rewards, the system must generate adequate and perhaps increasing economic benefits. But financing patrimonial state apparatus creates special problems because the political requirements of control and reward undercut the rational prerequisites of economic activity. Although the appropriation of office *may* support vigorous entrepreneurial activity, the state inevitably becomes less effective in generating public revenue and therefore less able to maintain the positions out of which patrimonial control can be sustained." (*Ibid.*: 15)

In these terms we can explain why the personnel of the Zairian state are increasingly driven to abuse their position and amass vast personal wealth. The result is a weakening of the administrative apparatus and decreasing control by the state of the processes of production and distribution, diminishing the degree of capitalist domination.

Although the primary exports of African countries are produced under capitalist relations of production and the great majority of men participate in wage labour for at least some period of their lives, 'capital's problematic control over the total process of production and reproduction poses severe limits to the domination of capital' (Cooper 1983: 17). This problem existed for colonial as well as for post-colonial states (Cooper 1981: 32). With the weakening of the state's administrative capacity in Zaire since independence, various class sectors have begun to compete to appropriate surplus. The state is not able to monopolize this surplus, so cannot close off opportunities for accumulation and socio-economic mobility. In such a situation investigation must focus on:

17

> the struggle between direct producers and capital over the conditions of labor in the sphere of production and over the distribution and realisation of the product, up to the moment of complete expropriation and direct control of production by capital. (Bernstein 1977: 69).

We will now look at the consequences of the incomplete penetration of capital and the weakening of the state: the articulation of capitalist and non-capitalist modes of production, the expansion of the second economy, and the autonomy of petty producers. We will review the theories concerning these phenomena, which, as we shall see, manifest the ongoing process of class formation. They reveal the dynamic reality of class relations: the struggle between producers and capital, the resistance to oppression, the mechanisms of upward mobility and the attempts to close class boundaries, all of which play a role in the emergence of local, productive capitalism.

## THE ARTICULATION OF MODES OF PRODUCTION

The term 'mode of production' is used here to refer to both the economic base of production and the political, juridical and ideological superstructure required to reproduce the relations by which production is organized.[4] The persistence of non-capitalist modes in articulation with the capitalist mode affects the process of class formation in Africa: these modes provide alternative means of subsistence to wage labour so that labour is neither 'free' nor alienated from the means of production. We will show that in Zaire this articulation not only provides subsistence alternatives, and in so doing impedes the process of proletarianization, it also provides for some people means for capital accumulation for investment in productive enterprise.

The concept of 'articulation' originates with French economic anthropologists writing in the sixties and early seventies. They modified Marxist theory, applying it to non-capitalist societies, to their transformation by the penetration of capitalism and to the incompleteness of this penetration (Meillassoux 1972, 1981; Godelier 1972; Terray 1972; Rey 1973; Dupré and Rey 1973).[5]

These anthropologists show that colonial states took over political power in already existing modes of production, undermining control of relations of production in these modes and the mechanisms for reproduction of that control, and creating the necessary labour force for capitalist production by forced labour, taxation, land redistribution and extensive programmes of road and rail construction. Colonial economies produced primary commodities for export to supply the industries of the metropole; they did not bring about local industrialization and expand the economy. Most Africans continued to exist as subsistence farmers, having access to land and participating in the relations of production of non-capitalist, small-scale societies. Wage labourers retained ties with rural society and could return there to work the land. In this way non-capitalist modes, though subordinated to capitalism and transformed in specific ways by commodity production, persisted in articulation with it: the direct or 'subsistence' producers were not fully expropriated because they still had access to land, and the full development of capitalism did not take place. This condition is very evident in Zaire.

Assessments of the significance of this articulation of capitalism with non-capitalist modes have been various. Since this feature so distinctively characterizes the Zairian economy and is a significant factor in the class formation described here, a brief outline of some of the arguments is appropriate. Some writers see the articulation of modes of production as a transitional stage. In their view the failure of capital to separate direct producers from their means of production restricts the extension of capitalism beyond industry into agriculture and results in restricted and uneven development. From this persepctive, incomplete penetration of capitalist relations of production and the persistence of non-capitalist forms that block capitalist development are the cause of underdevelopment (Rey 1973; Taylor 1979: 223). Another view is that neither the complexity of articulation, nor the multiplicity of the modes of production articulated necessarily result in backwardness, but rather the specific manner in which the articulation is achieved (Roxborough 1979: 68).

A contrast to the understanding of articulation as a transitional phase is the perception that not all systems penetrated by capitalism will necessarily undergo change to become fully capitalist; they may remain in a persistent state of articulation (Foster-Carter 1978: 225). A case study of such a situation is presented in superb detail by Emile Vercruijsse. He finds that Ghanaian canoe fishing has been transformed by the penetration of capitalism but has not been completely assimilated into capitalist production. To the contrary, it has retained many features of a traditional form of production and the dissolution of the traditional mode is not likely to progress further to the point where labour becomes a commodity freely exchangeable for money. The domination of the modern fishing industry is, however, established, since it sets the limits within which canoe fishing can operate and develop (Vercruijsse 1984).

Vercruijsse and others emphasize that articulation helps the development of capitalism in peripheral economies because non-capitalist systems provide a cheap labour force for capitalism and lower its cost of reproduction. Capitalist employers pay wages sufficient only to meet the direct subsistence needs of workers and depend on non-capitalist systems to provide supplementary subsistence, to support dependants and to provide for workers themselves in times of sickness, unemployment and old age. Not having to pay welfare benefits lowers the cost of labour, so that capital pays for labour power below its cost of reproduction; the labour supply is produced and reproduced outside the capitalist mode of production (Meillassoux 1972, 1981; Wolpe 1972, 1975; Rey 1973). From

19

this perspective, articulation with non-capitalist modes is functional for capitalism because it provides a source of cheap labour power, opens up new markets, counteracts the declining rate of profit through capital export, and secures raw materials (Goodman and Redclift 1982: 61).

We need not suppose that subordinated non-capitalist modes form a vast reserve army of labour. In the classical capitalism described by Marx the reserve army of labour did not need to be very large to keep wages down. According to Roxborough, 'all the evidence suggests that unemployment and underemployment in Third World countries is above this level. Moreover, only a small percentage of the unemployed or partially employed ever join the ranks of the industrial proletariat' (Roxborough 1979: 89–90). Cooper endorses this comment: 'capital's inconclusive assault on Africa created a guerilla army of the underemployed rather than the juxtaposition of the disciplined troops and the reserve army of the unemployed of industrial capitalism' (Cooper 1983:18; see also Berry 1985:11).

The critical issue here is whether the reproduction of relations of production in non-capitalist modes is destroyed by the penetration of capitalism.[6] Peter Geschiere reasserts Rey's and Terray's emphasis that analysis in terms of modes of production must start from the forms of exploitation. In the lineage mode of production, exploitation occurs in the relations between the elders and young men, women or slaves, and varies according to the different degree of the elders' control over production. Geschiere stresses Rey's point that the regrouping of the direct producers in the relations of exploitation is the crucial moment in the reproduction of any particular form of exploitation (in capitalism this moment is the buying and selling of labour power; in the lineage mode of production it is the circulation of men and women between local units for the profit of the elders). As long as the impact of the market and money economy reinforces the regrouping of the producers in the old units of production, then the old mode is still dominant; if the regrouping allocates labour to new units of production then capitalism dominates (Geschiere 1985: 82–6).

Geschiere's approach is in line with the argument that whether capitalism destroys or preserves non-capitalist modes is an historically contingent question. Capital draws upon non-capitalist economies in different ways at different stages of development, arising from specific historical circumstances (Bradby 1975: 129, 135). Stages in the implantation of transitional forms of production in canoe fishing in Ghana, for instance, can be explained if we relate them to the development of the small-scale production of cocoa for the world market and of the wage labour force for mining and capitalist cocoa farming (Vercruijsse 1984:12). The preservation of non-capitalist modes profoundly affects the development of both the form of capitalism and of class structure. Despite the arguments over the articulation of modes of production, the concept most accurately describes the realities of Zaire and of Africa in general, and

20

enables us to improve on a picture of an 'otherwise nondescript coping of peasants' (W. MacGaffey 1985: 57).

The articulation of modes of production has two consequences of particular significance for the class formation that we will describe in Zaire. One is that the role of the merchant or trader is greatly enhanced so that merchant capital develops extensively. The other is the difficulty of obtaining a reliable workforce for capitalist enterprise.

Where there is not full specialisation in commodity production, traders make profits because producer prices are cheap: the direct producers and the unit of production are reproduced by subsistence production of crops grown for their use value. The exchange value of the commodities produced is lowered because the 'reproduction of the producers is "subsidized" through use-value production drawing on the labor of all members of the household above a certain age' (Bernstein 1977: 72). Traders make profits on goods bought at these low prices. Such profits have been a means of capital accumulation for some of the entrepreneurs in this study.

The trader makes profits essentially as a 'linkman' between modes (Taylor 1979: 226). Norman Long calls traders brokers between different modes of production. In rural Peru, the hallmark of success of agricultural entrepreneurs is their 'ability to combine different types of social relations deriving from different modes of production and from different institutional contexts'. Transporters moving produce by truck from the rural areas to the urban market in return for consumer goods, 'tend to evolve close links with marketing entrepreneurs in both the village and town contexts, and are continually seeking to expand and consolidate these commercial networks' (Long 1975: 275–6).

In a society based on simple commodity production, in which independent producers own the means of production, the rudimentary elements of capitalism exist: wealth can be held as money, the precondition for systematic accumulation; as soon as commodity production expands to a point that a specialized class of traders can form, capital can emerge in the form of merchant capital (Kay 1975: 63–8). Accumulation, however, is not the mere amassing of wealth; it must be put back into circulation to multiply. But merchant capital in general has no direct control over the labour process and is dependent, in any particular instance, on the class which does. It cannot increase the value of the commodities it handles. In order to acquire surplus value and make a profit traders must engage in unequal exchange in which they sell at higher prices than they buy: 'This profit like that of all capital finds its real origin in the sphere of production as the unrewarded product of labor' (*ibid.*: 88). However, 'one of the main restrictions on the rate of accumulation of merchant capital is that it can only appropriate a portion of the surplus and *is unable to prevent other classes taking a share*' (*ibid.*: 70, my italics). This feature of merchant capital is a factor in opening up opportunities for social mobility in Zaire.

The transition from commodity production and merchant capital to manufacturing and industrial capitalism has varied greatly in different countries. From one perspective merchant capital in underdeveloped countries has repressed general economic development in proportion to its own independent development; the profits of trade are used to expand trade and not the forces of production, and thus drain part of the surplus out of the sphere of production (*ibid.*: 95). But this view ignores the possibility that capital accumulated in commercial ventures may be invested in productive enterprise, opening up new lines of production (Furtado 1964: 81–92). This certainly occurs in Zaire.

The second consequence of the articulation of modes of production of particular interest here is the difficulty of capitalist employers in obtaining steady and reliable work from workers who, as Cooper puts it, retain access to land, who make efforts to bring resources back to the countryside or devote them to petty trade or production back in the city, and who pose serious challenges to capital and the state (Cooper 1983:11).

> The interplay of small workshop, rural village, and large factory creates alternative means of livelihood, alternative ambitions, and alternative relations of production to the subordination of labor to capital. (*Ibid.*: 41)

In this situation it becomes difficult to reproduce relations of capitalist production. Cooper makes the point, with reference to the lowering of the cost of reproduction of the capitalist workforce by non-capitalist modes, that 'the very processes that cheapen the *physical* reproduction of the workforce might make *social* reproduction – the extension of capitalist relations of production – all the more difficult' (*ibid.*: 29).

The challenge posed by workers and petty producers to capital and the state may take the form of political action of some kind, or of violent rebellion, but it is increasingly the case that it takes the form of participation in that part of the economy variously referred to as the second, parallel, informal, underground, black or irregular economy. This phenomenon is increasing in scale world-wide and has attracted much attention from scholars and the media. There is as yet, however, little agreement on its significance and precise definition. The data from Zaire suggest that it can be seen as a manifestation of class struggle: its activities constitute a means to survive economic hardship but also a means to resist the dominant class and the predatory state; they represent successful efforts to evade controls and constraints and may provide opportunities for the accumulation of wealth; and they are a primary means for the state-based class to consolidate its position. The expansion of the second economy in Zaire is an indication of the difficulty the state has in controlling the extension of capitalist relations of production and their social reproduction. It is thus a measure of the decreasing significance of the state for class formation.

## THE SECOND ECONOMY

The second economy here refers to economic activities that are unmeasured and unrecorded. Some of its activities are illegal, others are not illegal in themselves but are carried out in a manner that avoids taxation or in some way deprives the state of revenue.[7] These are activities supposedly controlled by the state but which in fact either evade this control or involve illegal use of state position. By this definition the second economy is as much a political as an economic phenomenon. It is a manifestation of class struggle, as well as of coping strategies to deal with economic exigency. This approach provides a framework for comparison of second economies in different parts of the world. Alejandro Portes maintains that the historical process of the ups and downs of the class struggle unifies the phenomenon of the 'informal economy' in both advanced and peripheral economies (Portes 1983: 164). Variations in its form in particular countries can be seen to reflect different stages of the development of capitalism or socialism,[8] different processes of class struggle, and different adjustments to economic hardship.

Defined in this way the second economy is different from what is generally referred to as the 'informal sector', on which a voluminous literature exists. In African studies Keith Hart first distinguished the informal sector of the economy in Ghana, and introduced the distinction between formal and informal income opportunities, both legitimate and illegitimate (Hart 1973: 68–9). The literature on the informal sector since Hart, however, has dealt chiefly with the self-employment of the urban poor and the migrant population (see Sethuraman 1976: 73–5; Moser 1978). Some have defined this sector of the economy in terms of the characteristics of small enterprises (ILO Employment Mission in Kenya 1972), or by their size (Hugon and Deblé 1982), or scale (Bujra 1978: 49). But the parameters for criteria of this kind can only be set arbitrarily.[9] Definition in terms of individuals (Green 1981) is even less satisfactory since the same individual may operate in both the formal and the informal sectors.

Focus on the small-scale activities of the socially disadvantaged omits activities, included by Hart, which often are on a very large scale and carried out by those at the top level of society; they include political corruption, smuggling, bribery, and speculation. The definition of the second economy used here includes all the informal income opportunities mentioned by Hart, the activities of the rich as well as of the poor, those which are carried out on a large as well as a small scale and at all levels of society.[10] It is empirically the case that the boundary between the official and the second economy is ill defined and shifts. We are not concerned with categorizing activities as belonging to one or the other but with the relation between the two. For a particular individual a tension may exist over the decision to participate in the one or the other; this tension is political.

The second economy has come to include such a huge sector of the economy in some countries of Africa that a radical re-evaluation of what is actually going on is in order. In Uganda, for example, *magendo*, the black market economy, is estimated at two-thirds of, or even to exceed the GDP (Green 1981; Prunier 1983: 62); in Ghana *kalabule* exists on a similar scale (Chazan 1982); in the southern Sudan it is a crucial element of the economy (Prunier 1983). In Senegal, by 1965, 'losses' and acknowledged fraud in the central marketing board were more than the annual net profit. Lax accounting, dishonest agents and inadequate supervision made possible a network of private appropriation in the nationalized marketing sector (Cruise O'Brien 1971: 274). In 1980 more than half of Senegal's peanut harvest was smuggled out, resulting in a loss of 200 billion CFA frs. in tax receipts (Lemarchand 1986). Unmeasured economic activity on such a scale seriously distorts assessments of the state of the economy in these countries; the fact that so much goes on autonomously of the state has significant political implications.

That economic activities independent of the state exist on the huge scale found in Zaire and other African countries challenges the importance accorded to the state in the literature on class formation in Africa. Kasfir has strongly emphasized the new potential for class formation in Uganda as the *magendo* economy increases in response to shortages created by state failure. He questions the domination of the state in class formation when wealth from *magendo* has concentrated in the hands of a few on a previously unimagined scale (Kasfir 1984: 85).

In Reginald Green's view the *magendo* economy is so large that it has generated its own class structure and become a 'submode of production' (Green 1981). In an argument that can be transferred directly to Zaire, Kasfir points to weaknesses in Green's position, concluding that the pervasiveness of *magendo* does not mean that it results in a separate economy or class structure. To the contrary, position in the state brings access to resources and such access is crucial for certain activities in the second economy. It allows state personnel to consolidate their class position with massive accumulation of wealth in activities such as smuggling, bribery and embezzlement, and speculation and middleman activity: state and *magendo* are intimately related, both contribute to the process of class formation. The emergence of significant black markets, nevertheless, has fundamentally altered this process (Kasfir 1984: 90–103).

The personnel of patrimonial, administratively ineffective states, such as Zaire, must squeeze wealth out of their position in the state apparatus in order to maintain the patronage which is an important basis for their power. But the great increase in uncontrolled economic activity that follows the decline of administrative capacity brings higher returns to labour, permitting considerable accumulation and the potential for investment in productive or distributive enterprise for those outside the state. Colin Leys has commented on the effects of money made by coffee smuggling from Uganda to Kenya:

> Clearly the scale of capital concentration which may be achieved through these forms of modern primitive accumulation does not guarantee that such capital will be invested productively...Nonetheless the significance of these transactions for the long-run potential for further accumulation by indigenous capital remains profound. (Leys 1978: 253)

In response to the predatory state and the pillaging activities of state personnel, subordinated classes organize the system of production and distribution that make up the second economy. Its activities provide alternatives to wage labour and thus the means to avoid proletarianization. The degree of autonomy of petty producers and the significance of this autonomy for the undeveloped countries of Africa has, however, been disputed.

'PEASANT AUTONOMY': HOW POWERFUL IS SMALL?

In situations of the incomplete penetration of capitalism and its articulation with non-capitalist modes, the potential exists for autonomy for small-scale producers. Is this autonomy sufficient to affect capitalist development and class formation? Goran Hyden proposes that 'small is powerful' and that an 'uncaptured peasantry' renders illusory the power of those who rule and therefore constitutes the root cause of underdevelopment. In Hyden's view, small-holder African peasants who own their own means of production are sufficiently independent of other social classes to restrict development. He describes a peasant 'economy of affection', in which familial and communal ties and patronage are the basis for organizing activity, providing opportunities for social action and production outside state control (Hyden 1980).

Hyden, however, exaggerates peasant autonomy. Kasfir points out that peasants obviously cannot withdraw entirely into self-sufficiency. They need cash to pay taxes, and to buy hoes and goods such as salt, soap and cloth. In fact peasants are creations of the capitalist economy. Moreover, Hyden ignores the capacity of classes to use the state apparatus to exploit peasants: the 'economy of affection' masks class relations in which patronage is a form of class domination (Kasfir 1986).

The question of the dependence or autonomy of peasant producers in peripheral capitalism centres on the issue of whether 'capital can achieve effective control of the production process without undertaking its immediate organization and dispossessing the direct producers' (Goodman and Redclift 1982: 68). Bernstein argues persuasively that capital achieves control over petty producers through their needs for the products of capitalism.

According to Henry Bernstein, simple commodity production is a form of production in which the household, or other unit of production,

25

produces use values for its direct consumption needs and, in addition, commodities that are sold for cash to buy needed items. These petty producers retain control over the means and organization of production and are not, therefore, proletarians. They are, however, in varying degrees, dependent on the exchange of commodities for the reproduction of the producers and of the unit of production. The independence of the producers is thus circumscribed, both at the level of exchange through prices and at the level of production. Falling prices for commodities produced, relative to prices for bought commodities, result in reduced levels of consumption or intensified commodity production or both. Capital can thus put a 'squeeze' directly on production; the household is forced to intensify its labour to keep up the supply of commodities it needs to reproduce itself. The more commodity relations and a cash income become conditions of reproduction, the more powerful the control that capital can exercise, though still without having to organize and supervise the production process (Bernstein 1977: 64–5).[11] In Zaire people are drawn into the money economy by their need for tools, medicines and health care, manufactured goods and school fees, as well as by the imposition of taxes. 'The monetization of elements of this cycle of reproduction of petty producers through the substitution of commodities and the corresponding withdrawal of labour from use-value production, provides scope for the mercantile and political agents of productive capital to intensify commodity relations' (Goodman and Redclift 1982: 89–90).

Forms of resistance to this squeeze include attempts to withdraw at least partially from commodity production or attempts to find alternative sources of cash, such as migration for wage labour, and evasion of imposed terms of exchange through smuggling and other forms of illicit marketing to realize higher returns to labour (Bernstein 1977: 69). Resistance, however, cannot result in autonomy; the independence of petty producers is circumscribed by their need for the products of industrialization, which they cannot achieve themselves. Furthermore, not only rural producers but also artisans of underdeveloped countries are dependent on modern productive industry: the small enterprises of the urban 'informal sector' have expanded simultaneously with the spread of industry, partly because although industries have not provided sufficient employment, they have provided a range of other income opportunities (Kitching 1982: 100).

The play of squeeze and resistance opens opportunities for social mobility; social differentiation develops as the income of some petty commodity producers rises. As Robert Brenner puts it,

> The historical evolution or emergence of any given class structure is not comprehensible as the mere product of a ruling class choice and imposition, but...represents the outcome of class conflicts through which the direct producers have, to a greater or lesser extent, succeeded in restricting the form and extent of ruling class access to surplus labour. (Brenner 1977: 59)

Kitching has emphasized the need to accord more importance to struggles *among* Africans in the process of capitalist development, rather than to foreign domination. He does so in the context of the lively debate[12] that has been raging in the scholarly journals about whether or not dependent capitalist development has been occurring in Kenya. The debate began because Colin Leys re-evaluated his study of Kenya based on dependency theory (Leys 1974), and rejected the idea that colonialism, imperialism and multinational capital prevented development. He favoured a more open conceptualization that made a place for capital accumulation and struggle among Africans in the process of development (Leys 1978; see also Swainson 1977, 1980). This revision derived from the work of Michael Cowen on agricultural petty commodity production and accumulation.

Kitching summarizes Cowen's work to show that in Kenya peasants are not a uniformly impoverished mass of subsistence farmers subordinated to the labour demands of settlers but accumulate through acquisition of land and through increasing agricultural commodity production, a situation that clearly exists in Zaire also. But such increasing petty commodity production for the domestic and the export market imposes limits on the development of both indigenous and multinational capital. These limits, however, are contradictory: increased incomes of smallholders support the labour force in low-paid wage labour (thus subsidizing capital); these same low wages, however, provide no incentive to increase labour productivity and producer incomes only rise slowly. They thus restrict the growth of the domestic market and also of capitalism. Small-scale production thus inhibits the development of manufacturing, but it is supported by sections of both indigenous and foreign capital which trade, process and market the commodities produced.

Kitching uses this argument to demonstrate the fallacy that transnational capital is a monolithic cause of underdevelopment. He points out that it is not a question of what foreign capitalism will allow but what Africans can *obtain*: 'This will be determined in activity, in the struggles of some peasants against others, of workers against bosses, of sections of indigenous capitalism against sections of transnational capital' (Kitching 1985: 141; see also Berry 1984: 6). Class is not the only dimension of such struggles: gender, ethnicity and other modes of differentiation are also significant.

Much has been written about *how* surplus is appropriated in the conflict between state and petty producer, in the articulation of modes of production and in the 'informal sector' of small, unenumerated urban enterprises, but the question of *who* exactly appropriates this surplus has received much less attention. In Zaire it turns out to be individuals in a wide range of class positions. The results of this situation for class formation are a central theme of this study.

To sum up, this study of the emergence of local productive capitalism in

27

northeast Zaire draws on dependency theory to explain Zaire's place as a peripheral capitalist economy in the world system, but goes beyond this theory to explain Zaire's particular degree and kind of capitalist development in terms of domestic class structure, of its historical roots in the colonial experience and of the nature of the state and of the forms of resistance to it. In this analysis, the theories of Marx, Weber and Schumpeter all illuminate the observed processes of class formation and capitalist development.

### CULTURAL PLURALISM, PATRON-CLIENTAGE AND CLASS FORMATION

Any analysis of domestic class structure must also address both the cultural pluralism that in many ways dominates the everyday life of any Zairian citizen, and the ties of patron-clientage that exist at all social levels. Officially ethnic affiliation no longer features in documents and records, but the continuing significance of ethnicity and its intersection with class in the process of social stratification is quite evident.

Crawford Young points out that urbanization intensifies cultural pluralism because it brings a wider range of groups into more frequent interaction and competition (Young 1976: 27).

> Class as a basis for ordering the social universe is intersected by cultural pluralism, understood as multiple units of social affinity within a territorial society, based upon commonalities of language, ethnicity, religion or region ... an exceedingly complex amalgam of multilayered and interpenetrating identities, themselves in the process of evolution. In essence it is a self-versus-other relationship, where particular categories are defined according to characteristics that differentiate them from relevant others. (Young 1982:73–4)

Cultural identity is subjective, overlapping, situational. 'We' is defined by 'they': the relevant other in a social setting is central in shaping role selection, although this selection is not infinitely elastic. Groups are not defined by innate permanent cultural characteristics; the set of customs associated with a particular group may change over time while the identity of the group persists (Young 1976:41). As Ronald Cohen puts it, 'the identities to members and categorizations by others is more or less fluid, more or less multiple, forming nesting hierarchies of we/they dichotomizations' (Cohen 1978: 395).

In Zaire it is evident that some ethnic groups enjoy a privileged position in the class structure. Young has shown that in the colonial period ethnic categories developed through the classification and creation of territorial subdivisions and through unequal opportunities for social mobility among different cultural groups, creating widespread perceptions of an ethnic stratification and the crystallization of stereotyped ethnic attributes (Young 1982: 78–9). Groups changed and came into being in response to political situations and long term social changes. They varied widely from a highly developed degree of self-awareness to one that is amorphous and barely manifest (Young 1976: 3–6, 12–13, ch. 6). It is evident in Kisangani that members of the groups that attained a more favourable position in the colonial period are disproportionately represented among those in more favourable positions today.

Verhaegen's comment, that 'the tribe, or ethnic group, corresponds in part to a distinct professional sub-group, which retains an economic position and a particular educational infrastructure, marked by a dominant religious culture, or even by a particular missionary congregation' (Verhaegen 1969:xviii), fits Abner Cohen's characterization of ethnic groups. In his view such groups have continually

> re-created their distinctiveness in different ways, not because of conservatism, but because [they] are in fact interest groupings whose members share some common economic and political interests and who, therefore, stand together in the continuous competition for power with other groups. (Cohen 1969: 192)

In Kisangani Nande traders form a particularly good example of an ethnic interest group acting in the absence of formal political power and influence.

Ethnicity then, cannot be dismissed as false consciousness, a weapon and contrivance of the dominant classes of Africa in pursuit of their own interests; for this to occur there must first be something there to manipulate (Staniland 1985: 180). The intersection of ethnicity and class is a matter for empirical investigation. In Zaire ethnicity is a salient factor in the process of class formation: it is used not only to gain access to the state and to further the interests of the dominant class but also as a basis for the organization of resistance and protest, of political action, and for structuring specific interest groups lacking a formal institutional power base.

Ethnicity is also one basis for the patron-client ties that typify Zaire and other underdeveloped countries. Patron-client relations are dyadic relations characterized by unequal status, reciprocality and personal contact. They are prevalent where impersonal guarantees of security, status and wealth are weak, so that individuals seek personal substitutions and attach themselves to 'big men' who can provide protection and the means for advancement. Richard Sandbrook and others hold that such patron-client politics is a preferable model to that of social class (Sandbrook 1972: 109). But, 'far from being an *alternative* to class analysis, an approach to dependent economies which emphasises clientelism can greatly help to understand some of the mechanisms of class control which help to maintain dependency' (Flynn 1974:134). The weakening effect of clientelism on class organization is a mechanisms of class control deliberately imposed and maintained from above (*ibid.*: 148–52). For René Lemarchand, 'The crux of the issue is not whether ethnic or class analysis has greater explanatory power than clientelistic analysis, but at what point in time, and through what combination of circumstances, class or ethnic cleavages are liable to alter, combine with, or supersede patron-client ties.' How do class, ethnicity or clientelism interact with each other? (Lemarchand 1981:12).

# 2

# The political and economic context: from colonial oppression to the fend for yourself present

By the eve of independence in 1960, the Belgians had produced in the Congo the most industrialized country in Africa south of the Sahara, except for South Africa.[1] They constructed an economy oriented to the production of primary mineral and agricultural products for export, supported by a road, rail and navigable waterway network and abundant hydro-electric power. The principal instrument of this penetration of capitalism was a ruthlessly effective state administrative apparatus, backed by military force. But Belgian colonial policy allowed Africans little participation in administration or the profitable sectors of the economy, so that development of any indigenous commercial enterprise was severely restricted. The administrative capacity of the colonial state contrasts with that of the post-independence state, but the roots of the economic crisis which has beset Zaire can be found in colonial policies and in the nature of the colonial economy. The process of class formation and class struggle since independence needs to be set in this historical context.

## The penetration of capitalism and development of an export economy

> Through the combined efforts of bureacracy, capital and Church, each of which fashioned a formidable organizational structure in its own centre of activity, a remarkable colonial system was constructed, unparalleled in the depth of its penetration into the African societies upon which it was superimposed and in the breadth of its control of nearly the whole spectrum of human activity. (Young 1965: 32)

The colonial trinity organized the penetration of capitalism in Zaire. The intensity of its occupation and organization left an enduring legacy for the post-colonial society and economy, and therefore needs to be described in some detail.

Belgian administration was distinguished by the extent of its interference in people's lives; officers of the territorial service spent twenty days of each month in the bush enforcing the annual compulsory cultivation required from the population and supervising the maintenance of the network of unpaved roads (Young 1965: 10–12). The bureaucracy required more white administrators in relation to its population than any other African colony except Dahomey and Mauritius; in 1913 the Congo employed 2,450 state officials, with 252 more attached to the railways, whereas only 1,743 ran the entire German colonial empire in Africa and the Pacific (Gann and Duignan 1979: 177, 184). The administrative apparatus was thus very dense; the removal of its coercion and supervision at independence resulted in the collapse of many activities that it had organized, such as road maintenance, health and soil erosion measures, and cultivation of certain crops.

The church received the full cooperation of the administration. The missionary effort was essentially Belgian and Catholic. At the end of the colonial period there were 669 Catholic mission posts with nearly 6,000 European missionaries. The church established most of the schools; the state not only subsidized the mission schools but also paid for the missionaries. Land grants to the missions were usable for commercial purposes as well as self-support; the church commanded considerable resources and was extremely powerful (Young 1965: 12–14). It retained much of its power after independence and the Catholic church today remains one of the most effective organizations in the country (see Schatzberg: forthcoming, ch. 7).

The colonial administration cooperated as closely with the big companies as with the missions; throughout colonial history the Congo economy was dominated by a few large companies. The Leopoldian state had taken two fundamental steps to control the means of production: it appropriated land not 'effectively occupied' by Africans and then required the local male population to collect marketable products; first monopolizing purchase rights and then imposing production of a specific volume of agricultural products (Peemans 1975a: 169–70). King Leopold's concession was ten times the size of Belgium. The Belgian Congo continued these policies, establishing a regime that linked state capital with private monopolies in a way unparalleled in other European empires. It thus attracted investment not only because of its wealth of natural resources but also because of the unusual degree of administrative support offered for obtaining land and labour. After 1910 it granted five huge concessions to Unilever and many smaller ones to other agro-industries (Gann and Duignan 1979: 125; Jewsiewicki 1983: 98). The multinational companies which have so dominated Zaire's economy were thus entrenched very early on.

The plantation companies in the central basin were followed by the mining companies for copper and other minerals in the south, gold and tin in the east and northeast, and diamonds in Kasai. Union Minière began to produce copper on a commercial scale in 1911. After 1920, economic expansion was primarily in mineral exports; by 1924 three quarters of the

32

value of exports came from mining (Buell 1928: 509). Three-quarters of capital investment between 1920 and 1932 was in mining and its infrastructure; mineral exports increased sixfold between 1920 and 1930, whereas agricultural exports only tripled (Bézy *et al.*, 1981: 20). Both gold and diamond mining were very labour intensive, using unskilled techniques that were later to support illicit, small-scale, independent production. By the end of the thirties the labour force for the gold mines was 90,000, equalling 40 per cent of total mine labour. After World War II shaft mining replaced the exhausted alluvial gold mining. Diamonds in the western mining zone of the Kasai tributaries were manually mined by digging shafts and trenches; and the eastern zone employed industrial techniques of mass mining and extensive mechanization after the market opened up for very small diamonds for machine tools (Vellut 1983: 142).

In the period up until the forties, the colonial state and capital transformed production, firstly by the appropriation by the state of land held to be unoccupied, which was allocated in vast concessions, and secondly by mobilizing a labour force. Labour recruitment in the Congo was carried out under more direct compulsion than in other African colonies. Initially the Free State exacted levies of soldiers and contract workers from each district, and imposed taxes in kind: quotas of rubber, porterage, paddlers and food or wood. This labour tax of the Congo Free State was extraordinarily onerous. A decree of 1903 exacted forty hours of labour a month from the population, for which they were supposedly paid; in practice they were underpaid and subject to additional obligations. The example of one *chefferie* shows the extent of the burden thus imposed. The hundred huts of Bumba had to supply monthly five sheep or pigs (or fifty chickens), 60 kilograms of rubber, 125 loads of manioc, 15 kilograms of maize or peanuts and 15 kilograms of sweet potatoes. In addition, one man out of ten had to be a labourer at the government post: one had to serve in the military annually; and the whole population had to work one day in four on public works (Buell 1928: 430).[2]

The Belgian colonial government replaced the labour tax by the head tax in 1910, forcing people into wage labour to earn the necessary cash, but communal labour was nevertheless still required. In 1922 Governor-General Lippens issued a circular stating that 'it is a mistake to believe ... that once taxes are paid and other legal obligations met, the native may remain inactive' (quoted in Buell 1928: 539). Communal labour was of two kinds: unpaid, which involved keeping the village clear of brush, building a jail and dispensary and carrying out health measures; and paid, which consisted of road maintenance and building bridges, schools and European rest houses. The pay, however, was even less than that given by trading firms. This compulsory labour was limited by law to sixty days a year, only five in any one month, but the decree was not honoured in practice and more labour was demanded (*ibid.*: 499–500). Mwabila comments that the reasons for the deficiencies of the contemporary labour force must lie partly in the long history of grossly inadequate remuneration for long and arduous labour (Mwabila 1979: 51).

The church also assisted in the organization of a workforce. The year of training at a mission station for catechists served, in addition to its religious purposes, to socialize them into the colonial economy. Life in the religious community instilled the values of hard and disciplined work, performed on schedule, and of respect for authority. Each mission post was a miniature agricultural, craft and commercial enterprise. Free land concessions, tax exemptions and access to labour that was often free (because being trained), resulted in an economic empire that made the church almost financially autonomous. In 1927 the missions employed nearly as many workers as did small-scale private enterprise. Furthermore, the missions introduced their converts to the value of consumer goods, such as bicycles, sewing machines, furniture and durable construction materials (Jewsiewicki 1981: 3–4).

In the process of mobilizing labour, the *Force Publique*, the colonial militia, was a brutal coercive tool. Initially, in the period of the Congo Free State, it consisted of Africans brought from other countries; it was greatly expanded under the colonial government. The pay was low, even less than that of railway workers, and recruitment was mostly by conscription. Recruits selected by local chiefs were mostly the impoverished, slaves or local undesirables; they constituted a weak foundation on which to build the national army after independence. In the colonial period, the *Force Publique* operated as a combined police and military force; administrators could requisition troops and order police operations against the local population (Buell 1928: 496–8).

Colonization and the penetration of capital thus modified pre-existing production systems of shifting agriculture, transferring part of the labour force to capitalist enterprise, diminishing intensive food gathering and fishing, instituting compulsory cultivation, new crops and a new agricultural calendar, and destroying the complex balance of traditional fallowing systems. The need for cash for the head tax, other taxes, fines, bridewealth and European goods imposed the use of money and drove people to sell agricultural products and earn wages. Low minimum prices were never exceeded by monopoly buyers (Jewsiewicki 1983: 112–15), however, and pay was so low it could easily be exceeded by gathering and selling wild products (Buell 1928: 544). The miserably low wages of today had their precedent in the colonial period, but the colonial administrative apparatus was more ruthlessly effective in compelling people to work.

Nevertheless, labour supply on a sufficient scale to meet the needs of the mines, railway construction and plantations was a continuing problem. The administration was increasingly involved in the recruiting process, which often included the use of force or was done under false pretences: eventually controls were imposed on forced recruitment (*ibid.*: 503–7; 546–50). Labour was undertaken under contract and desertion brought fines or imprisonment. The result of combining labour contract and compulsory labour or forced recruiting, however, resulted inevitably in abuses and what frequently amounted to involuntary servitude. Desertion among Katanga's mine and railway workers amounted to 13.78 per cent before 1924 and to 15 or 20 per cent in other areas. In the South African mines it was only 2 per cent indicating a lower degree of compulsion (*ibid.*: 553–4). During the 1930s, the big companies, such as Union Minière, sought to stabilize their workforce by providing health care, housing, education and training by discipline and regimentation. The gap between stabilized labour and non-permanent auxiliary workers was maintained by differences in salary, clothing and housing. Infant mortality in the Union Minière fields dropped from 315 per thousand in 1929, to 58 by 1955, whereas the high rates characteristic of the majority, who lacked the medical facilities provided for company workers, did not change (Vellut 1983: 153–6).

In 1917, forced labour took another form with the introduction of compulsory cultivation of cotton and food crops, such as manioc, sweet potatoes, rice and corn, to provide food for mine and industrial workers. These crops were sold at fixed and not world market prices (Gann and Duignan 1979:130, 204). The success of this effort is evident in the fact that although most colonies in their early years imported more than they exported, the reverse occurred in the Belgian Congo: until the end of the 1920s exports exceeded imports in value (*ibid.*: 138). Compulsory cultivation was instituted primarily for fiscal reasons but it also integrated subsistence producers into the capitalist economy. Referred to as 'travaux obligatoires à titre educatif', it was designed to promote development by changing the mentality of the rural masses and organizing them into productive labour (Mulamba 1974: 4–5, 55–7). The population was liable to sixty days of compulsory cultivation a year until 1955, and for forty-five until 1960, a regulation enforced up to 1957 (Young 1965: 11).

At first the colonial state did not suppress traditional commercial structures. Customary chiefs, acting as intermediaries, were the principal beneficiaries, but rural producers realized enough of the commercialized surplus to pay for more than their taxes. When prices were favourable in regions near to transport, rural producers increased production of export crops, to the point that they were able to buy food instead of growing it. This situation did not last: the colonial administration opposed the liberalization of commerce, seeing the development of an autonomous economic base as a threat to authority (Bézy *et al.*, 1981: 16–18). In 1919 the Commission for the Protection of Natives advocated native agriculture as a means of combating depopulation; some European businessmen saw it as a means of increasing buying capacity. The government, however, wanted the production of export crops, except cotton, to remain with European plantations (Buell 1928: 522). 'A policy of free trade inside the colony would have provided an economic base for many social groups and for links between them (i.e., African peasants and petty African traders), and made the political control of them more difficult' (Peemans 1986: 70). A situation favouring some petty producers was not to arise again until after independence and the collapse of the state apparatus.

As the administration gave priority to labour recruitment, the control of petty trade and holding down producer prices to prevent attractive alternatives to entering the labour market, the role of chiefs became increasingly that of intermediaries in labour recruitment. The administration extended its control by the appointment of *chefs medaillés*; the *chefferie* became the instrument for mobilization of economic surplus through the increase of compulsory cultivation. For petty producers the production of commercial crops became an obligation; any tendencies towards the development of a market economy were suppressed (Bézy *et al.*, 1981: 21–32).

With the expansion of compulsory cultivation in the thirties the state came to exercise direct control over much African village production and thus fully controlled African labour. After 1930, the Depression changed the economy: Belgian industrial investment was reduced, workers returned to their villages and mineral exports dropped. The agricultural market for rural African products disappeared. A more centralized administration than had hitherto existed was made possible by an influx of Belgian capital, an increase in the number of civil servants and the reform of the army. By 1934–5 European companies monopolized processing and marketing to guarantee cotton, rice and palm kernel supplies to the factories, and increased road construction after 1935 brought rural communities into closer contact with markets (Jewsiewicki 1983: 101–15). The Congo survived the world depression because it increased its agricultural exports: they rose by over 60 per cent between 1930 and 1935, while the value of mineral exports remained stagnant (Peemans 1975a: 186). African producers, however, were restricted to the production of agricultural products at fixed prices, while foreigners had an effective monopoly of the industrial processing of these products, thus profiting from the added value. Thus African agriculture deteriorated relative to that of foreign settlers (*ibid.*: 190).

To sum up, the characteristics of the colonial system in the period 1920–40 had powerful long-term consequences. The privileged relationship between the state and the big companies, by which the state extended the structure of centralized control, constrained the development and nature of local initiatives. Public resources became increasingly dependent on a few activities, particularly mining. Other resources were essentially extracted from rural areas that were in reach of the formidable apparatus of the colonial state. The stultifying effect on the rural economy of the dependence of production on state control was manifested after independence, when the apparatus of this control disintegrated (Bézy *et al.*, 1981: 35; Peemans 1986: 71). Despite such a conclusion on the overall economic legacy of colonialism, however, it should also be noted that concern for the welfare and development of the local population was sincerely furthered by some high-minded administrators and particular state policies (Malengreau 1950).

In the period 1940–45, World War II caused a mobilization of the economy to satisfy the need in Europe and the United States for raw materials. During the war the number of days of compulsory cultivation was increased to 120 a year (Jewsiewicki 1983:123). Almost all the rural areas were encompassed in this authoritarian system and agricultural exports contributed a growing share of total exports (Peemans 1986:71). The acreage under cotton cultivation increased from 70,000 hectares in 1933 to 375,000 in 1944. From 1939–44 obligatory palm cultivation increased from 18,000 hectares to 35,000 hectares, rice from 50,000 to 132,000, manioc from 157,000 to 340,000. The enormous demand for labour increased the number of wage workers from 489,000 in 1938 to almost 800,000 in 1945. The powerful social tensions this expansion produced was manifested in strikes and mutinies in 1944–5 (Bézy *et al.*, 1981: 36).

The post-war years till 1955 were favourable for a growth in exports led by the mining sector. This expansion increased public revenues and spending and stimulated the expansion of the service sector, of employment and of internal demand. Some import substitution industry was started and some redistribution in welfare policies initiated, but they were dependent on the demand and prices of raw materials in the world market and primarily benefited white collar and privileged industrial workers. Nothing changed the stagnation of African agriculture, in which 90 per cent of the population engaged. Increase in marketed agricultural output in these post-war years was mainly from small enterprises owned by European settlers. They became the main outlet for wage labour in the 1950s. No base existed for an African rural petty capitalism or peasant agriculture, since the peasants were insulated from market mechanisms. 'Capital accumulation had no roots and no endogenous dynamism among the African rural world. It rested entirely upon the colonial state power and the support it gave to settler agriculture and agroindustrial companies' (Peemans 1986: 72).

Deep structural tensions underlaid this prosperity of the fifties following the economic expansion of the war period. The new development policy by the enlightened wing of the colonial administration aimed to eradicate the harsher measures for mobilizing manpower and to stabilize the system over the long term by promoting the development of an African middle class. The financial houses saw long-term security for their investments in such developments, but settlers in the rural areas opposed measures to improve the lot of petty producers, fearing loss of manpower and an increase of competition (Peemans 1980: 265–8). The expansion of the internal market from the development of an African middle class was essentially an urban phenomenon; migration to towns increased, rural areas stagnated and the agrarian crisis deepened. The colonial economy did not have a solid internal base; it was essentially an export economy, subject to the uncertainties of the international market for primary products. The increase in agricultural production between 1930 and 1960 was due to enforced expansion of acreage under cultivation, but the decreasing fallow periods and overpopulation were exhausting the soil. The roots of the post-colonial agricultural crisis can thus be found in colonial agricultural policy since 1920 (Bézy *et al.*, 1981: 42–3).

The growth of the African elite that comprised the incipient middle class had long been held back by Belgian policies, which resulted in serious deficiencies for the management of the country after independence.

## The African elite

The African elite of the colonial period lacked education, administrative experience and management skills. The education available to them was poor, they could not rise above the level of clerk in the colonial bureaucracy and they were excluded from large-scale business and commerce.

The Belgian Congo had one of the highest literacy rates in Africa, but, although primary education was widespread, secondary education was minimal. Until 1954 almost all education was in the hands of the missions. The aim of primary education was to train a child for regular work in agriculture and other pursuits considered suitable for the native, and to instil the precepts and values basic to the maintenance of the colonial order. Primary schools were the key agents in the socialization process for agricultural work and wage labour. The majority of children did not advance far in the educational system; having learned to read and write in African languages and having absorbed the values of the colonizers, they were returned to their rural villages of origin to transmit these values. Only a few completed six years of schooling, which included vocational training to be agricultural or medical assistants, teachers or clerks; only these few were permitted to learn French, the language for social advancement in the colonial order (Mudimbe 1981: 372–3). By limiting education to elementary and professional schools, by promoting civic and moral behaviour through work, discipline and healthy leisure activites and by training women in household tasks to foster family life, the colonizers sought to get higher productivity from their workers (Peemans 1980: 263).

The Belgians, unlike the British and French colonialists, had been slow to train an African elite capable of participating in administration and government: the civil service had only just begun to Africanize before independence. In the thirties a centre to train medical assistants and agronomists was formed at Kisantu in Lower Zaire, affiliated with the University of Louvain; not until 1947 was administrative and commercial training added. By 1958 a total of 184 students had completed the programme (Lacroix 1972: 22–32). Not until 1948 was secondary education outside seminaries introduced, and most of it was geared to vocational training for teachers, clerks and technicians. For the select few who were admitted to the six-year academic programme, conformity rather than brilliance was the criterion for advancement. Only in 1954 was secondary education under secular authorities, based on the Belgian system, introduced. The University of Lovanium in Kinshasa did not open until that same year, followed in 1956 by another in Lubumbashi (Elisabethville). It was, however, very difficult for the products of the colonial school system to pass the university entrance requirements; most gave up and found the low-level jobs for which their education had prepared them (Mudimbe 1981: 373–7).

Thus on the eve of independence in 1959, African school attendance totalled 1,502,588 in primary schools, but only 13,583 in secondary schools and higher education, and 17,142 in technical and agricultural schools (Young 1965: 200). There were 749 Congolese university students (Lacroix 1972: 106), but only 20 Congolese held degrees and 445 post-secondary professional training (Mudimbe 1981: 379; Young 1965: 200). Thus at independence in 1960, Zaire suffered from a gross lack of qualified and experienced personnel for government, administration, management and the professions. This situation was directly attributable to Belgian policy which created an efficient colonial administration to ensure a well-run system to serve Belgian interests, but which blocked access to administrative responsibility for Africans, to prevent interference in the organization of these interests.

The Belgians also frustrated African participation and management experience in the economy by constraining the development of indigenous enterprise on any scale in various ways. It was very difficult for Africans to obtain credit because they could not own land under individual tenure, a necessary collateral for loans. By 1959, the *Société de Crédit aux Classes Moyennes*, a government loan association for small- and medium-scale enterprises, had given only 118 out of 2,493 loans to Africans, 0.5 per cent of the total value of loans (Kannyo 1979: 100). Few opportunities existed for capital accumulation: rural producers suffered from taxation, expropriation of land for plantations and mining, and forced labour to produce food for the army and the labour force; prices for agricultural products were fixed at low rates and wages were very low. African farmers were forced into non-profitable sectors, whereas white settlers cultivated export crops; on the eve of independence 95 per cent of palm oil production, 87 per cent of coffee, 90 per cent of rubber, 97 per cent of tea, 35 per cent of tobacco and 99 per cent of cocoa, were European owned (Mukenge 1974: 137).

A major barrier to the development of African business in the colonial period and after independence was competition from foreigners, mostly

Greeks and Portuguese, who had their own close networks of business connections and mutual assistance. Since Africans lacked the legal status to deal with banks and European export firms, foreigners dominated the wholesale and import trade. African-owned retail businesses run by men did flourish in African urban areas of Kinshasa, however, where Europeans were forbidden to do business. For years these businesses evaded taxation but in 1954 the government discovered this evasion and ruined many of them by retroactive taxation (*ibid.*: 468). But a trading class began to emerge at the end of the colonial period. A 1956 survey of Leopoldville (now Kinshasa) found 7,000 self-employed, though only a handful had accumulated substantial wealth (Young 1965: 201).

The African elite of the colonial period was thus not based in the economy. It was primarily a bureaucratic elite comprised of those who worked as clerks in the Belgian administration and in the low levels of parastatal and private companies. Access to this elite was through education. In the early years of the colonial era it was primarily the sons of those who attached themselves to the Belgians, such as soldiers, domestics and mission workers, who were able to get primary education. These primary graduates found clerical jobs in the administration or the big companies and became urban dwellers. The children of the urbanized were advantaged in entering the universities since secondary schools preparing for university entrance were located in towns and it was extremely difficult to enter them from village primary schools (Young 1965: 196). Certain ethnic groups were favoured in establishing such advantages; their privileged incorporation into the urban economy laid the foundations of later ethnic conflict.

In some parts of the country the colonial elite also included some traditional office holders, but this was not the case in Kisangani because the population of the city was largely drawn from the surrounding forest peoples who lacked highly structured political systems. There was no equivalent in the Belgian Congo of the emphasis in the British system on educating chiefs' sons, nor did chiefs prosper. The rural customary chiefs in Congo local government were poor in comparison to the urban elite and their children were disadvantaged in getting into urban schools (*ibid.*: 185–95).

The educated class were known as the *evolués*; they were considered to have evolved socially and economically beyond the level of the masses. They consisted of clerks, agronomists, nurses and teachers, priests, university students and wealthy entrepreneurs (Nzongola 1982: 65). The lifestyle of this educated class was urban and distinctively different from that of rural dwellers and the uneducated: marriages tended towards the Western pattern, residence and friendship patterns crossed ethnic lines, membership in *evolué* association, such as alumnae associations, was common, and work relations were contractual and impersonal. The *evolué* wanted a status distinct from the general population and closer relations with Europeans, and bitterly resented the failure of Belgians, despite their promises, to accord him different treatment from other Africans. After World War II Belgian attitudes began to change and Africans who were literate, did not practise polygyny and were not convicted of certain offences could apply for a *Carte de Mérite Civique*, which, after humiliating investigation, conferred a separate legal status and the right to be subjected to European rather than customary courts and rights to property. But as integration still remained only partial, these *'immatriculés'* became increasingly disillusioned and, from 1956 on, participated intensively in nationalist politics. The first proposal for radical political change came from a European, but the second came from an *evolué* group in the *Conscience Africaine* manifesto, followed by the ABAKO counter manifesto asserting the need for political action. Thereafter independence came with a rush, hastened by the failure of the Belgians to fulfil *evolué* aspirations (Anstey 1970; Young 1965: 75–87).

At independence control and ownership of the economy remained in the hands of the big foreign mining and plantation companies and transfer of political authority resulted in the divorce of economic and political structures: 'From its bureaucratic genesis, the elite had derived one real vested interest: the state' (Young 1965: 203).

## The local level: colonial Kisangani

The history of Kisangani in the colonial period shows the early development of the present pattern of the city's exploitation of its hinterland and its character as a centre for transit and distribution, rather than production. Arab caravans probably came to the area in 1879 in search of ivory and slaves (Bontinck 1979: 24). In 1983 Stanley arrived to found a station for the Free State and in 1884 the Arabs established a permanent settlement under Tippo Tipp (*ibid.*: 28–9). The site of this early settlement was strategically important because river transportation was interrupted by rapids, later known as Stanley Falls. Stanley's trading post and military camp later grew into the city of Stanleyville, situated on both banks of the river just below the Falls. It was at first the frontier between the Arab and Belgian spheres of interest but war broke out for control of the ivory trade in 1896 and continued until the defeat of the Arabs in 1897 (Jewsiewicki 1978: 6–8). The legacy of this period of history is the *Arabisé* Islamic community in Kisangani, the Arab influence in the oldest buildings of the city along the river, and the Swahili language. Since Arab penetration Swahili has been a lingua franca in eastern Zaire; Kisangani is on the western boundary of its use. Lingala is generally used to the west of the city.

Stanleyville became important as a control point for transportation at which goods were transhipped from rail to river in 1903–6, with the construction of the railway up river to Ponthierville (now Ubundu). In 1913 the city became the administrative centre of the newly created

Oriental Province. Africans, however, with the exception of servants and soldiers, did not become part of the town until the Belgians established the *cités indigènes*, or African quarters, in 1920; by 1921 their population was about 6,000 (De Saint Moulin 1975: 33). The old colonial administration buildings and the villas in Makiso are relics of this period. The next few years saw the increasing importance of the province, and thus of the town. Agriculture (especially cotton) developed in the northern savannas and palm plantations in the forests. The exploitation of gold and tin reserves began, and a road network was constructed. The province became the biggest rice producer in the colony, the heaviest production coming from Stanleyville district. By 1930 rice and coffee were processed in the city; soap and soft drinks factories were in operation; and construction activity was intense, served by brick and tile factories and sawmills (Jewsiewicki 1978: 17–23).

The central role of the town, however, was as a centre for distribution of imported merchandise, for which the wholesale trade began to develop in the mid-1920s. The orientation of transportation towards the river route to the port of Matadi on the Atlantic estuary of the Zaire favoured domination and direct importing by the big Belgian wholesale houses. Kisangani became more important as an import than as an export centre. The commercialization and processing of agricultural products mostly bypassed the city. Cotton and palm oil from the north, for example, were exported via Aketi (see Map 3, p. 83). Far more goods were brought in than were sent out.

> This situation places Stanleyville in a favorable position in the chain of colonial exploitation of the interior. Being the principal importer of the region the town drains the money acquired by the Africans of the interior through the sale of their labor or its products. But the huge profits realised by the firms of the town benefit it only a little. It is itself the victim of the colonial economy. Almost all profits are transferred to Europe since processing industries exist only in an embryonic state. (*Ibid.*: 25)

In these early years, therefore, Kisangani played a typical part in the colonial economy as a transit and distribution centre. Foreigners primarily benefited from its opportunities for making money. African manufacturing or industry could not develop in the city because Africans were denied individual title to land; at this time no possibility existed for the rise of an African bourgeoisie.

In 1931, howeyer, an African urban population began to stabilize with the creation of the *centres extra coutumiers* (CEC), when the *cités* were changed to semi-autonomous urban units administered by Africans together with a European official. Ten years' residence, or birth in town, brought the status of permanent city resident (Pons 1969: 35–6). As a result African consumption, urban African society and African economic activities began to develop the town (Jewsiewicki 1978: 31).

The early fifties were the city's economic high point. The economic development in the province and the growth of cotton cultivation put money in the hands of Africans and attracted merchants. Wages doubled between 1949 and 1959, helping to stimulate commerce (*ibid.*: 41). Some consumption industries were established by Europeans in the 1950s: two breweries, an oil mill (now closed), two manioc mills, factories for cement, cigarettes (both closed after the rebellion of 1964 and never reopened), mineral water, cosmetics, paint and varnish; construction industry; metalworks and a printing works. In 1955 a hydro-electric power station was built on the falls of the Tshopo River on the north side of the city.

African commerce started to develop after World War II: in 1949 there were forty-five African firms (4 per cent of the total); by 1956 there were 1,972 (over 50 percent) (*ibid.*: 38). These firms were almost entirely engaged in the retail consumer trade; wholesale, semi-wholesale and large stores, however; were all foreign owned. Africans also began to enter the transport trade at this time.

This favourable state of affairs did not last, however. Cotton cultivation stagnated, the price of tropical products dropped and provoked a retreat in European commerce; credit difficulties reduced the size of African operations. Under the Belgians the town was essentially a transit and redistribution centre. The poverty of its population and that of surrounding rural areas did not attract industries of transformation for local consumption, nor did it supply a market for local agricultural production (*ibid.*: 44).

In the colonial period, therefore, despite a short period of improvement in the fifties, few opportunities existed for Africans to benefit from the commercial opportunities of the city or from the rich resources of its hinterland. Its main economic function was to drain natural resources for the profit of the metropolitan economy; only after independence was this situation to change.

THE YEARS SINCE INDEPENDENCE

> The capitalist West's role has been malevolent and destructive in destroying indigenous African economy and culture, replacing them with a foreign-oriented economy and oppressive class structure, and installing a colonial— and later supporting a neo-colonial—state with an oppressive administrative apparatus reflecting foreign orientation and interest. (D. Gould 1978: 10)

Zaire's colonial legacy included the policy of concentrating on the development of non-agricultural resources rather than on the development of a rural base for accumulation, and a gross lack of preparation of personnel to manage the affairs of state. The first meant that the new state lost control of an essential element in the development of autonomy from metropolitan power; the second resulted in weakening the administrative capacity of the state (Bézy *et al.*, 1981: 46–7). Both were to have far-reaching consequences.

## The post-colonial state

Independence in 1960 brought the disintegration of the institutional basis of the state. The army mutinied; Katanga, the richest province, seceded; the country was swept by rebellions. Before a year had passed, most trained personnel had abruptly left: by January 1961, 10,000 Belgian administrators and 5,000 teachers were reduced respectively to 2,668 and 308 (Malula 1980: 170).

Rapid decentralization of the state took place in the first five years after independence in the patrimonial politics of the First Republic: the number of provinces was increased from six to twenty-one in 1962; government was dominated by a number of leaders with their own military forces; and intense competition for public office brought an expansion of government personnel (Willame 1972: 27–30). State expenditure on this expanding bureaucracy increased steeply, but, at the same time, revenue decreased because the state was incapable of collecting its taxes and because mining and mineral production dropped 24 per cent and commercial agriculture 40 per cent between 1959 and 1966–7 (Bézy *et al.*, 1981: 204). Settler agriculture ceased almost completely in this period and agricultural exports were reduced by two thirds between 1960 and 1965. An important feature of the period, however, was the increased trade in foodcrops in the hinterland, supplying large cities; the share of trade in the GNP climbed from 9 to 13 per cent. In most areas, however, marketed agricultural output disappeared almost completely, as the share of agriculture in the GNP dropped from 22 to 8 per cent (Peemans 1986: 73).

This period ended with the rebellions of 1964–5 and the coup in which Mobutu took over as head of state in 1965. He recentralized the government, assuming the power to appoint and dismiss its members and to legislate by decree. He reduced the number of provinces to eight in 1966, dissolved parliament, abolished the independent judiciary and founded the single party of the MPR (*Mouvement Populaire de la Révolution*) in 1967. Provincial offices became purely administrative; to prevent the build-up of ethnic and personal power bases, officials were appointed to regions other than their own and were directly accountable to the president. In 1969, following student unrest, the JMPR, the youth wing of the party, was put in charge of all student activities. By 1970 the party and the state were fused (Schatzberg 1980a: 100–1), their organization consisting of the Political Bureau, Congress, the Legislative Council (of Peoples' Commissioners), the Executive Council (of twenty-five state commissioners appointed by the president), and the Judicial Council.[3] Administrative reforms in 1972 and 1973 further centralized authority and diminished local and regional autonomy (see Schatzberg 1982).

The first five years of the new regime saw an increase in the role of the state in the economy and some economic growth. In 1966–7 the state took over Union Minière, the giant Belgian coppermining company, turning it into a 100 per cent state-owned corporation, GECAMINES, although management and marketing were left to the Belgian company, SOGEMIN (for details of the long-term costs to Zaire, see Young and Turner 1985: 288–96). The devaluation of 1967, to restore the parity between the official and the black market rate of the Congolese franc, increased the profits of the big commercial and export companies and the state's indirect tax revenues, which doubled between 1964 and 1970. Real wages dropped by 20 per cent as a result of this devaluation. Rising discontent and increased copper prices led to salary increases in the private sector and for high officials in the public sector, which in turn stimulated the manufacturing industry to an increase of 40 per cent in 1967–8. The number of employees in the public sector continued to rise, increasing by 15 per cent between 1968 and 1972, but nevertheless public expenditure in goods and services increased in relation to salaries (Peemans 1975b: 515–17). The public, compared to the private, sector expanded its role in capital formation; investments, however, reflected the political and social preferences of the regime for prestigious, luxury or military expenditures, such as an ultra-modern radio and TV station, a satellite telecommunications system, the Inga dam and the Inga-Shaba power line, and the Maluku steel mill (for details of these last two fiascos, see Young and Turner 1985: 296–301). Agriculture was totally neglected.

After the takeover of ownership of Union Minière, the state participated systematically in the productive sector, increasing its economic base for negotiation with foreign capital; its operations increased from 23 per cent of the GDP in 1966 to 39 per cent in 1970 (Bézy *et al.*, 1981: 69). A new cooperative relationship arose: the state took over ownership of large enterprises but allocated management to a consortium or multinational. The 1969 Code of Investments liberalized the conditions for foreign investment, providing for tax exemptions and facilitating exports, as part of the new interdependence between the state and international financial capital. However, the new investments that resulted, among them the Goodyear tyre and SOTEXKI textile factories and cement and wood factories, made only a mediocre contribution to the national product: they were highly capitalized and therefore needed large outlays of foreign exchange for imported materials, as well as foreign experts, who then repatriated their incomes (*ibid.*: 97–9). After the fall of copper prices in 1974, dependence on external loans for financing investment and the increasing foreign debt indicated the involvement of the state in international financial capital (Peemans 1975b: 517–18).

The centralization of political power was accompanied by a concentration of economic revenues in the hands of the small and privileged circle surrounding the president and owing him personal allegiance, that had replaced administrators and specialized ministers in decision taking.

The post-independence dominant class initially lacked an economic base; it derived power from position in the state and alliance with the representatives of Western capitalism who retained ownership of the principal means of production. However, members of this class soon acted to establish an economic base. They used their position in the state to gain access to economic resources, although they did so in an 'essentially illicit or semi-licit manner in recognition of the politically illegitimate character of their conduct. This normative aspect sets definite limits on what the politico-administrative class can do with state power and partly explains their concern to establish an independent economic base outside, although in close relation to, the state' (Kannyo 1979: 15).

The use of the state to acquire an economic base for the new dominant class was an evident objective of the regime from 1966 on. In 1973 the Zairianization decrees were passed: the state took over big agro-industrial and commercial enterprises, and about 2,000 small- and medium-sized wholesale and retail businesses, small factories, plantations and farms belonging to foreigners were handed over to Zairians. Compensation was supposed to be paid at the rate of 10 per cent a year over ten years, but this measure was not enforced and often not carried out. The majority of new owners were politicians and administrators or their friends and relatives, the most powerful acquiring the most extensive holdings (for details see Young and Turner 1985: 326–50; Schatzberg 1980a:ch. 7; D. Gould 1979: 98–102). The consequences for the economy were disastrous: few of the new owners had serious business intentions, aptitude, managerial skills or experience; they spent revenue on personal consumption, sold what stocks they had and, in many cases, went bankrupt. To give one particularly outrageous example: a thriving and prosperous chicken farm in Lower Zaire was simply dismantled for the sake of its roofing iron. Laments about the lack of goods in the stores and the steep rise in prices were general. The new owners often failed also to pay their personnel, their taxes or their debts at the bank. Some Europeans sabotaged any possibility of orderly takeover by depriving their enterprises of viability before handing them over (Depelchin 1981: 34–5). The big wholesalers began to refuse to supply goods on credit. 'The acquirers soon became a hated category of people ... and there was a dramatic increase in class consciousness in the wake of the 30 November measures' (Schatzberg 1980b: 243). By 1974 commerce and agriculture were seriously disrupted and state revenues had declined drastically.

The strategy for the reconstruction of the state clearly envisaged the development of a public sector strong enough to serve the economic interests of the rising new class, but this strong state was hardly more than a superstructure of privilege, a place where political mechanisms concentrated natural resources. It did not change the structures of the unequal development and peripheral capitalism established in the colonial period; the economy continued increasingly to be dominated by the export of primary products, particularly minerals, and the agricultural surplus constantly declined (Peemans 1975b: 520–1).

This agricultural decline followed the weakening of state administration in 1960–5 and the relaxing of the colonial system of obligatory cultivation. Export agriculture, with the exception of coffee and fibres, was organized by the big companies, but they were heavily dependent on petty producers, who had supplied, for example, more than half the needs of the oil mills. There were great regional differences in this decline: food production benefited from the abandonment of export crops, especially cotton, in some areas; in others alternative markets for export crops developed through smuggling networks (Bézy *et al.*, 1981: 115–18, 155). Nevertheless, between 1958 and 1972 mining products increased from 33 per cent to 41 per cent of production, while agriculture declined from 40 per cent to 22 per cent (Peemans 1975b: 521). 'The regime, as authoritarian and repressive as it was especially in the rural areas, was unable to replicate the efficiency of the colonial state in using constraints for increasing the agricultural surplus, and to manage the centralised network of transport which ensured the evacuation of agricultural exports' (Peemans 1986: 77). The feelings of the population are well summed up in the words of a village chief:

> All the things that give us *mpashi* (trouble) are the things that the state used to look after. The state looked after the palm oil presses to make sure that they worked. The white men put things in the stores, and the state helped them so that things were always there. When the white men were here, we had medicines in the dispensaries. What is the problem with the state now anyway? Where is this independence that we have now? (Ewert 1977: 189)

## Economic crisis

The failure of Zairianization plunged Zaire into the economic crisis into which it has been spiralling ever since. The other major causes of this crisis were the 1974 drop in the price of copper and the tripling of world petroleum prices, the rise in price of industrial imports and the steady erosion of agricultural production caused by government policy. By 1972 imports of food were equivalent to 45 per cent of local production, instead of the 1 per cent they had been in 1958. The rebellions and the deterioration of roads and transportation had contributed to this situation, but a major cause was the indifference of the government (Peemans 1975b: 525). Between 1970 and 1978 agriculture received only 1 per cent to 3 per cent of current government expenditures, 2 per cent to 3 per cent of capital ones (Huybrechts and Van der Steen 1981: 277) and producer prices were ridiculously low.

This disastrous economic situation resulted in heavy pressure on the government to extend control over the economy. In January 1975, the president and the Political Bureau 'declared war on the national bourgeoisie'. They denounced the ten plagues they had themselves visited on the country, including greed, self-serving behaviour, inflation, and social injustice, and announced radicalization, or 'the revolution within the revolution'. The state took over all large-scale commercial, agricultural and industrial enterprises with a volume of business of one million zaires or more or of strategic national importance. It did not take over ranches or plantations, and multinational corporations established under the investment code of 1969 were not affected. Government officials were forbidden to engage in all commercial activity except agriculture and stock-raising (Lukombe 1979: 35–7). The president named about a hundred directors-general to head the state-owned enterprises but 'regrettably the choice was made not as a function of competence in management but rather on the simple consideration of whether the individual had once been a politician or had been, or still was, a friend of one' (*ibid.*: 39). Although officials were ordered to give back businesses held in their own names, their children over twenty-one could retain them or they could be held in the name of relatives; attempts to get officials and administrators to give up their Zairianized goods failed (Schatzberg 1980b: 248–9). 'The president symbolically rapped the knuckles of the new elite he had substantially encouraged 13 months earlier and yet expanded it' (D. Gould 1978: 31). In March 1975 the state took over about 120 primarily Belgian owned companies dating from the colonial period, principally textile mills, breweries, cigarette factories, cement works and construction firms. 'The upper layer of the state bourgeoisie had converted the January war on itself into a March preemptive strike against a formerly untouched sector of the economy' (Young and Turner 1985: 356). A few years later the bitter comment in Kisangani's daily paper on the government's failure to solve problems was that the political bureau had done nothing to remove the plagues it had denounced; 'to the contrary, several more have been added' (*Boyoma* 4 February 1980).

In an attempt to redress the continuing disastrous economic situation, the president announced the policy of retrocession in September 1976, in which businesses were to be returned to their former owners. Radicalized firms were to be retroceded entirely; mismanaged Zairianized ones were to be restored to their former foreign owners in a 40 per cent share with new Zairian partners (see Young and Turner 1985: 357–9). These partnership opportunities gave the political-administrative class yet another chance to increase their stake in the economy (D. Gould 1978: 33; Schatzberg 1980b: 257).

Zairianization and radicalization seriously disrupted the economy. The infrastructure deteriorated from neglect; marketing and credit with foreign suppliers were broken off; financial mismanagement was widespread; and production declined, most sharply in construction, mining and agriculture. In addition to these problems, imports were halved between 1974 and 1978, following the huge drop in copper prices from an average of US $1.20 per pound in 1967–74, to only 61 cents 1975–8. The results were lack of raw materials and spare parts for industry and manufacturing and of fertilizer and pesticides for agriculture; shortages of fuel, trucks and spare parts; gross scarcity of manufactured goods of all kinds; a drop in tax revenues on foreign trade, which had previously accounted for more than 60 per cent of government revenue; and difficulty in meeting external debt obligations incurred by heavy borrowing for the prestigious or politically expedient investments of 1970–3. Decreased confidence in Zaire resulted in the drying up of private sources of finance (World Bank 1980). In addition the Angolan civil war closed the Benguela railroad from 1975 on, making it difficult for Zaire to export the copper on which its economy is so dependent; and copper production was disrupted by the two Shaba wars of 1977 and 1978. The 'most significant bankruptcy, however, was in the eyes of its citizenry: the real degree of ascendency acquired in the ascendency and expansion phases eroded almost to the vanishing point' (Young and Turner 1985: 362).

By 1978 the crisis had resulted in an output about 17 per cent below the level of 1974, and imports 50 per cent below; a manufacturing sector operating at only 40 per cent of capacity; inflation of almost 100 per cent; and real wages and salaries at one quarter of their 1970 level (World Bank 1980: 111). By 1979 industry was working at only one-quarter to one-half capacity. In 1980 Zaire's foreign debt stood at over US \$5 billion. In addition, as Young and Turner point out, corruption constituted an enormous drain on public resources, to the amount of at least \$5 billion in the seventies (Young and Turner 1985: 401).

However, some people benefited from the crisis. Decreased supply and acute scarcity resulted in rampant speculation, which favoured those who controlled strategic points in the distribution network.[4] Thus agricultural production is not encouraged because imports allow opportunities for huge profits.[5] State monopolies of energy, transport, marketing and land ownership offer opportunities for embezzlement detrimental to the functioning of the system but bring immense potentialities for wealth for those in control (Rymenam 1980: 52). Attempts at reform that do not address the political basis of the problem are therefore doomed to failure; the five Mobutu Plans, 1976–83, to stabilize the economy with the help of extended credit from the IMF and teams of foreign experts, have had little effect (see Callaghy 1984: 198–200).

To conclude, the lack of development of the productive and manufacturing sector has meant that control of the economy by the state-based class has been vested much more in control of distribution and of imports than of production. In contrast, the emergent capitalism to be documented here is beginning to concentrate in production as much as in distribution.

## The absolutist regime and the new class structure

Mobutu's absolute power is backed by force and is primarily exercised through three structures: the single party, the MPR, which counts all

49

citizens as members; the Political Bureau, the chief organ of the party, composed of ministers of state, high civil servants and political commissioners; and the Office of the Presidency, which manages ministerial departments, state industries and public services directly. The other major institutions of government are the Executive, Legislative and Judicial Councils.

The MPR is more of a propaganda element of the state apparatus and less institutionalized and less a political machine than the parties of most African states (Callaghy 1984: 8). It pervades all institutions and sectors of Zairian life. Its main activities consist of marches, mass rallies and communal labour, *salongo*. This is, in essence, a direct continuation of the colonial policy of forced labour 'enveloped in a thick cloud of "revolutionary cant"'. Tasks organized under *salongo* include building and repairing roads and bridges, constructing and maintaining state buildings, the houses of officials and sometimes schools and hospitals, and cleaning streets, public areas and drainage canals. The lack of enthusiasm for these tasks reflects the population's perception that they consolidate the power of an increasingly unpopular regime (*ibid.*: 299–301).

The Presidency is the most powerful institution of the state and the principal instrument for carrying out the president's will. Security affairs and those of key economic importance (such as GECAMINES) are directly controlled by it (Young and Turner 1985: 167). The coercive agents of state control are the secret police, the gendarmerie and the army. The secret police (CND) brutally suppress any evidence of dissent, maintaining efficient and accurate information gathering networks (Schatzberg: forthcoming, ch. 3). Fear of their network of informers, the 'enemy within', greatly increases the suspicion amounting to paranoia that so tragically divides the population against itself; it decreases the chances of mounting any effective and organized opposition to the regime.

The gendarmerie and army are best described as occupying forces; their genesis in the brutal colonial *Force Publique* endowed them with the worst possible tradition. They are an ineffective instrument of the state's coercive power, because uncontrollable and of very limited capability (see Young and Turner 1985: ch. 9). The army performs poorly in any military confrontation, despite extensive foreign training programmes, and Mobutu always has to call upon external help. The security forces and the territorial administration also fail to collaborate effectively. Ordinary soldiers earn no more than unskilled workers; junior and non-commissioned officers have salaries equivalent to the middle levels of the civil service. But housing is poor and wages often not paid, especially in the interior, so the soldiers extort means for a living from the population (*ibid.*: 125–6). Callaghy and Schatzberg give appalling documentation of the abuses, brutality, armed robbery and pillage that they perpetrate (Callaghy 1984: 293–8; Schatzberg: forthcoming, ch. 4). In Kisangani in 1979–80 such incidents were frequent. The security forces are thus the basis of the state's control over civil society, but are at the same time a source of insecurity because they offer only the most tenuous obedience to civilian leadership; neither the commissioners nor the magistrates can effectively control them.

Callaghy describes Mobutu as a presidential monarch who has 'adapted a colonial state structure and patrimonialized it by creating an administrative monarchy which is used to recentralize power' (1984: 5). The patrimonial elements consist of the centralized authority of the president; the legitimation of his position and routinization of power by a mixture of charismatic, patrimonial and legal-rational doctrines; and his support by officials and administrators whose positions depend on their personal loyalty to him. Politics is highly personalized; the ruling class has developed out of the state, using state power to create an economic base, but not thereafter expanding production, and territorial administrators, the president's direct representatives, control all key groups of the society via the party (*ibid.*: 45–56).

Government institutions undergo frequent changes. In 1972, as part of the process of centralizing and personalizing power and fusing party and state, the Council of Ministers was replaced by the Executive Council subordinated to the Political Bureau. In 1974, the party school, the Makanda Kabobi Institute, was created and 'Mobutism' proclaimed the new official doctrine (*ibid.*: 172–3). In 1977, under pressure for electoral reform from the international aid donors, the members of the Legislative Council and eighteen of the thirty political commissioners were elected; the councillors of the urban zones,[6] instead of being appointed as previously by the Legislative Council, were also elected (see Van der Steen 1978; Young and Turner 1985: 204–7). The system was in addition democratized by the *Interpellations*, occasions on which peoples' commissioners could interrogate state commissioners. These hearings were shown on national television; they revealed some scandalous activities, which resulted in several prosecutions[7] in 1980, and aroused much public interest. Reaction was swift. In 1978 Mobutu had named six additional members to the Political Bureau so that the appointed equalled the elected members, but in 1980 he abolished elections of any of them, reserving their appointment to himself, and announced that any questions in the *Interpellations* must first receive his authorization. Constitutional reforms in the same year added a Central Committee to the organization of the party, an advisory body that eclipsed the Legislative Council; its 121 members are appointed by the president.

Some commentators on Zaire have adopted the perspective of dependency theory. They describe its problems in terms of unequal exchange, in which a political-administrative bourgeoisie assists the multinationals to transfer wealth to the industrialized countries, and hold the view that underdevelopment and dependency are self-perpetuating (Gran 1979; D. Gould 1977, 1978). Others see Zaire's dependence as primarily technological. In this view, the state-based class controls the economic activity of the country; foreign technical aid and military cooperation (and even intervention) give this class the means to maintain its power. Technological imperialism with the multinationals as its agents has replaced the direct exploitation of workers and resources of the colonial period, and local development is stifled (Verhaegen 1978, 1979, 1984). These assertions of the significance of foreign domination have been challenged on the grounds that they lack concrete documentation, that in certain regions in the colonial period there was some African agricultural capitalist development and that it is the class struggle within Zaire, rather than foreign influence, that will determine the course of the country's future development or underdevelopment (Vellut 1979). From this perspective, the cause of Zaire's failure is the 'project of self-aggrandisement' of the state-based class as it pursues its own narrow personal and class interests (Callaghy 1984: 56). This class has not served neo-colonial economic functions since 1975: 'It does not extract or produce effectively for monopoly capital' (Callaghy 1983: 79).[8]

The new dominant class in Zaire (as opposed to the subordinated class, in a model corresponding to Marx's division of society into 'bourgeoisie' and 'proletariat') is made up of several distinct sectors, or fractions, defined in terms of their position in the system of relations of production.[9] The state-based sector consists of three major categories. The first is the Presidential Clique, made up of members of the president's family and a few others. This clique comprises a few dozen persons at the head of the most important economic enterprises or in control of the political and military organization; their incompetence is general and they have unlimited possibility for corruption since their impunity is total and guaranteed. The second category is the Reigning Brotherhood, composed of favoured individuals from the president's ethnic group or region of Equateur and representatives of other regions and groups known to be politically loyal and docile. Numbering several hundred, they occupy almost all important administrative, political and economic positions. Periodic rotation in these positions is the rule; massive embezzlement is possible; impunity is not total but return to favour is rapid; entrance is marked by spectacular presents from the president, such as cars and houses. The members are surrounded by satellite cliques from their own ethnic groups. The third category is the Aspirant Bourgeoisie, including thousands of middle-level officials and administrators, university graduates and professors. Their access to sources of corruption is real but limited and they do not enjoy impunity (Rymenam 1977. See D. Gould 1979: 102–3; Callaghy 1984: 184–5).

Callaghy calls this state-based class the 'political aristocracy'. Loyalty to Mobutu is the ultimate requirement for entry and continued membership. Like an absolutist monarch Mobutu rules through this political nobility, his chosen patrimonial instruments, who engage in true court politics. This ruling group is not a 'bourgeoisie' in any true sense because it is not a productive social class; it is a political aristocracy because its basic values, its power, and its economic base result from its relationship to the state (Callaghy 1984: 184–5).[10]

Those with ultimate political and economic power rapidly became fabulously rich by siphoning off the state's revenues for their personal benefit. Several have acquired fortunes of over $200 million (Rymenam 1980: 48); Mobutu's uncle Litho got $35 million in just the eight months that Nguza Karl-i-Bond was prime minister (as reported on CBS TV, 4 March, 1984). The scale of this process of self-enrichment, as the Presidential Brotherhood pursue their 'relentless quest' for new mechanisms of capital export, has been amply documented (see Young 1983: 124–6; Blumenthal 1982). It is evident that repatriation of the overseas holdings of just a few of the Presidential Cluiqe would pay off the national debt. Mobutu himself is considered to be one of the richest men in the world. Young and Turner provide the details of his vast fortune and estimate that one-third of the national revenue is in some way at his disposal (Young and Turner 1985: 178–83).

This class sector does not control production, it merely levies a tithe on economic circuits through control of strategic points of economic distribution (Rymenam 1980: 51). Many of its members acquired productive holdings in Zairianization, on a sometimes enormous scale, but they had neither the inclination nor the competence to maintain and develop them. The arbitrary selection of those in authority and power and their general incompetence, as well as their corrupt practices, paralyses administration.

The political aristocracy is placed in the system of productive relations through its cooperation with, and ties to, Western capitalist interests, whose representatives form a sector of Zaire's dominant class. Since independence, the multinational companies have retained control or ownership under varying terms of the big mining and agro-industrial enterprises; they also own the majority of the larger wholesale houses distributing manufactured goods.

The foreign commercial class of wholesalers, retailers and plantation owners makes up another sector of the dominant class. Distinct in terms of its smaller-scale and individually owned, or partnered, enterprises, this class includes the remnants of the colonial settler and small business class.[11] It was displaced in the violent events following independence and in Zairianization; its numbers decreased and the assets of departing foreigners were taken up by nationals. Some of these foreigners returned and a significant number remain in various forms of partnership or rivalry with members of the political aristocracy or of the new indigenous commercial middle class.[12]

The emergence of an African middle class, the local bourgeoisie revealed in the data from Kisangani, is denied by some writers and its beginnings confirmed by others. J. L. Vellut mentions the existence of such a class in some areas, as cited above; Mukenge Tshilemalema found that a number of African merchants in African urban areas in the colonial period had accumulated a sizeable amount of capital (Mukenge 1974: 468); Elinor Sosne writes of the beginnings of an African planter class in Kivu at the end of the fifties (Sosne 1979: 193); M. Anselin found that the middle class in Elisabethville mostly engaged in distribution and had no influence on the economic development of the city (Anselin 1961: 108). This class does not, as yet, present any challenge to the political aristocracy for control of the state.

The petty bourgeoisie, or sub-bourgeoisie, consists of 'increasingly marginalized and frustrated' clerks, teachers, junior officers and non-coms in the armed forces, collectivity and locality chiefs (Young and Turner 1985: 122).[13]

We can follow previous analysis and divide the subordinate class into sectors also: the working class, of both urban and rural wage earners; the petty producers ('the peasantry'), cultivators of commercialized commodities tied to communally owned land; and the *lumpenproletariat*, the unemployed and those not integrated into capitalist production and distribution (Demunter 1972: 92–7; Nzongola 1970: 378–80; Comeliau 1965:90–8).

Only the political aristocracy has developed consciousness to the extent of sustained organization and action to promote its interests. It thus constitutes a 'class for itself'. Other classes, lacking such organization, are 'classes in themselves', but there are clear signs of developing consciousness and even the beginning of organization in some of these other class sectors. The Belgians restricted and controlled the development of trades unions and the Congo had very low rates of unionization compared to other African countries (Nzongola 1982: 74). During World War II, urban riots were set off by workers and soldiers protesting through strikes and mutinies. In 1941 Union Minière workers went on strike; in 1945 in Matadi striking dockworkers demonstrated; and in 1944 soldiers mutinied in Kananga (then Luluabourg) (Young 1965: 289). According to Jewsiewicki, since these strikes were not organized on an ethnic base, they indicate the growth of some class consciousness and organization for action among the working class. In 1946 strikes were banned. Development of class consciousness declined with the rise of ethnically based political parties in the anti-colonial struggle (Jewsiewicki 1976: 67–9). After independence there were three trades unions which in 1967 were merged into one, later to become UNTZA, which was financed by the state with the leadership essentially coopted. Mwabila's study of industrial workers in Lubumbashi in 1970 found very little class consciousness; allegiance was oriented towards the boss and feeble towards the trade union (Mwabila 1979: 9). LaFontaine points out that unions, at first hampered by the prohibition on strikes, found economic conditions and the high rate of unemployment made strike action ineffective because of the plentiful supply of alternative labour (LaFontaine 1970: 165). Strikes in Shaba and Kinshasa industries

1976–7, at the peak of the economic crisis, however, indicated a growing willingness of the workers to defy the regime and engage in class action to protect their interests (Kannyo 1979:198; Young and Turner 1985:131).

This outline of colonial and post-colonial events furnishes the context in which to investigate Kisangani's entrepreneurs. It shows that the particular kind of economy, the weak administrative capacity of the state and the nature of the dominant class that have developed since independence are determined by both historical and socio-economic factors: in part by Belgian policies for keeping Africans down by denying them educational opportunity or training and experience in government and management; in part by the colonial economic legacy, Zaire's place in the world economy and the effect of world recession; and in part by the boundless greed of those who took over the government after independence.

# 3

# Business and class in Kisangani

The central and very recent role played by the colonial state and foreign
capital affected the genesis of the African capitalist, and especially the
African industrial capitalist, to the extent that many observers have doubted
his very existence—until one day he is encountered, buying out an import
agency in Accra, establishing a factory in Nairobi, or owning a block of
apartments in London. (Leys 1982: 122)

A bustling commerce is immediately evident in Kisangani; the size, scale
and number of businesses, and the diversity of people arriving and
departing at the airport or by truck or river boat invite investigation.
Inquiry soon showed that representatives of the class sectors one would
expect to find in large-scale business do indeed tend to dominate in
particular areas: international capitalism is present in the big import-export
houses and the local branches of multinational companies; members
of the political aristocracy own large wholesale or agri-businesses or are
partners with foreigners in national level companies; and the foreign
commercial middle class, the majority of them Greeks and Asians,
specialize in a variety of businesses. Unexpectedly, however, a number of
nationals, both men and women, who do not hold political position and
who are relatively independent of politics, also own substantial enterprises: they are the beginnings of a local capitalist class investing in
productive as well as distributive enterprise. Much of what they produce is
for local consumption, and they manage their concerns in rational capitalist
fashion and plough back their profits into expansion.

This chapter will detail the kinds of businesses owned by representatives
of these different class sectors and describe the socio-economic context for
the emergence of indigenous capitalism, including the importance of ethnic
variables. The new class is taking on what is generally referred to as a
'middle class lifestyle', and is reproducing itself as a class by investing in
inheritable productive property and real estate and educating its children.
The next chapter will focus on the processes of its emergence.

Identifying substantial enterprises and their owners in the city was no
easy task. Because no comprehensive or reliable list of businesses existed I

56

compiled my own.[1] It included twenty-eight outlets of national and international wholesalers, with both foreign and Zairian owners; twenty-three firms owned by Zairian politicians and military officers; twenty-five Greek, twenty-four Asian, six Belgian, five Portuguese and a few other foreign-owned enterprises; and thirty-two businesses owned by nationals, both men and women, who were not political office holders. Thirty-two seems a relatively small number. (I subsequently found a few more individuals who could be added for whom I do not have precise information.) The number is substantial enough, however, if compared to the number in the other categories of the large-scale business owners of Kisangani just listed; it amounts to 22.3 per cent of the total.[2] Thus a significant percentage of the owners of substantial businesses in the city are entrepreneurs who do not hold state position and who are relatively independent of politics. One must say 'relatively', because to get anything done in Zaire it is necessary to have political connections of some sort.[3]

I also found another group of nationals, all Nande from Kivu, who did not hold political office and who all specialized in exporting vegetables from Kivu to Kinshasa, via Kisangani, where they had depots and wholesale outlets. With the exception of one man, they did not appear on any of the Kisangani lists I used. They all belonged to the Chamber of Commerce (ANEZA) in Butembo, a town in Kivu, and operated substantial concerns. But, though recognized as an important part of the town's commerce, they are a group apart in Kisangani; they will be discussed as a special case in Chapter 6.

THE BIG WHOLESALE HOUSES: MULTINATIONAL CAPITAL

The list of wholesalers in Kisangani I was given by the Town Hall numbered thirty-four. I subsequently found out that four of these firms had gone out of business and that the report sent in from the same office at the request of the central government for the budget gave their number as forty. The list I compiled also totalled forty; it is given in Table 3.1.

The multinational firms on this list and the majority of the big national ones, which are owned by foreigners, represent the Western capitalist interests that dominate the Zairian economy. Even though many of them were radicalized, as indicated, and subsequently with retrocession took on Zairian associates, they still primarily further the interests of Western rather than Zairian capitalism. They make little contribution to local development: their huge profits are sent overseas and their high capitalization results in a relatively small contribution to employment. Eight of them are local branches of multinationals. Details on a few indicate the difficulties that any local capitalism must face in the sectors dominated by the formidable size and resources of these enormous companies. As Bromley and Gerry have pointed out, goods produced by 'modern', capital-intensive technologies, not only have considerable cost, quality or

57

Table 3.1 *Wholesalers in Kisangani 1979–80*

| Firms | Goods sold | Owner |
|---|---|---|
| *Multinationals* | | |
| SEDEC* | textiles, general | Unilever |
| BATA* | shoes | British |
| TABAZAIRE* | cigarettes | Belgian etc. |
| BATZAIRE* | cigarettes | British American Tobacco |
| MARSAVCO* | household goods | Unilever |
| SAPRO | tools, general | subsidiary SEDEC |
| Phillips | electrical | Dutch |
| Goodyear | tyres | American |
| *National companies* | | |
| SGA (ex-Congo-Frigo)* | food, clothing | Zairian politician |
| Interfina* | general, alcohol | Belgian |
| Economat du Peuple* | food | Government |
| SOLBENA* | clothing, textiles, plastics | Jewish |
| Nogueira* | general, food | Portuguese |
| Hasson and Frère | clothing, textiles | Jewish |
| Alhardeff* | textiles, etc. | Lebanese American |
| Habib et Cie. | general | Lebanese |
| CHANIMAT* | electrical | Zairian |
| CODITEX | textiles, food | Zairian |
| Kreglinger | general | Zairian |
| Issia Frères | shoes, rice, palm oil | Zairian politician |
| Zaire Prestige* | general | Zairian politician |
| TRANSCOMPRO | used clothing, pans | Zairian |
| Ets. Tropical | general | Lebanese |
| Groupe UNICOM | general, soap, bakeries | Zairian and Asian |
| BELTEXCO | general, textiles | Asian |
| Mboliaka | general | Asian and Zairian |
| FAMACO | general | Asian and Zairian |
| GOLKO | general | Asian and Zairian |
| *Parastatal* | | |
| DCMP | pharmaceutical | |
| *Local firms* | | |
| Ibrahim Haji | general | |
| KINTRADING | clothing and cloth | |
| SOCOZAKI | general | Asian—some |
| SOCOAFRICA | general | with Zairian |
| Mundeke Kepo | general | partners |
| ALIMA | general | |
| SORAM | general | |
| MAMY | semi-wholesale | |
| Kazabel | textiles | |
| Tala Awa | general | Zairian |
| Mfaume | general | |

* = radicalized

performance advantages over local handicrafts, but they are backed by the media and the changing tastes and needs fostered by the change to the money economy. Not only is local enterprise subject to the competition of firms established on the spot, transport technology has exposed them to goods manufactured by the world's lowest cost producers and smuggled in, 'dumped' or sent by aid programmes (Bromley and Gerry 1979: 16).

SEDEC is the commercial branch of Unilever. Established in Zaire before 1920, it had taken over about 20 per cent of the distribution of imported products by independence. It now has branches in seven out of the country's nine regions. Its car division, the sole representative for General Motors, supplies 25–30 per cent of the Zairian market; the company is also the agent for Frigidaire and Electrolux (Willame 1980: 17). The multinational base and large-scale organization of this huge company enables it to dominate the expanding market among the new dominant class for appliances, electronic gadgets and other imported household goods.

TABAZAIRE is the largest cigarette manufacture in Zaire. It is a branch of the Belgian TABACOFINA which joined German, Dutch and English companies in Rembrandt Tobacco, a South African multinational, in 1972. It has done little for the local economy: it relies on imports of tobacco which, despite its tobacco farms in Shaba, doubled from 1965–74; it is also highly capitalized, employing only 1,000 workers. BATZAIRE, established in Zaire in 1951, is the second largest cigarette producer. It originated in a merger of the American Tobacco Company and British Imperial Tobacco in 1902 and is now the biggest cigarette manufacturer in the world. BATZAIRE imports both paper and tobacco; although it has cultivated tobacco in Kwango-Kwilu since 1966, it imports 40–60 per cent of its tobacco from the United States. Like TABAZAIRE, it is highly capitalized, employing only 469 workers in 1970 and 896 in 1978. From 1970–8 its profits tripled (*ibid*.: 25–8).

The BATA shoe company is Zaire's only large producer of shoes. This multinational originated in Czechoslovakia and is now based in Britain. It set up a factory in the early fifties which produced 4 million pairs of shoes in 1960 and 10 million in 1979, despite a slump after Zairianization. BATA completely dominates the shoe market. By 1972 it had seventeen wholesale depots, fifty-six branches and supplied 1,800 retailers. Unlike most multinational companies in Zaire, it is an industrial manufacturer, doing more for the economy than the others. It employs over 1,000 workers and in 1977 set up its own training programme for African personnel (*ibid*.: 30). In Kisangani, in addition to BATA's own branch, there are two retailers and one wholesaler for BATA products.

The largest industry in Kisangani is SOTEXKI, the textile factory started in 1973 and employing 1,501, including forty-three expatriates. It is a multinational, 60 per cent owned by the French company Beaujolin, financed by loans from Chase Manhattan Bank, German, French and Belgian institutions, and managed by a Swiss firm (*ibid*.: 53–4). It is highly mechanized and capitalized, and was established under conditions that ensured the return of its investment in two years.

In addition to multinationals, twenty wholesalers are branches of big national companies or of local ones that have branches elsewhere as well. Table 3.1 shows that, like the multinationals, these companies are mostly foreign owned, but seven of them belong to nationals, including three politicians.

## POLITICIANS AND MILITARY OFFICERS: THE POLITICAL ARISTOCRACY

Position in the political order enabled the politicians and high-ranking military officers in business in Kisangani to take over extensive holdings, especially in commercial agriculture. Table 3.2 gives an alphabetical list of twenty-three politicians and army generals who have businesses, or branches of their businesses, in Kisangani. This list is probably not

Table 3.2 *Politicians and military officers with businesses in Kisangani*

| Name and office | Business | Ethnic group |
|---|---|---|
| 1. Ali Idi Kunda Kisaka People's Commissioner Kisangani | Café Boyoma | *Arabisé* |
| 2. Badjoko wa Lileka Former provincial minister | PLANTARU: agro-industry, coffee, transport | Mungala |
| 3. Bambule ma Zambale People's Commissioner Aketi | PLANCOM: coffee plantations and export | ? |
| 4. Bangala Basila People's Commissioner Tshopo | Ets. BABAS: coffee plantation, coffee mill, commerce | Lokele |
| 5. Bondjala Maingolo People's Commissioner Tshopo | rice and rice mills, coffee plantations, rubber, butcher shop | Topoke |
| 6. Bosongo wa Bosongo People's Commissioner Tshopo | Ets. BOLINGA: transport, commerce, coffee plantations | Lokele |
| 7. Derikoye Tita Avungara People's Commissioner Ango | Ets. Derikoye: import/export, commerce, coffee plantations, retail store | Azande |
| 8. Diomi Ndongala Political Commissioner Kinshasa | Diomi Import | Kongo |
| 9. Djona Mbitima People's Commissioner Lower Uele | DJONAGRI: coffee plantations and export, ranches, commerce | Mungbetu |

60

Tabel 3.2 *(Contd.)*

| Name and office | Business | Ethnic group |
|---|---|---|
| 10. Duga Kugbe Toro<br>People's Commissioner<br>Kisangani | COMPRODUITS:<br>commerce, coffee<br>plantations | Mungbande |
| 11. Issia Amundala<br>People's Commissioner<br>Tshopo | St Issia Frères<br>(shoes), coffee planta-<br>tions, cocoa | Musoko |
| 12. Kirongozi wa Kanyonyo<br>People's Commissioner<br>Kisangani | Ets. KIWAKA:<br>(hardware), coffee<br>plantations | Mobali |
| 13. Kisombe Kiaku Muisi<br>Political Commissioner<br>Kinshasa | ZAIRE PRESTIGE:<br>coffee buyer | Kongo |
| 14. Kithima bin Ramazani<br>Political Commissioner<br>Kivu | EXCAVEZA:<br>coffee exporter, rubber<br>and coffee plantations | *Arabisé* |
| 15. Lengema Dulia<br>People's Commissioner<br>Kisangani | CRISTALEAU (soda),<br>butcher shop, coffee<br>plantations, rubber,<br>palm and cocoa | Lokele/Topoke |
| 16. Losembe Batwanyele<br>Former Minister of<br>Education (1969–70) | PEMESA (fishery),<br>coffee and palm<br>plantations | mulatto |
| 17. Nendaka Bika<br>Political Commissioner<br>Upper Zaire | PLANKUMU (coffee),<br>fishery, forestry,<br>manufacturing, etc. | Mubua |
| 18. Utway Mungamba<br>People's Commissioner<br>Tshopo | coffee, rubber, palm<br>plantations | ? |
| 19. Yambuya Bandombele<br>People's Commissioner<br>Kisangani | Ets. Yambuya (furniture),<br>commerce, ranch, mills,<br>plantations: coffee, palm | Lokele |
| 20. Zamundu Agenong'ka<br>Political Commissioner<br>Upper Zaire | OTMABER (fishery),<br>coffee and palm<br>plantations | Topoke (adopted) |
| *Military officers* | | |
| 21. Gen. Bangala Otto wa<br>Nyama | TRANSCO-SOCOPLA<br>(runs airport restaurant),<br>coffee plantations | Lokele |
| 22. Gen. Singa | casinos, coffee plantations | Luba |
| 23. Gen. Tshinyama | Ets. Les Tshinyama<br>(vegetables) coffee plantations | Luba |

*Sources:* Van der Steen 1978; *Boyoma;* informants and observation; list of plantation owners of Upper Zaire, Agricultural Division, Administration de Territoire.

exhaustive and the number of businesses given for each one is only partial but it gives some idea of the vast scale of the economic holdings this class sector has acquired. None of these individuals are women, because very few hold political position in Zaire.

Politicians and military officers are heavily involved in commercial agriculture, in particular in coffee. Twenty-one of the twenty-three in Table 3.2 have coffee plantations or are coffee buyers; eleven of these have rubber, palm or cocoa plantations as well, or commercialize rice or vegetables or own cattle ranches. Twelve have commercial enterprises of some sort, including wholesale shoes, butcher and hardware stores and import/export businesses. Other businesses are in manufacturing, such as furniture and a soda factory. Three own commercial fisheries on Lake Mobutu with wholesale depots in Kisangani; two have transport businesses and others own hotels, restaurants or casinos.

These men have largely used the power, influence and connections of their official positions to take over business enterprise on a vast scale. Official lists of plantations show the extensive coffee, rubber, palm and cocoa plantations Zairianized or taken up after foreigners abandoned them in the troubles following independence. Control of the state apparatus has since enabled members of this class sector to manipulate legislation in their favour and gain access to scarce resources; details of these activities appear in Chapters 5 and 8. The multiplicity and scale of their enterprises are illustrated by details on the holdings of a few of them:

No. 15, Peoples' Commissioner Lengema, acquired large holdings in Zairianization, including CRISTALEAU (the city's soda factory), a butcher business and plantations comprising 911 hectares of coffee, 150 of rubber, 15 of palm and 25 of cocoa. He is involved in management or ownership of over ten companies, owns a hotel and is a large owner of real estate (according to a well-placed source in the Land Title office).

No. 2's company, PLANTARU, consists of agro-industrial and transport enterprises, furniture-manufacturing and a garage. Badjoko wa Lileka was a provincial minister and acquired a large number of plantations in Zairianization in Upper Zaire; official lists show that he took over a total of around 3,000 hectares of coffee, 1,167 of rubber, 227 of palm and 100 of cocoa. He employs up to 2,000 nationals and 22 expatriates. His two transportation companies have 40–5 trucks and a 1,200-ton barge. He also owns real estate in the city on a large scale.

No. 17, Nendaka Bika, Political Commissioner for Upper Zaire, who founded and headed the secret police 1960–4 and held several ministerial posts thereafter, is one of the largest business owners and wealthiest men in Zaire. In 1979 he held a champagne breakfast at Zaire's principal hotel to celebrate his tenth billion in Belgian francs (at that time the equivalent of about three billion dollars). Two-thirds of his holdings are in Upper Zaire. His *Groupe Nendaka* consists of fifteen companies. They include industrial fisheries, sawmills and forestry concessions, engineering companies, land and river transport and agri-business, retail stores, a paint factory and hotels. He Zairianized over 2,000 hectares of coffee and 1,000 of palm plantations. He employs as many as 3,000 nationals and 15 expatriates.

The power of the new dominant class after independence came from political position, not from a base in the economy. The details given here show the extent to which some members of this class have used political power to move into the economy. In 1965 a survery of those holding key political positions in the country, showed that the majority (95 per cent) had previously been bureaucrats and that few of them had outside occupations that allowed reinvestment of the profits accumulated in their political careers. Many sat on the boards of foreign companies and had opportunities to be involved in commercial enterprise. 'Yet those who do so never develop their enterprises to a profitable degree' and small plantations and land managed by relatives are 'never organized as a profit-making venture in the capitalist manner' (Willame 1972: 172–3).

Now that this class has taken over much of the economy, these comments still apply. Zaire's abysmal economic performance attests to the mismanagement of businesses, plantations and factories by their new owners. From 1974 onwards, the government's regional economic reports were full of statements on the bad effect on the local economy of the neglect of plantations and the decline and bankruptcy of enterprises belonging to acquirers. Lists of unmaintained plantations included several of the names in Table 3.2. The workers of many of them went unpaid for months and even years. By 1980 Nendaka's industrial fisheries on Lake Mobutu had almost ceased producing and his plantations were reported to be overgrown and poorly kept. Badjoko's plantations were producing 3,000 tonnes of coffee annually, only half of the amount that 3,000 hectares could produce, according to the estimate of one Greek planter that a properly managed coffee plantation produces 2 tonnes of coffee per hectare. This same planter told me that the politician who Zairianized his four plantations in Upper Zaire produced from them in one year only 100–20 tonnes, instead of the 1,000 tonnes they had formerly produced. This acquirer's fishery too had closed down by 1980.

Office holders who used their political power to move into the economy and acquired vast holdings do not operate in the true capitalist spirit and are not primarily businessmen. They are not involved in the good management of their enterprises, nor do they reinvest their profits locally. Instead they pillage what they have taken, amassing vast wealth from their mismanaged but extensive holdings and spending it on themselves. These parasitic practices suck wealth out of the economy rather than expanding it.

This situation creates a great need for efficiently organized productive enterprise to sustain the economy and to keep up with local demand; the independent entrepreneurs fill this need in the economy. They have to contend, however, not only with the domination of multinational capital but also with the easier access to resources enjoyed by holders of political office, and with the decay of the economy and its infrastructure resulting from corrupt and illegal activities. In addition the independent entrepreneurs face formidable competition from another category of local businesss owners in the city, the foreigners.

### THE FOREIGN COMMERCIAL CLASS

This class makes up 34 per cent of the substantial business owners in Kisangani. It consists mostly of Greeks and Asians; a lesser number are Belgian and Portuguese and there are a few others. A number of Greek refugees from Greece's civil war were settled in Upper Zaire after World War II; more arrived in 1955 fleeing from Nasser's Egypt. The Asian community in Kisangani originated from the Indian labour imported to work on the Mombasa-Lake Victoria railroad between 1895 and 1901. After it was finished about 6,000 out of 32,000 decided to remain. They were denied land rights in Kenya and therefore mostly lived in towns and engaged in commerce, spreading through Uganda and Tanzania and into Zaire (Delf 1963: 11–13). In Kisangani in 1952 they numbered 200–300 (Pons 1969: 21); by 1979, in the estimate of a prominent Asian, their numbers were down to 125–200, many having left after Zairianization. There are only a few Portuguese and Belgians in business in Kisangani because most Portuguese settled in Lower Zaire and Belgians were mostly administrators rather than businessmen. The city also has a small colony of West and other non-Zairian Africans, known as 'Sénégalais'.

The largest groups of foreign businessmen in Kisangani, the Asians and the Greeks, specialize in different kinds of business. Asians, as is evident in Table 3.1, are heavily involved in the wholesale and retail trade. Greeks are mostly in the wholesale fish trade, the hotel, restaurant and entertainment business, or in retailing.

Asians own twenty-four businesses: thirteen are wholesalers with retail outlets; eight have retail stores, two of which are pharmacies; two manage transit depots for businesses elsewhere; and one has a transport business. BELTEXCO, one of the wholesalers, is a big national company with a branch in Kisangani. It also has a subsidiary, ALUKIVU, which makes aluminium cooking pots locally, employing twenty-one workers, and has a potential capacity to produce 2,000 pots daily. Both are under the same Asian manager.

Greeks own twenty-five businesses. Six own fisheries in association with their Zairian wives or Zairian partners; six own hotels, restaurants, nightclubs or casinos; six own stores, including two for hardware and one for auto spares; two deal in coffee, two are in the wholesale vegetable trade from Kivu; and the others own a paint factory, a construction business and a barbershop. Greeks specialize in the fish trade because they obtained a monopoly on the commercial fisheries of Lake Tanganyika in the colonial period. They also monopolize ownership of casinos, with two in Kisangani (one in partnership with a military officer) and eleven in Kinshasa.

Both the Greeks and the Asians form distinct communities based on language, culture and religion. The Asians (Shiite Muslims), are mostly from Pakistan; they speak Gujerati and their community centres on the mosque. There are a few Hindu families, most of whom work as technicians for SOTEXKI, the textile factory, who were recruited through its branch in Tanzania. The Asians keep to themselves, and have little contact with the local Muslims. They generally intermarry and place restrictions on their women: girls may not go out alone, wear short skirts or nail polish, or talk freely outside the house. Children are sent to the Belgian primary school in Kisangani, then to relatives overseas for secondary education.

The Greek community centres on Kisangani's Greek Orthodox Church. Children go to a small Greek primary school, then to secondary school in Greece or Cyprus. The community is less closed than that of the Asians. Greeks are said to marry African women more often than Asians; I knew of five Greeks with African wives but of only one Asian. Many more Greeks live in the interior, where they own plantations and stores, than in the city.

The term *Sénégalais* now refers to people from Mauritania, Sudan, Nigeria, Guinea, the Republic of Central Africa and Senegal. They originated in the small foreign elite of 'coastmen' living in Tshopo zone (then Belge 1) in the colonial period, who were recruited as clerks by British and French firms for developing trade with English-speaking Africa (Pons 1969: 32, 42n.). They are to some extent integrated into the Islamic community in Tshopo zone. The Belgians did not allow these West Africans, who arrived in Kisangani after World War I, to settle with the other Muslims but forced them to live in Tshopo, where they eventually built their own mosque (Bibeau 1975: 229). These traders do not have their families with them and travel frequently. In Kisangani some twenty of them will rent a house but only a few will live in it at any one time. They are highly organized into efficient trading networks and very rapidly move gold, diamonds and the goods imported in exchange.

In 1959 foreigners numbered over 5,000 in Kisangani; by 1967 they were down to 400 (Pons 1969: xxi) but, as shown in the population figures in the Appendix, they had increased again to 1,266 by 1973. Zairianization caused a drop to 737 but by 1979 they numbered 1,472. Overall these figures show an enormous decrease in numbers after independence, but foreigners still, nevertheless, constitute a formidable presence in the business community of the town.

The predominance of certain nationalities over others among foreign businessmen is explained in part by historical circumstances, in part by differing opportunity costs. An Asian or a Greek, but not a Belgian, is willing to live in Kisangani or in a town in the hinterland, and sell fish or cloth in a little store, because wages and standards of living are lower in Pakistan, Greece or Cyprus than in Belgium. A Belgian is accustomed to a much higher standard of living in his home country than a Greek or an

Asian and must make correspondingly much more money in Zaire: his opportunity costs are higher. Pons quotes a Greek who told him in 1967 that 'he and his brother had in two and a half years in Kisangani made as much for themselves as they would possibly hope to make in a lifetime of hard work in Greece' (Pons 1969: xxi).

## THE INDEPENDENT ENTREPRENEURS

The thirty-two nationals owning businesses who do not hold political position own manufacturing businesses; plantations, farms and fisheries; processing plants and sawmills; wholesale and retail businesses; transportation and garages; nightclubs and real estate. Table 3.3 categorizes all the businesses owned by them; all are in the official economy. The figures refer to numbers of businesses of a particular type.

Forty-eight of these businesses (48.5 per cent) are in production, in commercial agriculture and processing, manufacturing, food production, and one in construction which is rentier capitalism. Fifty-one (51.5 per cent) are in distribution and services, in commerce, transportation and entertainment.

Most of these productive enterprises supply the internal local market. Furniture and work uniform manufacture, fisheries, bakeries, meat, rice and palm oil are all for local consumption. Rubber plantations supply the Goodyear factory in Kinshasa, and sawmills the local furniture factory and construction companies. Coffee and timber are primarily for the export market. Development of production for the internal local market is also indicated in the plans some of these entrepreneurs had for expansion in the future. They envisaged a pharmaceutical factory, expansion of livestock rearing for the local meat market, manufacture of jewellery, and sisal plantations for the manufacture of sacks.

These men and women, therefore, participate almost as much in production as in distribution. They thus represent a change in the situation perceived by previous commentators on Zaire's class structure, who maintain that no economic bourgeoisie is forming in Zaire (Rymenam 1977: 9; Verhaegen 1978: 376–7; D. Gould 1978: 34). These Kisangani entrepreneurs produce for the local market as well as for export; in true rational capitalist fashion they invest their profits in expansion of their businesses, rather than spending them in conspicuous consumption or keeping them in foreign bank accounts. They constitute the beginnings of a class of local indigenous capitalists, an embryo true national bourgeoisie, contrasting with the parasitic capitalists of the political aristocracy. These entrepreneurs are taking on the attributes of a capitalist class and ensuring their reproduction as a class: they invest in inheritable productive property and real estate, employ wage labour on a considerable scale, engage in rational capitalistic management of their enterprises, have access to the capital market, enjoy a middle-class lifestyle, and give their children a

Table 3.3 *Businesses owned by independent entrepreneurs*

| Commercial agriculture and processing | | | Manufacturing, food production and construction | | |
|---|---|---|---|---|---|
| plantations—coffee[1] | | 18 | furniture | | 2 |
| —palm | | 3 | work uniforms | | 1 |
| —rubber | | 2 | bakeries | | 2 |
| —rice | | 1 | fisheries | | 3 |
| ranches and farms | | 4 | construction | | 1 |
| | | | | | — |
| coffee mills | | 3 | | Total | 9 |
| rice mills | | 3 | | | |
| forestry | | 2 | *Transportation* | | |
| Sawmills | | 3 | transport | | 6 |
| | | — | car and bicycle sales | | 2 |
| | Total | 39 | garages | | 2 |
| *Commerce* | | | | | — |
| wholesale[2] | | 6 | | Total | 10 |
| retail—Kisangani | | 15 | | | |
| —interior | | 6 | *Entertainment* | | |
| import/export | | 4 | night clubs | | 2 |
| distance commerce[3] | | 6 | beer depot | | 2 |
| | | — | | | — |
| | Total | 37 | | Total | 4 |

[1] Includes four coffee exporters 1980.
[2] Three partnered with Pakistanis.
[3] To Kinshasa or the interior.

good education. Details follow and more will be given in the case histories of Chapter 4.

This local capitalism emerging in Kisangani appears to be typical of indigenous capitalism elsewhere in Africa, which is generally to be found in the border area between petty producers and big foreign firms: in saw-milling, furniture-making, baking, building materials and motor transport, all areas in which the capital required for entry is not large and the technology is relatively simple (Iliffe 1982: 75). By expansion in these sectors, Kisangani's entrepreneurs avoid competition from multinationals.

Details of the expansion of the business holdings of two entrepreneurs illustrate the process by which this kind of local capitalism expands:

> Mr L.'s first enterprise was a partnership in 1971 in an auto business assembling trucks. In 1975 he invested his share of profits in buying a workshop manufacturing work clothes and school uniforms. He expanded the business to include a retail store. In 1977, he separated from his partner and acquired a cycle outlet, selling motor bikes, scooters, bicycles and spare parts. He is the representative for CYCLOR and also sells Yamahas and Vespas. He goes to Kinshasa every month to arrange imports.
>
> He also has other lines of business. He sells alcohol wholesale as

representative for a Kinshasa firm of Belgian importers and in 1979 he started a pig farm, to produce meat for the local market, after studying pig raising at a Chinese aid project in Kinshasa. His four pigs had increased to forty by 1980 and he was seeking capital from SOFIDE (the World Bank funded development bank) or from Canada to improve his farm by building pens according to the Chinese plan, because pigs fatten quicker if penned in. He feeds his pigs on residue from the local brewery, water hyacinths from the river and manioc which he grows. In 1980 he started a rice mill, paying Z55,400[4] for a rice husking machine which will husk 500 kilograms an hour. He will use the residue for fattening his pigs. He also bought a manioc mill. His other investments include a coffee plantation, from which he expected to begin exporting and earning hard currency in 1981, and a boutique jointly owned with his wife, which she manages. He employs forty-one people, not including the boutique, and has a monthly turnover of Z300,000–400,000.

Mr B. inherited a coffee plantation and other commercial businesses from his father who was killed in the rebellion. Mr B. was at a Belgian university at this time. In 1973 he Zairianized a furniture factory from a Belgian for which he paid with loans from the bank. He has continued to have good relations with the bank because he presents his accounts and pays back loans on time. The business went well and he started a bakery and bakery store in 1977. In 1979, he invested in a forestry concession and he has an export-import business in Kinshasa, exporting timber and coffee. In 1980 he expected 250 tonnes of coffee to be sorted and dried at his Kisangani plant. He was planting corn, rice and manioc crops as he felled his timber. His factory produces plush-upholstered sofas and armchairs, beds, cupboards, glass-fronted cabinets, tables, chairs, bookshelves etc. Customers come from towns in the interior as well as Kisangani. The factory has Belgian machinery but though he imports some spares, he has a workshop to manufacture others. Local sawmills provide wood. He imports cloth and foam rubber from Kinshasa, not only for his factory but also for sale to other local furniture makers. In 1980, he planned to travel to Montreal and Chicago seeking partners to put up capital to expand his businesses. He employs 219 people in Kisangani and his plantations, including 3 Belgians and 1 Frenchman, and 21 in Kinshasa. In Kisangani he has five trucks, two cars and a Land Rover; in Kinshasa he has three cars, one truck, a pickup and a Land Rover.

He attributes his success to hard work, good organization and management, and to keeping in close touch with all that is going on in the business. He does not choose his employees because they are foreigners or nationals: 'it is the man who counts, how he works, whether he has a head for business or not. I can tell if he is any good in three months.'

Both these men have diversified as well as expanded their business holdings, a typical pattern in circumstances of political insecurity and economic dependence. Investment of profit in their businesses, the use of local materials for pig feed and sawmills, the production and processing of agricultural products for local consumption and an emphasis on good management are features in the enterprises of these two men that signify they are typical bourgeoisie.

The independent entrepreneurs compare favourably for size in business with both foreigners and politicians, some having smaller concerns some larger. I was only able to obtain a few rates of monthly turnover; it is a touchy subject because so much business takes place outside official channels and is unrecorded by the state. For this reason, I did not feel I could ask to see company book and records. But putting number of enterprises and the few available figures together with number of employees and vehicles owned, it is possible to make some comparisons of size. Increase in the number of workers and in the quantity of the means of production marks the transition from petty commodity to small capitalist commodity production (Le Brun and Gerry 1975: 2).

One of the largest of the independent entrepreneurs has a wholesale business with branches in Kindu and Kinshasa as well as Kisangani. He has sixty-four stores in the interior, and also owns a coffee plantation. He employs 800 workers altogether, owns eight trucks and has a monthly turnover of 1 million zaires. Mr L, in the case history above, has a turnover of Z300,000–400,000. The largest transport concern among these entrepreneurs owns twelve trucks. The smallest business owner has only one shop, but trades to Kinshasa besides. In comparison some foreigners have more, some less than the larger of these entrepreneurs: one local Asian wholesaler has a monthly turnover of about 2 million zaires; another, in partnership with a Zairian woman, up to a quarter of a million; for one in semi-wholesale (*demi-gros*, wholesale on a small scale), it is Z175,000.

These businessmen and women invest in real estate, some of them extensively. Their reasons for doing so reflect an insecure and unstable political situation. Some of them say specifically that it is a more secure investment than trade or manufacturing:

> A woman retailer who travelled extensively on business said her aim was to invest her profits in buying houses and renting them out before attempting to expand her business any further: 'Property in houses lasts through troubles and is more sure.'

> A retailer and nightclub owner who built a row of five stores with a building for his nightclub and a large house for himself behind them, commented: 'It's the best thing I've done in my life.' He felt that there are always troubles but if stores got looted the buildings would remain and bring in income from rent; they would endure even if the business failed, and preserve his wealth for his children. He will use two out of the five stores himself, but will rent out the other three at Z600 a month, which will bring him in Z7,200 annually.

When asked to rate real estate holdings of those on the list of substantial business owners, a source in the Land Title Office categorized three of the independent entrepreneurs as having large holdings, nine as medium (one of these I know owned ten houses), and eleven as small. Nine were unknown to him.

Owning real estate is extremely lucrative in Kisangani and many of the city's court cases concern the title to abandoned houses. People want to be able to rent them out to the government or to big companies who provide housing for their employees; rents are often paid in cash, which makes them tax free. Houses rent for Z200–50 a month, villas for Z500–1,000. Rents rose spectacularly from 1976–80: one three-bedroom apartment went from Z250 to Z500, to Z1,000 a month. The large buildings in the centre of town, with apartments above and stores below, owned by politicians, officials and military officers, thus bring in enormous sums of money. Such development of rentier rather than productive capitalism is considered to be a check on the development of capitalism (Iliffe 1982: 69). Paul Kennedy, in a study of Ghanaian entrepreneurs, found that those

> who channeled a higher proportion of their profits into house building than into plant, materials or equipment, who began spending money on houses quite soon after going into business, or whose second and third enterprises did not involve rational linkages with or extensions to their first firms, were less likely to be successful overall. (Kennedy 1980:164)

Ownership of a comfortable house to live in is a feature of the middle-class lifestyle enjoyed by these entrepreneurs.

## MIDDLE CLASS CULTURE AND LIFESTYLE

Marshall Sahlins describes capitalist production as a cultural Process:

> It proceeds according to a meaningful logic of the concrete, of the significance of objective differences, thus developing appropriate signs of emergent social distinctions...The product that reaches its destined market constitutes an objectification of a social category, and so helps to constitute the latter in society; as in turn, the differentiation of the category develops further social declensions of the goods system. Capitalism is no sheer rationality. It is a definite form of cultural order; or a cultural order acting in a particular form. (Sahlins 1976:185).

Richard Jeffries, discussing different classes in Ghana, observes that each class has a distinct style of life and that people only mix regularly with those of similar economic and educational status (Jeffries 1978: 183).

The new commercial middle class in Kisangani has taken on the culture and way of life developed by the post-independence dominant class. It is evident in type of house and house furnishings, ownership of a car or motor scooter, style of dress and leisure activities. The expense of this lifestyle attests to the wealth of the members of this new commercial class.

Since independence the new government bureaucrats, professionals, company managers and university professors have taken over the villas in the European residential area of Makiso, or built themselves houses in similar styles. Businessmen and women have done the same. These homes are spacious, surrounded by lawns and flower gardens with ornamental shrubs and trees, usually enclosed by a high wall or iron fence, most of them guarded by a watchman and often by a large dog, whose ferocity is proclaimed by a sign over the gate.

Most middle-class houses have upholstered, factory-made living room suites, in preference to the wood and cane furniture found in the houses of the less well-off. Such a set of sofa and armchairs from the local furniture factory cost around Z3,000 in 1980. Rugs on the floors, pictures and ornaments and a variety of electrical appliances complete the comfortable and sometimes opulent style of house furnishing. Members of the middle class invariably own TV sets; in 1980 a large set retailed for Z8,000, a small for Z2,700. Many people have electric fans, refrigerators and radios; some also have freezers, stereo record players, tape recorders, calculators and various other gadgets and imported goods. The list of prizes for the raffles of the Lions and Lioness clubs is a good index of favoured consumer items. The 1980 prizes included a kerosene refrigerator, an electric sewing machine, a ladies bicycle, an electric stove, a kerosene stove, a radio, a dress length of *wax* print, a set of tools, car tyres, bicycle tyres and curtain cloth. In 1979 the first prize was a ticket from Kinshasa to Brussels. Other prizes included a motor scooter, a radio, a fan, a camera, watches, a mixer and an electric razor.

The preferred dress style also fuels the demand for imports. Although suits and ties were outlawed in 1972, in the name of authenticity, and replaced by the tailored *abacos*, men prefer imported European and American shirts and foreign made belts, wallets and other accessories. Women wear embroidered blouses and colour-toned wrap-around skirts, or a complete outfit, in *wax* print. In 1980 prices for imported Dutch *wax* ranged from Z320 to Z1,200. An abundance of jewellery, such as gold necklaces, bracelets and earrings, and matching shoes imported from Europe and costing Z300–400 a pair, complement these outfits. Some women prefer Western style dresses in imported fabrics and the latest fashion. The luxury boutiques and tailoring establishments of the new commercial middle class have arisen in conjuction with these tastes, which act as distinctive markers of social differentiation.

Certain kinds of pictures and ornaments are also part of this culture. The paintings hanging on living-room walls represent several distinct genres: scenes of African life, landscapes and sunsets, and colonial oppression. This popular art is one of several new national art forms which currently appear in the houses of the well-to-do in Zaire, and which are distinct from the traditional art of different ethnic groups. (For a detailed description of the paintings of Shaba popular art, see Fabian and Fabian 1976.) Particular to Kisangani is a series of representations of the terrible events of its past, such as execution scenes from the rebellion, paratroopers dropping from planes to an airport runway defended by rebels with bows and arrows and blocked with oil drums, or a bloody battle scene of the mercenary uprising. After the demonetization of 1979, a painting appeared for sale in the market of a man who had hoarded his money in a trunk, despairingly throwing it all away. New art forms include the modern art of noted painters and sculptors of the Fine Arts Academy of Kinshasa and, at a more mundane level, the craft production for the tourist market which includes both crude and beautifully made objects. In Kisangani ivory and ebony carvers produce such pieces for sale locally.

People in Kisangani use certain locally made household items, such as baskets, mats, small ornamental pestles and mortars, raffia shopping bags and pottery cooking pots and jugs. This demand sustains some local craft production in Kisangani and in the rural areas. But a distinctive feature of the middle-class lifestyle is the preference for imported manufactured household goods, especially electrical appliances. The desire for certain imported products while creating a market for those involved in distributing them, creates a barrier for those attempting to produce household items locally. One man peddled ingeniously made basketry lamps, lampshades, planters for the ubiquitous houseplants, wastebaskets and crude pottery ashtrays and vases door-to-door, but had difficulty finding customers, because people complained that his asking prices were too high although they were, in fact, very low compared to the prices of the preferred imported items. West African style machine-embroidered shirts produced locally have not supplanted the vogue for shirts imported from the West. Schmitz and Langdon have commented on the way such patterns of demand or 'taste transfers' can favour multinationals and block the development of certain sectors of local industry (Langdon 1975: 30–2; Schmitz 1982: 438).

Kisangani offers a variety of leisure activities as part of this distinctive lifestyle. The city has two casinos, mostly frequented by foreigners but with some Zairian patrons as well; four nightclubs, each with a specialized clientele; a range of restaurants and numerous bars. The French cultural centre puts on plays, concerts and movies. *Boyoma*, the daily newspaper, reports frequent government cocktail receptions to mark special occasions and entertain important visitors. People go to dinner parties, dances, christening and birthday parties, weddings and other social events, some of which are reported in the newspaper.

The businessmen and women of this study live in the desirable residential neighbourhoods of the zones of Makiso and Tshopo (see Map 2). The class structure of the city is reflected in the housing and provision of public utilities and schools in the different zones. Makiso, the upper-class residential area, has more paved roads than the other zones, and is better provided with electric light and running water, as shown in Table 3.4. Tshopo has always been regarded as the most desirable residential neighbourhood after Makiso. Mangobo follows and Kabondo and Kisangani are the most disadvantaged.

In the Second Republic education became the qualification for entry into the dominant class, through employment in government, the professions or by big companies; 53 per cent of ministers and party leaders between 1965 and 1975 were university graduates. Increasingly schools became uneven in quality and opportunity depended on access to the best of them. The political aristocracy began educating their children in Europe as 'Powerful

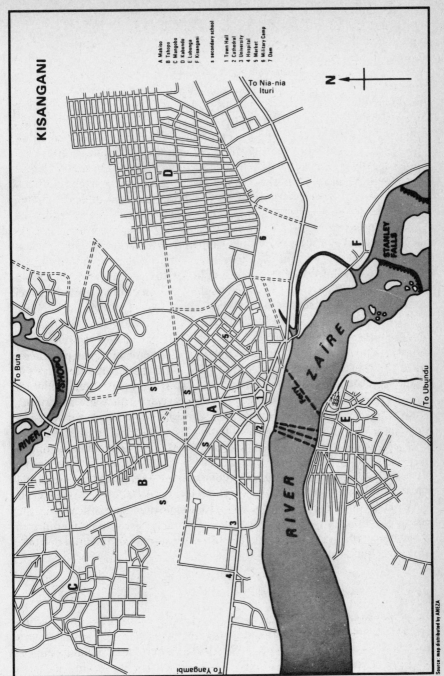

KISANGANI

A Makiso
B Tshopo
C Mangobo
D Kabondo
E Lubunga
F Kisangani

s secondary school

1 Town Hall
2 Cathedral
3 University
4 Hospital
5 Market
6 Military Camp
7 Dam

To Nia-nia
Ituri

N

To Buta

To Yangambi

To Ubundu

STANLEY FALLS

RIVER ZAÏRE

TSHOPO RIVER

Source: map distributed by ANEZA

Map 2. Kisangani

73

Table 3.4 *Public utilities in the zones of Kisangani*

| Zone | Houses with electric light | | % of lots with running water |
|------|------|------|------|
| | 1972 | 1975 | |
| Makiso | 352 | 516 | 94.7 |
| Tshopo | 16 | 82 | 54.8 |
| Mangobo | 3 | 62 | 50.0 |
| Lubunga | 10 | 19 | 7.0 |
| Kisangani | — | 55 | 1.9 |
| Kabondo | 4 | 2 | 1.1 |

*Source*: Nkongolo Bakenda 1975: 54, 58.

social selectivity processes [became] linked to the stratification of school quality' (Young and Turner 1985: 123, 135). In Kisangani the better schools, mostly in Makiso, are well supplied with materials and the fees are higher than for the schools attended by the children of the poor, which lack benches, doors or teaching materials (Verhaegen *et al.*, 1984: 136). In 1975 16.6 per cent of 325 secondary students came from Makiso, which has only 3 per cent of the population. Kabondo, with 32 per cent of the population supplied only 19 per cent, and Lubunga with 17 per cent of the population only 5.8 per cent (Kasongo *et el.*, 1977: 22). The figures are given in Table 3.5. The members of the new commercial class send their children to secondary school. Few have reached university age but two who have are studying overseas. One, a boy, is an engineering student in Brussels; the other, a girl, is in medical school there.

We have so far documented the formation of a small commercial middle class of local capitalist entrepreneurs in Kisangani, which has arisen despite inimical political and economic circumstances. The sector to which it is most closely juxtaposed in the class structure is the foreign commercial class. These foreigners were displaced to some extent by political strife and the Zairianization measures, but they still present strong competition in some areas and relations between them and the new indigenous capitalist class are complex.

RELATIONS BETWEEN FOREIGNERS AND NATIONALS IN BUSINESS

In some areas the foreign commercial class and the new national commercial middle class compete, in others they cooperate. To understand the relations between these two class sectors, it is necessary, as Paul Kennedy suggests, to look at a whole spectrum of conflicting and converging economic interests (Kennedy 1977: 183–6).

Competition generates conflicting relations. The foreign commercial class

Table 3.5 *Secondary school students by zone*

| Zone | No. in study | % | Population 1974 | % |
|------|------|------|------|------|
| Mangobo | 84 | 25.8 | 46,670 | 15 |
| Tshopo | 68 | 20.9 | 44,305 | 14 |
| Kabondo | 64 | 19.7 | 97,108 | 32 |
| Makiso | 54 | 16.6 | 9,794 | 3 |
| Lubunga | 19 | 5.8 | 51,662 | 17 |
| Kisangani | 16 | 4.9 | 32,926 | 11 |
| Others | 20 | 6.2 | 24,508* | 8 |
| Total | 325 | 100.0 | 306,973 | 100 |

*includes former collectivity of Lubuya Bera.

*Source*: Kasongo *et al.*, 1977: 21.

presents a formidable competitive block to the new class of independent local entrepreneurs because foreigners enjoy various kinds of advantages in business: Greeks and Asians have kin and business connections in other countries which bring access to foreign exchange and greatly facilitate importing and exporting; their enterprises are often family based, with a tradition and long experience of working in business; within Kisangani itself foreigners cooperate, forming a business community offering mutual assistance between members from which Zairians are excluded.

Asian enterprise is organized on a family basis, often using family members as managers or labour. Asian families are dispersed in several different cities in Zaire, in East Africa and in England, Canada and Pakistan; these dispersed kin networks provide assistance in exporting and importing goods, facilitate getting jobs and setting up business, act as insurance in times of political trouble and solve the problem of finding adequate education for children.

The five genealogies given in Figure 3.1 give examples of this dispersal of kin, and of business connections and employment based on kinship.

In four of them, A, C, D and E, groups of brothers have businesses in different cities in Zaire, in East Africa and in England or Canada, either singly or in partnership. In B, the men have married sisters, or are brothers-in-law, and have become business partners. Those in Kisangani use their relatives in Kinshasa to obtain goods for them, deal with the bureaucracy and personally supervise rapid transit through the docks. Relatives in Kivu or Kenya or Uganda assist in importing East African goods. Coffee, ivory or gold are often exchanged in these transactions to the East. Parents and other family members in Canada or England board children while they go to secondary schools that are better than those available in Zaire.

75

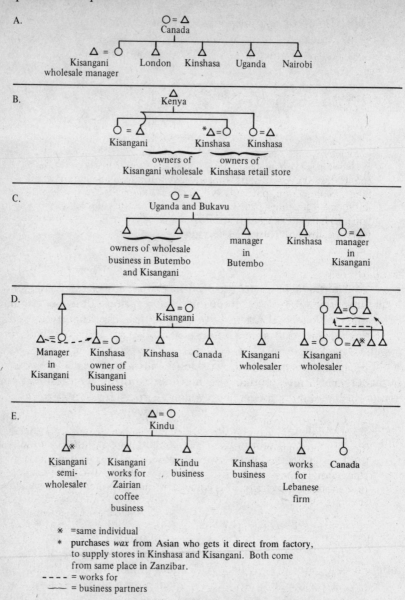

Fig. 3.1. Asian genealogies showing kin dispersal and business connections

These networks give Asians far greater resources and resilience than are apparent in their small communities, and help to offset their lack of political power and influence. When political disasters strike, as for example when businesses were taken away from foreigners in Zairianization or when Amin expelled the Asians from Uganda, kin who are established in a neighbouring country provide shelter and a job until it is possible to return or start out again in a new business and a new country. Kin networks are maintained by frequent contact through telephone calls or visits.

Another advantage that Asians have is that many families have been in business for generations. According to one of them:

> 70 per cent of Asians are businessmen. It runs in the family: you are brought up in it and learn to run a business by working for relatives, getting the knowledge and experience to start up on your own. Asians compete against each other, so you need some special tie to establish trust with a partner. You cannot just arrive and start from nothing but must have family or some other kind of connection, particularly in Zaire today where so much is illegal and unofficial—you must have someone you can rely on completely. For example, you may have to take goods without an invoice or use money acquired in illegal ways, so absolute trust is essential.

Like the Asians, the Greeks work with family members and maintain strong family ties. One Greek businessman had 150 relatives scattered in Kisangani, Isiro, Wamba, Beni and Kinshasa; all descended from four men who came to Zaire in 1932 from the same village in Cyprus; all keep in close touch and help each other out in difficulties and in business dealings by buying from each other and by selling things without charging a commission.

Foreign businessmen of all nationalities in Kisangani co-operate with one another, through mutual assistance in the form of interest-free credit and exchange of information. Two Asians gave details of this cooperation:

> *A wholesaler*: any member of the foreign business community can call on another for credit without interest. Newcomers will be given help to get started. Information is passed round on prices or on the situation in Kinshasa: if you go on a trip you pass word of anything of interest when you return. If someone offers you a load of goods you check with someone else to see if the price is right. It is completely informal, there is no committee or anything like that. One man came to Kisangani and was helped to start out but he spent the money on living high. After asking for their money back three or four times people withdrew help and he's gone: it's impossible to continue in business once this has happened.

> *A retailer*: foreign businessmen extend credit to each other: Jews, Portuguese, Greeks, Pakistanis, Indians, Lebanese, *Sénégalais*. Zairians are not included because they are not to be trusted. The majority of foreigners are trustworthy. If you ever lose prestige and trust for credit you are finished. [This retailer has credit with six or seven people in Kinshasa, four or five in Kisangani; they are all Jews, *Sénégalais*, Pakistanis or Greeks.]

Individuals in this foreign commercial class can make enormous amounts of money, but they are politically in a very insecure position and run high risks. The following history of a Greek shows how quickly it is possible for foreigners to make money in Zaire and also to lose it repeatedly. I heard similar histories from other foreigners in Kisangani; all show that it is worthwhile for a foreigner to start again after even phenomenal losses.

> Mr. A. from Cyprus has invested the thirty-two years of his working life in Zaire. In 1960 he owned two stores in a town in the interior, one of them dealing in goods for Europeans. In 1960 the mass exodus of Belgians and other foreigners left bills unpaid and stocks of food rotting in his store. He had to close it down but kept the other store going. By 1961 he had recouped his losses and was able to buy three coffee plantations and start up in coffee buying as well. By 1964 he had 700 tonnes of coffee, five foreigners working for him, fifteen trucks and five small cars and was expecting a harvest of 800 tonnes of coffee. Then came the rebellion and he lost all of it. He and his wife and children lived for four months terrorized by the rebels. When the mercenaries came Mr A. and his family left for Cyprus. Once again, after only four months, disaster struck and they were caught in the civil war. In 1968 he returned to Upper Zaire to try again and started up his shop and his coffee plantation. By 1973 he was again prosperous with two plantations (of 200 hectares and 60 hectares) are two stores in the town, five trucks, a Land Rover, a Range Rover and a Mercedes. At the end of that year he lost everything *again* in Zairianization: his shops, plantation and vehicles were taken from him by an ex-minister of the national government and by a provincial government minister. This time the family went to England. In 1978 after retrocession, Mr A. was offered partnership by the acquirer of his big plantation. On arrival in Kinshasa, however, he was told that the acquirer had changed his mind. He has since been engaged in a bitter struggle to get back the plantation to which he is entitled because it is mismanaged. 'We have suffered too much', he says.
>
> However, in spite of so much misfortune, he was able to start up in commerce again quite easily. In the spring of 1980, when goods were extremely scarce and Zairian merchants were having great difficulty getting them from the big wholesalers, Mr A. obtained Z20,000 worth of merchandise from one of the big multinational wholesale houses with which to restock his store in the interior, retroceded to him with empty shelves. He expected to get his money back in three to four months at 20–2 per cent profit. His status as a foreigner and past record of dealings with this company were enough to enable him to obtain goods when his aspiring Zairian competitors could not.

Peter Marris comments on the obstacle posed by these self-enclosed foreign business communities to the development of African business, and adds that:

> The problem is not so much to train Africans in the methods of European business, as to make European and African businessmen familiar with each other and each other's societies, and establish personal relationships. (Marris 1968: 36)

Such personal relations and familiarity are generally lacking in Kisangani. The comment of the retailer above was echoed in many derogatory remarks by expatriate businessmen about their Zairian counterparts.

Given their advantages, the foreign commercial class poses formidable competition for nationals.[5] This problem is compounded by the fact that

Zairians do not trust one another sufficiently to cooperate and unite in similar fashion. Against the statements of the Asians one can contrast others from nationals: 'you don't find cooperation and assistance among Zairians but a spirit of jealousy which holds us back; we are not together'. 'Pakistanis work in groups, Zairians on their own.' These judgements are confirmed in an article on business by Kiakwana Kiziki:

> The lack of trust between nationals in business is one of the most serious problems. They distrust one another to the point of refusing to form limited companies able to foster capital growth and increase the size of the enterprise, and therefore its efficiency. Lack of trust in their subordinates moves them equally to refuse to delegate authority, still a characteristic of most of these enterprises... (They) have more confidence in the integrity and honesty of a foreign businessman than in that of their compatriots. (Kiakwana Kiziki 1974: 101)

This lack of trust between African businessmen is reported elsewhere. Zambian businessmen are highly competitive and see each other as rivals. They are reluctant to give or take advice among themselves and seek it more readily from Asians (Beveridge and Oberschall 1979: 188). In Nigeria mutual suspicion and lack of trust in other Nigerians as partners prevents the establishment of larger, more impersonal but more permanent enterprises (Schatz 1977: 87). A general atmosphere of distrust prevails among Ghanaians; Kennedy finds the inability of Ghanaian entrepreneurs to form partnerships and companies a major obstacle to the emergence of a viable business community able to compete with foreigners (Kennedy 1980: 111–16).

Although the interests of the foreign commercial class are often in competition with those of the emergent indigenous capitalist class, they do not necessarily coincide with those of multinational capital:

> In so far as this kind of foreign businessman does not obtain the same privileges from the government as the large corporations, does not have access to the same capital and technological resources and may cater for the lower end of the consumer market... his interests and theirs are more likely to conflict than coincide. (Kennedy 1977: 186)

Sometimes relations between the foreign commercial class and nationals in business are characterized by various kinds of cooperation. Although some of the foreign commercial class repatriate their profits and benefit the local economy but little, others have lived in Africa most of their lives, may have African wives and intend to remain permanently. They have invested their life's work in their business; some do reinvest their profits locally, expanding both their enterprises and the local economy. Their interests then sometimes converge with those of the independent entrepreneurs. Retrocession, in particular, introduced several distinct forms of collarobation and sharing of profits between foreign business owners and the Zairian partners they had to seek out.

79

In one form the individual who is the Zairian partner in the retroceded enterprise is simply a 'frontman or woman', who serves to fulfil the letter of the low and has no managerial responsibility. Such persons have no particular skills or political connections to make them useful. They will, in some cases, be simply paid so much a month and be on the books as the partner in the firm; behind their backs they are said to be partners in name only.

The second form involves collaboration for political reasons. The Zairian partner will be a man who is either himself politically powerful or who has good political connections. Such access is a significant advantage in the operation of a business in Zaire's current situation. In such cases individuals of the foreign commercial class are advancing their interests by collaboration with the political aristocracy. An example in Kisangani is a wholesale business owned by two Asians in partnership with a Zairian who is well-connected to Ruakabuba, a political commissioner and uncle of Bisengemana, who was for years head of the Presidential Secretariat.[6] People in such positions can be of great assistance for the businesses of those who have connections to them. In this case the politicians increased the quotas of merchandise from the big wholesale houses for the wholesale business in question. This business began as a small Asian semi-wholesale store in a small town in 1976. In the three years after retrocession under partnership between two Asians and the politically connected Zairian, it expanded to a wholesale business with branches in Kinshasa, Kisangani and two other towns. The Zairian partner has, in addition, developed a large transport business and a huge coffee buying and exporting concern of his own.

The third form of partnership for a foreigner is with a national who is an active partner in running the business, a real cooperative and responsible business colleague. A case history of one particular foreign businessman who spoke highly of his Zairian colleague is an example.

> Mr H. came to Zaire in 1948, where his father had a construction company in Maniema. This enterprise was annihilated by the rebellion and Mr H. returned to Europe. His father, however, stayed, started a transport business and became partner in a sawmill in Kisangani. By 1969 business was going well and Mr H. came out to work for him. The father died in 1972 and the next year the businesses were Zairianized by two different acquirers. Mr H. stayed on and worked for the new owner of his transport business but by 1976 it was having severe problems. Mr H. then took up managing the sawmill, whose acquirer had given up and left. In 1979 the Bureau de Portefeuille ordered the business to be retroceded to him, with the condition he find a new Zairian partner.
> Meantime he had bought the transport business and its trucks from its acquirer and was running it with a Zairian with whom he got on very well. He asked this man to be partner in the sawmill. If the paperwork could all be worked out, they were going to join sawmill and transport company into one business which they would jointly own and operate in active partnership.

Such partnerships evidence the converging interests of the two class sectors.

An important feature of the socio-economic context within which the new commercial middle class is emerging is the multiplicity of ethnic groups which make up the population of the city.

ETHNICITY AND CLASS FORMATION

If the cultural pluralism of Zairian society were irrelevant for class formation, members of different ethnic groups would be equally distributed throughout the class structure. This however, is not the case in Kisangani, so that some exploration of the intersection of ethnicity and class is needed. In Kisangani significant variation existed between different peoples, in the history of their relations with the colonizers, in the process of their incorporation into the city and in the subsequent part they played in business and commerce. This situation conforms to a tendency, general in Africa, for particular ethnic communities to produce large numbers of entrepreneurs because of privileged access to modern advantages (Iliffe 1982: 70). This privileged access actively promotes advancement of members of the advantaged groups: more opportunities are available to them than to members of disadvantaged groups, also more influential and prosperous members to serve as patrons.

The African elite of the colonial period came primarily from peoples who were on favourable terms with the colonizers. Alliance with them was more important than traditional prestige for affording opportunities to move into the colonial elite; urban leaders did not emerge from among those of high rank in traditional society (Young 1965: 195; Clément 1956: 479). Favoured relations with the Belgians led to privileged urban incorporation and an advantageous position for access to the modern sector. Factors affecting these relations included a favourable geographical position in relation to colonial penetration, location near urban centres or on a major commercial axis, and presence or absence of particular forms of political and economic organization. Furthermore 'the colonial state, then, provided both an arena and an implement for the creation, consolidation and politicization of ethnicity' (Schatzberg: forthcoming, ch. 2). When power was handed over by the Belgians, its legitimacy, as Young points out, was determined by elections and the surest way for aspiring leaders to build their constituencies was to mobilize their ethnic clientele (Young 1965: 89. For details see *ibid*.: 292–8 and Lemarchand 1964: 192ff.).

After independence ethnicity modified the process of class formation. Class cleavages developed within ethnic groups but ethnic clientage served to maintain the class position of those who had succeeded in moving into the dominant class. Ethnic clientage also inhibited the development of class consciousness in sectors of the subordinated class and ethnic loyalties were manipulated to benefit those in the dominant class: 'As long as the little people are provoked into concern for ethnic differences, their capacity for solidarity and unity is hampered, thus maintaining the security of the dominant group' (D. Gould 1980: 102).

In Kisangani it appears that ethnic groups which achieved a favourable position in the colonial period have retained it to the present day (see Map 3). The most prominent group in the city, the Lokele, were traders and fishermen in pre-colonial times, travelling long distances up and down the Zaire River, exchanging fish for the products of the forest people and establishing small colonies. Since the river was a route for penetration by colonizers and missionaries, the Lokele were able to benefit from the setting up of the first schools in their riverine villages and also from serving as intermediaries in trade between the Belgians and the people inland in the forest. Their familiarity with trade and travel made the move into the city and adaptation to its commerce easy. Today they bring plantains, manioc, rice and palm oil from the villages of the Bakumu and Bamanga to Kisangani's market; in exchange they trade salt, cloth, fresh and salt fish, cigarettes and other European articles (Lokomba Baruti 1975: 67–71; 1972: 8–10). Traditionally the men fished and the women traded. Women worked in groups of two to four, generally family members, known as *linyala*, in which each member of the group contributed what they could but profits were shared equally. Unlike women in general in the city they thus worked together. This cooperation and their long familiarity with commerce seem likely to be factors in the domination of the market trade in Kisangani by Lokele women and their subsequent success in large-scale commerce, especially the trade of dried and salt fish to Kinshasa. One example of the cooperation of these women was a group that ran a stall for imported second-hand clothing and kerosene in the market in Kisangani and another in a village market out of town. They were related as follows:

A, B and D ran the stalls in Kisangani and A and C went to the village market twice a week. E also had a stall in Kisangani market.

The economic prosperity of the Lokele and their advantages in education, gave them a dominant place in the modern employment sector. In 1952 they comprised 18.8 per cent of the clerks and 43.8 per cent of qualified workers (Pons 1969: 93–4). Today most of them are in salaried employment or have turned their position in administration to their advantage in getting into business. They are prominent among local politicians, in business and in the retail as well as the market trade. Five out of the twenty three politicians and military officers listed in Table 3.2 are Lokele, and seven out of the thirty two independent entrepreneurs. Their good relations with the Belgians in the colonial period were the start

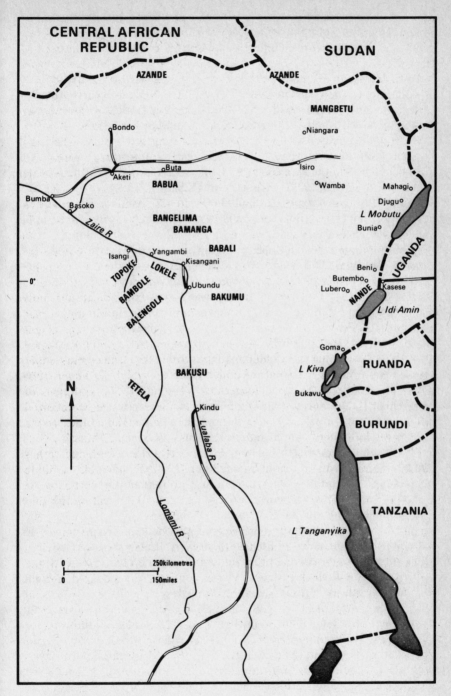

Map 3. Principal ethnic groups of North East Zaire

of their political and economic success; that this was resented was evidenced in the formation of a 'cultivators' cartel' in 1962, by which local producers sought to pre-empt the Lokele role of trade intermediary (Lokomba Baruti 1975: 84–5).

The *Arabisés* are also prominent in the city. They live in two communities in the zones of Kisangani and Lubunga and consist primarily of descendants of the Arabs and of their islamicized African followers from among the Bakusu and Tetela (who come from Maniema, to the south, see Map 3). The Arabs did not exercise political power over the local population of the areas in which they penetrated but formed alliances with local chiefs by intermarriage; gradually those associated with them began to speak, dress, eat and pray like them (Bibeau 1975: 187).

As the ruling class of the Arabized villages in Maniema, the Bakusu found new opportunities for advancement with the Belgian penetration, forming an elite that spread through Kivu and Upper Zaire. In the colonial period they outnumbered other ethnic groups in the administration and professions (Verhaegen 1969: 33–8). In the rebellion of 1964, when ethnic and social tensions coincided, much of the violence was directed against them (*ibid*.: 753). The Tetela were also part of the colonial elite (Young 1965: 558). Pons found that a number of *Arabisés* were full-time traders in 1952, and that they held a higher than average proportion of good jobs (Pons 1969: 93, 246). In 1979 two *Arabisés* were among the politicians in Table 3.2, four among the independent entrepreneurs, nine others were retailers and three were in other small businesses. They also concentrated in the pharmacy trade, allegedly because a Tetela official high up in the Ministry of Health ensured them supplies: six Tetela and one Kusu owned seven of the fifteen pharmacies in the zone of Makiso; the remainder were owned by foreigners, Luba and one Kongo.

The colonial African elite also came from the Babua, who lived 300 kilometres north of Kisangani (see Map 3). The Belgians prevented the Azande from conquering Babua territory; thereafter the Babua became collaborators and dominant in the local colonial administration (Monnier and Willame 1964: 127). They acquired the reputation of being good soldiers and substantial numbers were drafted into the army; their first settlers in Kisangani were discharged soldiers. Later they specialized as truck drivers, mechanics and masons. As one of the older groups in town they enjoyed advantages over more recent comers and held a higher than average proportion of good jobs (Pons 1969: 78, 93).

After independence this colonial elite dominated the new governing class. The first provincial government in Upper Zaire included three Bakusu, two Lokele, two Babua and one Tetela: eight out of a total of eleven (Epée 1971: 68). In 1962 the Lokele had four out of nine ministerial portfolios; in 1963 the new provincial government included four Lokele among its ten members (*ibid*.: 101, 110).

Other groups, in contrast, had poor relations with the Belgians. The

84

Bakumu from the east were receptive to Kitawala, an anti-European offshoot of the Jehovah's Witnesses, for which they suffered government repression. After independence they transferred their anti-colonial hostilities to the governing class and supported the rebellion (Verhaegen 1969: 21).

Isolated in their forest life to the south of the Topoke, the Bambole had little contact with the colonizers. They did not arrive in the city in large numbers before 1964. They have a low level of education, live mostly in the poor quarter of Lubunga in deplorable conditions and have a bad reputation for thieving and violence. They are mostly employed as barrow boys or small vendors, not in offices; many of their women are prostitutes. Excluded in this way from the dominant economic and administrative sectors, they are marginal in the city (Bongele Yeikolo 1975). The Balengola remained rural dwellers, arriving late in town, and are only employed as unskilled labour (Epée 1971: 26; Pons 1969: 245). The Babali and Bamanga are likewise marginal.

The Topoke from the south and west of Kisangani were little affected by wage earning or missionary penetration and did not enter wage employment until the 1930s. They began to move into the city after World War II as unskilled labour and were in a disadvantaged position to compete with other groups (Pons 1969: 79–81). Hostility to their Lokele neighbours led them to join the Simbas and kill many of their old enemies. Circumstances seem to have changed to favour them; many are now businessmen, intellectuals and university students (Bongele Yeikolo 1975: 144).

The majority of Kisangani's population is from these groups from the surrounding area, but members of certain ethnic groups from other regions are also prominent in government and commerce, chiefly the Nande, the Luba and the Kongo.

The Nande will be discussed in Chapter 6. Both the Luba from Kasai and the Kongo from Lower Zaire gained high status in the colonial period. At the time of European penetration, the slave trade caused gross dislocation of Luba society, so that many fled to the safety of European posts. In the 1920s they were recruited for railway construction and subsequently established farms along the railway or settled in the towns. They were targeted as suitable for missionizing by both Catholics and Protestants, so were well supplied with schools. Subsequently their high status and good reputation gained them preference with employers: 'no other group compared in its dispersion through urban Congo' (Young 1965: 258–61). In Kisangani today two Luba generals own large enterprises, two Luba are big retailers among the thirty two independent entrepreneurs, four own pharmacies, three are retailers, one is an optician and plantation owner, one a BATA distributor and there is a branch of a big Luba retail firm from Lubumbashi.

The Kongo from Lower Zaire likewise took advantage of European contact. In pre-colonial times they served as intermediaries in commerce from the coast to the interior. In the colonial period they produced cash

85

crops to feed the several urban centres in their region and were helped in moving into the new economy by railroads, a dense road network and large-scale missionary penetration (*ibid.*: 257). Two of the politicians in Kisangani are Kongo, four own stores, one is a wholesale trader and there is a branch of a large Kongo commercial agricultural business.

Those of mixed race (*mulâtres*) form a category, not an ethnic group. They do not often appear among the politically powerful; only one is on the list of politicians with businesses in Kisangani. They are, however, prominent in business. In the colonial period they were privileged as *gens de couleur civilisées* and admitted to European schools two years before Africans were (Mukenge 1974: 156). Some had wealthy European fathers to pay for their education; some Zairianized their father's businesses, thus keeping them in the family; and some of them also Zairianized the businesses of other foreigners. They were therefore well situated to become successful in business.

The dominance of the Lokele, *Arabisés*, Luba, Kongo and those of mixed race in commerce is reflected in the ethnic background of the thirty-two independent entrepreneurs: nine were of mixed race, seven were Lokele, five *Arabisés*, two Luba, two were from Bukavu, one each were Mobali, Mabudu, Nande, Mubole, Mongelema, Topoke, and one was from Bunia. The same dominance was repeated in the results of a count of retail stores and small businesses in the zone of Makiso, the commercial and administrative zone of Kisangani, as follows:

| | |
|---|---|
| Lokele | 29 |
| *Arabisés* | 27 |
| Foreign | 21 |
| Other Zairians | 11 |
| Luba | 9 |
| Nande | 8 |
| Mixed race | 7 |
| Kongo | 4 |
| Not known | 15 |
| | |
| Total | 131 |

These findings indicate that the more advantageous positions in the class structure attained by some ethnic groups in the colonial period have been retained to the present time, offering their members greater opportunities for advancement.

We have shown that despite circumstances generally regarded as unfavourable for the development of local capitalism, an indigenous capitalist class is in process of formation. The next two chapters will show how these businessmen and women were able to surmount the difficulties confronting them; how they found opportunities to get started in business, successfully accumulated capital and expanded their enterprises. Clearly the economy stands in need of rationally managed and expanding enterprise producing for local consumption; the question to which we must lead is whether such a class having started to form can continue to do so in the face of competition and domination by foreign capital and in confrontation with a state and state-based class of the kind that exists in Zaire.

A market stall

Building and stores owned by one of the independent entrepreneurs

Wholesale businesses of the foreign commercial class

Building with stores, offices and apartments owned by a politician

# 4

## Opportunities for capital accumulation: the emergence of an indigenous bourgeoisie

When changes are actually in process, they are defined as social *problems*, rather than as social *opportunities*. (Obbo 1980: 5)

The parasitic capitalism that developed in Zaire after independence and the pillaging, consumption-oriented ethic of the political aristocracy provided very unfavourable conditions for the development of a true national bourgeoisie. Yet, as we have seen, despite such inimical circumstances, a local indigenous capitalist class has begun to emerge in Kisangani. The detailed data on individuals presented in this chapter show the part played in this process by the indigenization of foreign capital and by opportunities for profit making in the articulation of capitalist and non-capitalist modes of production. Personal histories of Kisangani businessmen and women show how they acquired enterprises, achieved success in business, and accumulated capital. The histories also reveal the social background of these entrepreneurs, their sources of venture capital and details of their relations with family and kin. These case studies show the process of class formation taking place in the actual experiences of individuals. Comparison with other parts of Africa shows similar processes occurring elsewhere.

Various opportunities for accumulation of capital and acquisition of businesses occurred in the sixties and seventies for those without position in the state. Formation of enterprises is not itself a measure of accumulation but it gives individuals the means through which to accumulate (Swainson 1980: 211). The critical factor is the use made of accumulated wealth. The political aristocracy have used their position in the state to move into the economy and acquire extensive enterprises, but they have plundered rather than expanded their acquisitions. The nascent bourgeoisie emerging in Kisangani, however, displays true capitalist spirit: these entrepreneurs are concerned with good management and reinvestment of profit. Since they do not have the benefit of state position and its opportunities to increase wealth through pillage and appropriation, their possibilities for wealth and advancement lie in the development of their business concerns.

90

In the sixties, opportunities for acquiring enterprises came when foreigners fled the violence and other disruptions that accompanied and followed independence. The disorganization of the administrative apparatus of the state at this time made it possible for some individuals without political power and influence to acquire the abandoned businesses, real estate or plantations that were to be the basis for subsequent capital accumulation, investment and expansion. In the seventies the decrees of Zairianization and retrocession mostly transferred ownership of foreign concerns to those in the state or with political connections, but they also benefited, both directly and indirectly, a number of individuals outside politics. In addition to indigenization of foreign capital, profits made from the sale of commodities acquired at low prices in non-capitalist systems and sold for high prices in urban markets or for export resulted in rapid accumulation of wealth for some individuals.

## THE VIOLENCE OF THE SIXTIES

We have shown that in the colonial period few opportunities existed for capital accumulation by Africans and that the economy was dominated by foreigners. In the sixties, the violence and political troubles following independence caused many expatriates to flee, abandoning businesses, plantations and real estate. The extent of this exodus varied from one region to another: in Shaba (Katanga) the majority of the colonials stayed on for two years; in the east and northeast the Belgian presence almost vanished (Peemans 1980: 275).

Demands for independence in the late 1950s were met by the Belgians with complacence and a conviction that decolonization would be controlled and gradual. The riots of January 1959 in Kinshasa took them by surprise and the subsequent deterioration of authority and administration and the demands of militant nationalism resulted in precipitate granting of independence in 1960. Political chaos followed: within two weeks the army had mutinied, mineral rich Katanga province (now Shaba) had seceded, Belgian civil servants, planters and businessmen were leaving the country in panic and Belgian troops had intervened to quell distrubances. By the time a UN peace force arrived in July the European population, which had been 110,000 in 1959, was down to 20,000.

In the ensuing breakdown of government, hostility between prime minister Lumumba and president Kasavubu led to the arrest of Lumumba, whose supporters, headed by Antoine Gizenga, then set up a rival government in Kisangani (then Stanleyville). Disturbances in the northeast followed Lumumba's assassination in January 1961, as the Stanleyville regime extended its influence to Kivu and south to North Katanga and Kasai. In North Katanga alone, violent reprisals resulted in as many as 20,000 deaths (Young 1965: 352). In August 1961 Cyrille Adoula became prime minister and in January of the next year, with the arrest of Gizenga,

Kisangani ceased to be a centre for dissidence.

Despite localized disruption the economic infrastructure remained remarkably intact during this time: schools and administration functioned after the initial three months of independence; river and rail transport and mining production were maintained; production of cement, sugar and beer for the domestic market even increased (*ibid.*: 351). But the panic stricken exodus of half the foreign population resulted in the abandonment of stores, plantations, businesses and houses, giving nationals the opportunity to acquire them.

In 1964 horrific events took place in Kisangani which in 1980 were still all too vivid in the minds of the inhabitants. A series of rebellions broke out, in southeast Kwilu under Pierre Mulele and in the east and northeast under Gaston Soumialot and Nicholas Olenga. They expressed the disillusionment and alienation of the population and their perception that the privileged class had taken all the benefits of independence for themselves. In 1963 Mulele organized guerilla training camps in the forest for men of the villages to fight for a 'second independence' against the politicians, civil servants, teachers, soldiers and police who were seen to have replaced the Belgians as an exploiting class. In 1964 the rebellions broke out and by August the 'Peoples' Liberation Army', or 'Simbas', took Kisangani and formed a Peoples' Republic of the Congo. They attempted to eliminate the new exploiting class through executions and mass murders. It is estimated that at least 20,000 people died, most of them men. (For a detailed account see Verhaegen 1969; Young 1970; 1965: 582–98).

The violence of these rebellions had much more profound effects than the earlier disorders. Drastic disruption of social and economic structures accompanied the taking of Kisangani by the rebels and the subsequent occupation of the city by foreign mercenaries and the national army; it was then, people in Kisangani say, that 'the war against the people really began'. In 1967 the mercenaries revolted but were defeated; a year later the town was pillaged by the army. Case histories show that, as is often the case in the aftermath of disaster, some individuals successfully exploited this situation. The disruption of supplies and closing of stores and other businesses during this period of political upheaval led to shortages of all kinds and individuals with initiative and means to start an enterprise in the aftermath found they had a ready market and no competition.

Table 4.1 summarizes case histories of sixteen of the thirty-two men and women who are owners of substantial businesses in Kisangani and identifiable as members of the emergent commercial middle class. Number 7, 14 and 16 provide examples of individuals who got started on their successful business careers through opportunities occurring in this period of political chaos.

No. 7, Mr S., completed school in 1952, and at the age of eighteen started to work for a private company. In 1965 he decided to set up on his own and

Table 4.1 *Summary of case histories*

| Father's occupation | Education | Previous occupation, year began business | Business | Employees |
|---|---|---|---|---|
| **Men** | | | | |
| 1. village farmer | 3 yrs S | petty trade, 1973 | 4 retail stores nightclub coffee plantation | 30 |
| 2. village farmer | 6 yrs S | teacher political office, 1970 | furniture factory sawmill coffee, rubber, rice plantations; coffee, rice mills, timber, ranch | 300 now 185 |
| 3. employee private company | Univ. degree | own business, 1973 | furniture factory bakery agro-industry: coffee, maize, rice, manioc, timber export/import | 240 |
| 4. employee private company | 6 yrs S | ranch, 1970 | 4 luxury retail stores, ranch | 32 |
| 5. employee private company | 4 yrs S | accountant political office, ? | coffee, oil palm plantations; coffee and rice mills beer depot, stores in interior, pig and goat ranch | 125 |
| 6. customary chief | 2 yrs S | private company 10 years, 1960 | wholesaler (branches Kindu and Kinshasa) 64 retail stores in interior, coffee plantation | 800 |
| 7. Italian planter | 6 yrs S | private company 13 years, 1965 | bakeries, hotels partner in 10 businesses coffee plantations and export, wholesale and retail, garage, cars etc. | many |
| 8. Belgian businessman | 6 yrs S | private company 20 years, 1972 | manufacturing: work clothes; garage and bike sales, wholesale alcohol, pig farm, rice and manioc mills, coffee plantation | 41 |

Table 4.1 *(Contd.)*

| Father's occupation | Education | Previous occupation, year began business | Business | Employees |
|---|---|---|---|---|
| 9. Greek ? | 5 yrs S accounting | private company 6 years, 1965 | coffee plantations rice and coffee mills, fishery transport, 5 stores in interior | many |
| *Women* | | | | |
| 10. government employee | 3 yrs S | teacher 4 years, 1974 | retail store trade to Kinshasa and Bunia | 19 |
| 11. government employee | 2 yrs S | housewife, 1975 | retail store wholesale (with Asian partner, coffee plantation) | 15 |
| 12. government employee | 1 yr Univ. | housewife, 1979 | boutique, tailoring establishment (Greek partner) | 5 |
| 13. trader | 1 yr S | teacher, 1973 | retail and semi-wholesale, trade to Bukavu | 7 |
| 14. customary chief | few yrs P | ? 1961 | bar, nightclub, coffee plantation store in Bunia, partner with husband in fishery, transport, general commerce | 264 |
| 15. ? | 5 yrs S | travelling commerce, 1975 | 4 retail stores semi-wholesale commerce to Kinshasa transport | 50 |
| 16. ? | 6 yrs S | travelling commerce, ? | stores in Kisangani, Bunia, Kinshasa commerce to Kinshasa coffee plantation partner with husband in transport | ? |

S = secondary school, P = primary school

came to Kisangani, which was a ruin after the rebellion. Mr S. bought up abandoned houses, used them as security to get credit at the bank for capital to go to Kinshasa, buy goods and charter a plane to bring them to Kisangani.

He invested the money he made in buying a lot more real estate and started an import business, using his business profits and his real estate as collateral, to get hard currency from the banks.

In 1980 he was one of Kisangani's biggest businessmen. He owned real estate on a huge scale and had recently bought extensive plantations and become a major coffee exporter. His multiple business concerns included hotels, a wholesale company, bakeries, electrical stores, garages etc., in Kisangani, Kinshasa and other cities. In several of his businesses he had foreign partners.

No. 14, Madame F., is one of the forty children of a customary chief. She had only a few years of primary education but is reputed to be one of Kisangani's biggest businesswomen. She started in business by running a bar and by 1961 she had enough money to buy two coffee plantations from departing Belgians, using a loan from the government agency for business assistance, the *Société de Crédit aux Classes Moyennes*. She escaped the rebellion by going to Kinshasa, but returned in 1966, opened a nightclub and sold alcohol wholesale, both profitmaking businesses in the aftermath of the troubles when the city was full of soldiers.

She thus already had substantial business concerns when in 1965 she married an expatriate who owned a fishery. They operate their businesses in partnership, but she manages the ones that were hers. They own a transport firm (that until recently had eighteen trucks), stores in Bunia and Kinshasa and ten houses for rent (she told me with pride that she had personally supervised the building of six of them), as well as the fishery, plantations and nightclub. They employ 264 workers. She had a licence to begin exporting coffee in 1980. In her house she has photographs of President Mobutu presenting her with two gold medals for her plantations and businesses, an indication of her importance and reputation as a businesswoman independently of her husband. Their son is at secondary school; their daughter manages their Kinshasa store.

No. 16, Madame B., also one of the best-known businesswomen in town, completed secondary school, then went into commerce by buying a truck on credit and trading all over Upper Zaire, Kivu and Kasai. She started her business in Kisangani after independence when 'it was easy to get a store, there were so many left empty'. She is married to a Kenyan who made his money in transport and now imports fish, helped by a family connection in Mombasa. They are partners in business and very wealthy, and have invested their profits in coffee plantations and real estate. Like Madame F., she manages her enterprises in the partnership independently. She goes to Kinshasa once or twice a month, exporting fish, rice and beans on a large scale and importing food, cloth and other goods. One of their daughters is studying medicine in Brussels, two help with her store.

These individuals all founded their successful careers in business on enterprises acquired from foreigners fleeing from the violent events of the sixties and on exploiting the economic opportunities in the aftermath of these events. It is not possible to quantify precisely the rate of success and failure of those who acquired these, or other, businesses, but in 1980 these three examples at least among the substantial independent entrepreneurs had been helped in their business careers by the events of the sixties.

ZAIRIANIZATION AND RETROCESSION

More extensive indigenization of foreign capital occurred in 1973 when the Zairianization decree handed over retail and wholesale business, small factories, plantations and fisheries owned by foreigners to Zairians. Most businesses were allocated to those holding positions in the state, or to persons connected to them. The political basis of this selection process has been documented for Equateur and Shaba. In Lisala, Equateur, administrators, collaborators or relatives of Mobutu, wives of foreigners and those with ethnic links to the powerful obtained businesses. In Bumba, a larger commercial centre than Lisala, seven of the nine who acquired businesses had some position with the party; the other two were an army officer and a Kinshasa merchant originally from Bumba (Schatzberg 1980a: 131–5). In Lubumbashi in Shaba, the regional commissioner and his five closest collaborators were among the largest acquirers (D. Gould 1978: 28). In Kisangani also, politicians and military officers received many businesses, but the list of enterprises being retroceded to their former foreign owners showed a significant number of acquirers were not holders of state position. The process of retrocession was 80 per cent completed by 1979; 20 per cent were still disputed. The information on fifty-four enterprises that had been Zairianized showed that fourteen had been acquired by individuals with political or military position: a sub-regional commissioner from Shaba (two businesses); three people's commissioners from Upper Zaire (one had two businesses); a 'Chef de Bureau'; an economic councillor to the regional commissioner; an official of the Regional Economic Office; a former secretary of UNTZA (the national trade union); the divisional chief of the Land Title Office (two businesses); and two army generals. Forty other businesses were acquired by sixteen Kisangani businessman, two Kisangani businesswomen, six family members (five Zairian wives, one son mixed parentage), thirteen businessmen from elsewhere (all but two from Kinshasa), and by three with occupations unknown.

It is probable that the Kinshasa businessmen were frontmen, acting for politically powerful individuals, but, at the very least, twenty-four of the fifty-four businesses on the list, or nearly half, had been Zairianized by individuals without position in the state. Although some of these entrepreneurs went rapidly out of business, others did not. Thus in Kisangani Zairianization provided opportunities for economic mobility for some individuals who had a good head for business and serious intentions, in contrast to the results of Zairianization reported elsewhere by Gould and Schatzberg. Some of these Kisangani entrepreneurs bought their businesses outright from the former owners; others acquired them through ties to foreigners, either of marriage or, as in the case of those of mixed Zairian and European parents, of kinship. Some ambivalence existed towards takeover as a means of acquiring businesses, however; some of the businessmen I talked to made a point of emphasizng either that they were not acquirers, or that they had paid in full for their businesses. One man said that decent people felt reluctant to go and take away the business another had spent all his life building up. Schatzberg reports similar reactions in Lisala (Schatzberg 1980a: 152).[1]

Two histories of individuals who successfully developed businesses they acquired in Zairianization have been given above, p. 68. They are Numbers 3 and 8 in Table 4.1. Numbers 2, 9 and 10 provide three additional examples. Number 2 is an example of one who got his initial business through political position, but lost this position soon thereafter and now belongs in the commercial class.[2]

> No. 2, Mr A.L., went through secondary school, then became a teacher and afterwards an inspector of schools. He described himself as a 'victim of the Lumumbist rebellion', but he survived and entered politics briefly in 1970. At the same time he took up commercial agriculture, investing the money from his first harvest in husking machines for rice and coffee. His political position brought him two foreign businesses in Zairianization: a furniture factory and rubber and coffee plantations, previously owned by a Greek and a Belgian. He failed in politics but his businesses did well; in 1976 he invested his profits in a sawmill and another coffee plantation. At this time he had nine trucks and two tractors and employed 300 workers. In 1980 he had a rice mill and was forming a rice cooperative; he also had a forestry concession, 140 hectares of rubber, 210 hectares of coffee which produced 90 tonnes of coffee 1978–9, and a farm with twenty to thirty cows from which he planned to get milk and cheese. He was renting out two houses and building a third.
>
> In 1980 his business was floundering because of the economic crisis, in particular the difficulty and expense of getting spare parts, fuel, varnish and plywood from Kinshasa for his furniture factory; his workers were down to 185 and his trucks to two. He said bitterly: 'there is an economic crisis but the government does not know, to judge from its actions. They just continue to demand taxes and enforce regulations instead of controlling the price of fuel and importing spare parts.'
>
> Mr A.L., unlike most acquirers, made a success of the business he Zairianized, until he was overtaken by the general decline of the economy. He attributes his success to being on the spot to control and be involved in his business: 'I deal with everyone directly, not through intermediaries. A workman needs to see the boss around or else he gets discouraged.' So when he visits his various enterprises he talks to his workers, works alongside them and encourages them to bring their problems directly to him. 'If a man has a sick wife or child and needs money for medicine and the request for authorization has to go up through a whole hierarchy, the child will die in the meantime.' He also assures his workers that if they work and the enterprise prospers they will share in the proceeds.

Mr A.L., concerns himself with his workers and the proper management of his business. By just paying his employees regularly he is far ahead of the majority of acquirers, who, as frequently reported in *Boyoma* and government reports, fail conspicuously to fulfil such minimal obligations to their employees.

97

No. 9, Mr M., has a Greek father. He started out in transport with a truck bought for him by his Greek uncle. Later he bought two more on credit from the bank and contracted to work for the big wholesale companies. His business increased to ten trucks, and he invested his profits in fifteen businesses with the help of more credit from the bank.

In 1973 he Zairianized a coffee plantation from his Greek uncle, a big planter in the interior who had no children of his own. He also Zairianized a fishery for which he later paid. His businesses were successful and he invested his profits in a coffee factory which processes 16 tonnes a day, a rice mill which processes 150 sacks of rice a day, five stores in the interior and in a lot of real estate. He is said to be very rich, owns eight trucks and drives around in a Range Rover.

Clearly, in addition to Zairianization, Mr M.'s Greek relatives were a factor in his success. Madame K., the next example, owed the start of her considerable business directly to Zairianization.

No. 10, Madame K., had three years of secondary school. She traded on a small scale on weekends, learning from her mother. She then worked as a teacher for four years. She had a child acknowledged by a foreigner, which entitled her to claim his retail business in Zairianization. She paid for his store and three trucks, using Z2,000 of her own money: Z1,000 as a downpayment and Z1,000 to work with. She continued paying money to the bank each month until the business was paid for. She built it up successfully enough to buy five houses in 1976 and 1978, and also the building in which she has her store which includes another shop besides hers and two apartments above. She has nineteen employees. She ships 100–200 sacks of beans to Kinshasa every month or two, and travels there herself about four times a year to stock her store. She also trades to Bunia in the interior, where she has her own agent.

These individuals all benefited directly from Zairianization. Their success forms a contrast to the majority of acquirers, who failed. Among the examples I have collected, Zairianization opened up more opportunities than did the upheavals of the sixties.

Individuals who acquired enterprises benefited directly from Zairianization; others benefited indirectly. Many of the acquirers of foreign concerns went out of business or ceased to function effectively, so that competition in the retail business almost disappeared for the few stores that remained in existence under competent management. This situation resulted in the rapid expansion of a number of retail businesses.

Individuals who benefited indirectly in this way are rare in the commercial population partly because foreigners had dominated the retail trade but also because an unusual degree of talent, innovation and hard work seems to have been necessary for such success. Mukenge's study of businessmen in Kinshasa indicates that innovation is crucial in outdoing competition (Mukenge 1974: 49).

No. 4, Mr T., had a retail clothing store in 1972, when he was only twenty-three, but refused to take over businesses offered to him in Zairianization. 'After a while,' he said, 'I was almost the only Zairian businessman in town; everybody came to me and business flourished.' By 1976 he had four stores. He invested 'for security' in construction of two buildings of offices with apartments above, in the centre of town. He now has a purchasing office and two building lots in Kinshasa, on which he rents out three houses. He employs thirty-two people.

From the beginning Mr. T. showed a flair for perceiving and exploiting market openings. He also impressed the bank inspectors with his bookkeeping and the volume of his business, and had no difficulty getting credit from the banks and from his suppliers. In his first store he discovered that shirts sold best, so he stopped selling food and beer and concentrated on shirts, trousers and *wax* print cloth (sold in lengths for making blouses and wrap-around skirts). His stores are now luxury boutiques: one sells children's clothes, frilly embroidered infants' outfits and imported children's shoes; another has imported shirts and men's clothes; and a third sells gold and silver jewellery, toiletries and leather goods, such as briefcases, wallets and belts. The decor and design of his stores are reminiscent of smart European boutiques and outside he has neat flowerbeds and shrubs. He is, very astutely, exploiting the tastes and desires of the newly wealthy class for the consumer luxuries and surroundings of Europe. With his talent and imagination he has built on the favourable early start given him, indirectly, by Zairianization. I heard subsequently that he had opened a workshop for the manufacture of jewellery in Kinshasa and invested extensively in real estate there.

No. 15, Madame W., is married to a Zairian businessman, but they are not business partners: her enterprises are her own, managed by her. After five years of secondary school, she started in commerce in 1971 by trading manioc down river from Bandundu to Kinshasa. After two trips she had realized Z500 to put in the bank. She did not want her husband to know she was trading, fearing his interference, so her elder brother signed as her husband, giving her the necessary permission to open a bank account. On her third trip 100 out of 107 sacks of manioc were stolen. Her sister, a big trader, helped her to get credit from the bank for a forty-five day loan of Z2,500: she bought fresh fish (the much prized *capitaine*), an innovative item, and quickly sold it all at the dockside in Kinshasa, spending Z300 and making Z1,500, a profit of Z1,200. Since she paid the bank back in ten days, the bank manager was delighted and increased her credit to Z5,000. Another theft of 105 sacks of manioc, however, discouraged her and she decided to follow her sister in selling *wax* print cloth. She began to trade all over the country, travelling by plane and selling *wax* prints in Lubumbashi, Kisangani, Kivu and Mbandaka. By 1973 she had Z30,000 capital and had bought a house and a store in Kisangani. Her younger sister joined her to manage the store when Madame W. travelled.

In 1974 she started in transport, buying a truck and opening a store in Bunia, in the interior. By 1979 she had opened three more stores in Kisangani, one of them a luxury boutique selling imported *wax* prints, liquor, shoes and men's shirts. This store, like Mr T.'s, had a carefully designed decor: the shelves in the display cases were covered with pebbles on which a few pairs of shoes were arranged, interspersed with Christmas tree ornaments. She had fifty employees, including seven members of her family, and owned five trucks, four cars and four houses to rent out. In 1979 she ran a bus service for a while. She supplies her stores by going to Kinshasa every two months to buy from wholesalers. She gets a relative to buy *wax* prints for her in Brazzaville, travels to Ruanda on buying trips about once a month and also buys from the Kisangani wholesalers. Her son and daughter attend good Catholic schools. She and her husband share household and educational expenses for their children.

Madame W.'s business in Kisangani expanded rapidly because of the lack of competition after Zairianization. Her history reveals other factors contributing to her success. She received help from her family, both in starting out and in assistance in her business, and she is innovative in choice of goods and type of store. The profit she made on particular transactions and the rapidity with which she accumulated capital reflects the enormous differential between wholesale prices and the prices the consumer can be forced to pay; large profits are made shipping goods from one part of the country to another, where they are scarce, and charging a high mark-up. Her experience of massive theft is an example of one of the worst problems in transportation of goods. Her history also shows that a successful businesswoman can have good credit with the banks and can make unofficial arrangements to deal in foreign currency.

No. 1, Mr A., was selling goods up and down the river from a canoe in 1973. In that year he used money from four years of this trade to open a store. 'I started out at a good moment,' he says. 'It was a scandal: those who acquired businesses from foreigners just sold up the stock and spent their money.' He found a good market in these circumstances for Dutch *wax* prints which he bought for Z6–7 in Kinshasa and sold in Kisangani for Z14. He was soon going to Kinshasa once or twice a week. He studied the market and started selling records, bought for 40K in Kinshasa and sold for 80K in Kisangani, an innovation that paid off since they were cheap and in great demand and he was the only one selling them. In 1979 he had four retail stores and a discotheque, which he had started in 1978, and employed thirty-one people. He also owned a coffee plantation acquired after Zairianization.

These individuals all invested the capital they accumulated in expanding their retail enterprises, moving into manufacturing, production or transportation and in buying real estate. They all showed innovative entrepreneurial talent and a willingness to work hard for extremely long hours.

PLANTATIONS: ACCESS TO A PROFITABLE ECONOMIC SECTOR

The plantations handed over in Zairianization were of particular importance for capital accumulation, especially coffee plantations. Coffee growing is one of the most profitable sectors of the economy in Zaire. Coffee, known as 'green gold', became the most important source of foreign exchange after copper and cobalt between 1971 and 1981, averaging 40.5 per cent of agricultural exports and 6.4 per cent of total exports in 1970–5 (IRES 1977: 14). European planters dominated the coffee sector both in the colonial period and after independence; although many Belgians left in the troubles of the sixties, they were replaced by

Greeks. In 1973 however, Zairianization brought nationals access to this extremely profitable sector of the economy.

The official list of plantation owners for the whole region of Upper Zaire included thirty-two politicians, military officers and officials, all but a few of them local to the region, and twenty-three Kisangani businessmen and women, as well as many individuals from other parts of the region.[3] Only four of the individuals in Table 4.1 do *not* own plantations. Coffee plantations are the most valuable; of the thirty-two substantial independent business owners in Kisangani, nineteen owned coffee plantations, seven did not and for six I do not have information. But these data show the acquisition through Zairianization of extensive productive enterprise by these entrepreneurs.

Many acquirers mismanaged and neglected their plantations; coffee production dropped from 74,052 tonnes in 1972 to only 59,444 tonnes in 1975. In 1976, however, a world shortage produced a spectacular rise in the price of coffee. The shortage was caused by frost in Brazil, drought and floods in Colombia, and the Angolan civil war. Prices rose from 40 Belgian francs a kilogram in 1975 to 92 FB in 1976 and 240 FB in March 1977. There was a rush to get into growing, buying and exporting coffee: 'One sees the appearance here of a multitude of enterprises; traders, transporters, exporters, everyone has become interested in coffee' (IRES 1977: 4). Kisangani hotels reported an increase of 71 per cent in occupancy between 1976 and 1977 (*Rapport Economique Sous-Régional* 1977). People who had bought coffee at the old low price made fortunes selling it at the new high prices. The sub-regional commissioner from Lower Uele complained of an influx of businessmen from other regions to buy coffee who were not respecting the official price, and also that people were turning to coffee cultivation and abandoning food crops (*Boyoma* 18 March 1977). Production rose in 1976 to 108,613 tonnes as coffee became a primary means to accumulate wealth.

Zairianization generally contrasts with indigenization measures in other African countries because it brought nationals access to this extremely profitable sector of the economy. In Zambia, for example, foreigners found means to circumvent the economic reforms designed to effect indigenization of foreign capital, so these reforms were not directly responsible for the growth of African businesses. They did, however, indirectly encourage such growth because they hastened the foreign exodus from the more marginal areas of trade which were then taken up by Africans and they made foreigners feel less secure and therefore easier to compete against (Beveridge and Oberschall 1979: 253). In Nigeria and Ghana, indigenization of foreign holdings resulted in partnership of African entrepreneurs with foreign capitalists but without a move into production (Hoogvelt 1979; Hutchful 1979). In Senegal, foreign capital was withdrawn, with a few exceptions, from unprofitable sectors of the economy, only allowing local capital access to sectors incapable of furnishing opportunities for rapid accumulation (Amin 1971: 367–71). But more recently, despite lack of credit facilities, certain sectors catering to an expanding domestic market have been able to develop, such as wholesale butchers and fishmongers, fruit, vegetable, kola nut and rice traders. The result is the growth of some national capital (Amin 1981: 317–19).

In 1976, because so many acquirers in Zaire mismanaged or bankrupted their new enterprises, the decree of retrocession returned businesses to their former foreign owners. This decree provided new business opportunities for some Kisangani entrepreneurs, however, because the foreigners were obliged to take Zairian partners. Two of the women in Table 4.1 had entered such partnerships. Number 11 owned a retail store and was invited to be a partner with an Asian in a wholesale business which provided her with the opportunity to expand her activities beyond the retail store. Her husband partnered the Asian's brother in another business. Husband and wife acquired a coffee plantation in Zairianization, bought up another which had been abandoned, and invested in real estate. Number 12 is married to a prominent professional with many connections to Europeans, one of which brought her an invitation to become the partner of a Greek woman in a retail dress store. The Greek became ill and returned to Greece, though she still retained a share in the business. Number 12 proceeded to transform the store into a thriving concern, details of which will be given in Chapter 7. Thus retrocession, like Zairianization, has played a part in capital accumulation for the new commercial class through the acquisition and expansion of enterprises.

PROFITS FROM RURAL-URBAN TERMS OF TRADE

Rural producers of food and export crops subsist for very low costs in non-capitalist modes of production and get very low prices for their products. Transportation costs increased drastically with the rise in oil prices and the deterioration of the roads; delays and theft sometimes result in heavy losses for traders. Nevertheless, appropriation from petty producers has resulted in the expansion of merchant capital. Some traders by a combination of luck, enterprise and hard work are able to make large profits buying food and export crops at the low prices paid to rural growers and selling them at the much higher prices of the urban or export markets. Case histories show that profits made from such trade have been invested in productive concerns as well as in expansion of distributive enterprise or in real estate. Such profit making cannot be monopolized by foreigners or the agents of the political aristocracy; it has provided the means for upward mobility for men and women from various class backgrounds.

The profits in such trade can be considerable. Details of Madame W.'s first trading trips show how lucrative they were. She bought commodities produced under non-capitalist relations of production at very low prices, and sold them at the high prices of Kinshasa's market as follows:

Madame W. (No. 15 in Table 4.1) had Z45 for her first trip in 1971 from Idiofa, Bandundu, to Kinshasa. She bought fifteen sacks of manioc at 50K each, and sold them at Z5 each, so she made Z75 for an expenditure of Z7.50. She also bought Z20 of manioc puddings (*chikwanga*) at three for one likuta, which she sold for Z150. Her round trip ticket for the boat cost Z12. She returned with a profit of around Z200 after additional expenses, such as transport to and from the docks. On her second trip her purchases included 77 sacks of *chikwanga* and manioc. This time she returned with a profit of Z900, put Z500 in the bank, Z100 towards her household and had Z300 for her next trip.

One must take into account the high risks of this very profitable trade, remembering that on subsequent ventures she suffered large-scale theft. Competition is also very steep; others seek to realize similar profits and rush to trade in commodities particularly in demand. Nevertheless, considerable opportunities for profit sometimes occur; for some individuals who are fortunate and escape adversity, profits are sufficient to provide them with capital on a sufficient scale to permit investment in productive enterprise and real estate. More examples appear in Chapter 6.

We have discussed so far how personal histories have shown that the indigenization of foreign capital and the articulation of non-capitalist and capitalist modes of production have provided opportunities for capital accumulation. These histories also reveal details of the background and functioning of this new class.

THE NEW CLASS

We will turn first to the social and educational background of the entrepreneurs, and to their sources of venture capital, then describe their relations with kin, and end with a discussion of the generality of the data. These details complete the account of the emergence of the new class and make possible some comparisons with the development of local capitalism elsewhere in Africa.

The independent entrepreneurs in Kisangani come from diverse backgrounds. Table 4.1 summarizes personal histories of sixteen men and women of this class. Such a small number is insufficient to allow definitive conclusions about background but it gives some indications. This new class sector appears to draw its members from all classes; the fathers of these entrepreneurs ranged from village farmers and customary chiefs to employees of private companies and government officials.

Education varies considerably among these men and women. The data support the findings on educational background in studies of successful business entrepreneurs in Kinshasa and Lower Zaire. For the individuals whose histories are summarized in Table 4.1, education ranged from only a few years of primary school to university, but fifteen of the sixteen had secondary education of some sort. This is consistent with the conclusion of Mukenge's study of successful businessmen in Kinshasa, that success in business requires good bookkeeping skills and therefore education beyond the primary level (Mukenge 1974: 21). Diambomba's study of factors influencing performance among 200 entrepreneurs in Lower Zaire and Kinshasa found that the most successful had a background of on the job training and some formal education (Diambomba 1971).

These entrepreneurs acquired initial capital in various ways which can be categorized as follows: working for a big firm and trading on the side, saving wages and additional earnings; help from relatives or spouse; and savings from small-scale commerce in which any accumulation required talent and very hard work. The first is more usual among men, the last two among women. This and other data on the significance of gender in the process of class formation will be discussed in Chapter 7. The range of sources of venture capital also illustrates the variety of class background of these entrepreneurs.

Five of the entrepreneurs of this study (Numbers 5, 6, 7, 8 and 9 in Table 4.1) accumulated venture capital by working for private companies. Among Kinshasa businessman also, Mukenge found that the successful had had a good start from the salaries and status of their previous jobs. Working for a big firm brought not only salary but also opportunities to establish contacts with foreigners and government officials that were later useful for business (Mukenge 1974: 385).

> No. 7, Mr S., worked for several different companies for twelve years before setting up in business on his own. During this period of employment he also traded in fish and cigarettes, eventually saving enough money to buy a truck to expand this trade and accumulate his initial capital.

> No. 8, Mr O., worked for twenty years for a Danish multinational company. He invested his savings in 1972 in an auto business, in partnership with Mr S. They were the local dealer for Nissan, importing and assembling trucks, and were also the local outlet for Mazda and Datsun cars.

> No. 9, Mr M., acquired his venture capital by working for six years at the local brewery. He then went into transport in which he rapidly accumulated capital.

> No. 6, Mr T.A., worked for ten years for SEDEC, the big import/export branch of Unilever, and traded on the side, accumulating enough capital to set up a trading business in 1960. In 1978 he invested in productive enterprise by buying up two abandoned plantations, with the help of a loan from the *Société de Crédit aux Classes Moyennes*. By 1980 he operated at the national level in his wholesale and retail businesses.

Two of the men and five of the women among these entrepreneurs accumulated their initial capital in small scale commerce, in which any accumulation required innovative talents and very hard work. Details of the women will be given in Chapter 7.

> No. 4, Mr T., had some money from a cattle ranch in Shaba before he moved to Kisangani in 1970. A European friend lent him the extra capital he needed to set up in a small store selling French fries, cigarettes, soap, oil and

sardines. He worked very hard for long hours, sometimes till 4 a.m., for two years until he had enough capital to expand his business.

No. 1, Mr A., left secondary school after three years in 1968 to work for his brother-in-law, a Lokele trader selling clothes, soap and sardines by canoe to the riverine villages. At this time people were returning from the forest after the troubles and there was a great demand for clothing. Mr A used his aunt's sewing machine to make clothes. After one year he had Z100 and started trading on his own spending Z20 on a canoe, Z40 on a commercial licence and Z50 on goods from a wholesaler. He emphasized how hard he worked: all goods had to be carried to the river on his head, he had to paddle long distances, often at night, to get to markets early enough, or in rainy weather when rivers are dangerous. After three years, in March 1973, he had accumulated Z400, enough to rent and stock a store.

The issues of the employment of family members and its effect on the operation of businesses and of the degree to which obligations to the extended family hamper capital accumulation are often raised in the discussion of African capitalism. Sara Berry found that, in Nigeria, Yoruba without financial resources were able to mobilize labour among their dependants on promise of future assistance rather than cash wages, and were thus able to launch small businesses or farms without access to working capital. This did, however, limit their ability to control and expand their enterprises (Berry 1985: 11). In several of the cases detailed above, relatives gave some sort of assistance or training. Employment of relatives, however, is not so usual. Number 8, in Table 4.1, had his sons managing his different enterprises. His father was a European; political difficulties that he said arose from his mixed parentage made it necessary to rely on his children. Number 1 had his brother-in-law working as a disc jockey in his nightclub and a cousin also worked there. He tried using other members of his family as employees, but found it did not work out. Number 2 had his younger brother working for him for two years but that too was a failure. Number 7 had his brother-in-law managing one of his enterprises. Number 15 was unusual in employing seven relatives.

Employment of relatives is the exception rather than the norm. They are not considered to be necessarily more trustworthy and are, in fact, thought of as a problem because if they prove dishonest it is difficult to dismiss them or take legal action against them. Some businessmen make a point of keeping relatives out of their business concerns.[4] We see here a contrast with both Asian and Nande enterprises. One obvious difference in this respect between Asians and Africans in Kisangani is that Asians live in small, relatively closed communities, in which sanctions for default can be more easily applied than they can by Africans in the context of a large city population. The reasons for close cooperation of family members among the Nande will be discussed fully in Chapter 6.

Family obligations for support of dependent and less well-off relatives are another matter, however, and are widely undertaken. One businessman said that he was unusual because he drew the line at helping more than a select few of his closest relatives. Such obligations can be a considerable burden.

No. 14, Madame F., has taken on the total support of her deceased sister's five children and pays for them all to go to a mission boarding school. She regularly holds court in a room at the back of her house to deal with family problems, such as paying for medical care. When an uncle died in a town in the interior, she organized the wake for all kin resident in Kisangani. In keeping with tradition the women sat apart to keep watch all night. Madame F. presided, dressed like any village woman instead of in one of her usual high-fashion outfits, and sat on the floor in traditional fashion on a mattress. But instead of the customary refreshment, she provided generous quantities of Teachers Highland Cream whisky.

Just how burdensome family obligations can be is illustrated by the details of the household budget for one middle-class family, that of Mr L.H. a construction engineer.

Mr L.H. and his wife are Nande from Kivu; they came to Kisangani in 1973. He was well qualified, having trained in Canada for six months after qualifying in Kinshasa. His annual salary, then Z1,300, covered monthly purchase of ten sacks of cement for building a house, completed a year later. Additional income came from work on the side: he drew up plans and supervised construction of houses at Z2,200 a time. The sale of potatoes and cabbages sent by family members in Kivu also brought in some income. His wife got a degree at the university in Kisangani and subsequently took a job as a school secretary.

In 1980 their incomes were Z6,000 and Z3,900, but their financial obligations to various relatives were such that they found it difficult to make ends meet. Besides their three young children, her two sisters and a brother lived with them to go to school. They also sent money to Kivu for her widowed mother and his parents every month, paid for school fees and clothes for the five children of his deceased mother's brother, and provided plane fares for his younger brother to go to Kinshasa to attend the university.

In 1978 they built a bar-restaurant where they employed seven workers, and they planned a motel, but by 1980 beer was so expensive that they were running at a loss. They had a 3 hectare field out of town in which they grew manioc, sugar cane, bananas and pineapples to feed the family; they sold the surplus. They also kept rabbits, pigeons and chickens in their yard. They employed two farmworkers, two domestics and one watchman/gardener. Their major expenses per year can be approximated as follow:

| | |
|---|---|
| School fees and transportation for their children | Z2,618 |
| School fees and travel for children of relatives | Z1,130 |
| Wage bill if averaging Z1 a day per employee | Z4,320 |
| Electricity | Z120 |
| Total | Z8,188 |

Not included are contributions to parents, school supplies, clothing and food that they cannot grow. Their income from salaries totalled only Z9,900 to meet the expenses listed above and all others. Additional income came from the sale of fruit and vegetables and revenues from the bar when it was profitable. Relatives helped: the wife's sisters took care of the children while she worked, and also helped with the cooking; the husband's parents continued to send vegetables from Kivu every month for them to sell, in return for salt, kerosene, soap and oil shipped to Kivu by Nande truck driver friends.

My data indicate that several features of this family are typical of families of the commercial middle class. Husband and wife both needed to work to meet expenses. In addition a range of other income-producing activities was essential. This family produced much of its own food and had extensive cultivations outside the city. Kin in a rural area sent produce into town and received commodities in exchange. The family contributed to the upkeep of, or took complete care of, parents, siblings and children of relatives, which constituted a considerable drain on capital accumulation. They employed several domestic and other workers.

GENERALIZING FROM KISANGANI

How far can we generalize from these data on the emergence of a commercial class in Kisangani? Is such a class emerging in other parts of Zaire? Information from both Kivu and Lower Zaire indicate that it is and, in fact, show that such a class is not only emerging in regions distant from Kinshasa, out of reach of the central government:[5] multimillionaire businessmen who have not held any government position and do not wield political influence exist not only in Kivu but also in Lower Zaire close to Kinshasa. In addition some Kisangani businessmen have their head offices in Kinshasa itself as they progress from business at the local to the national level. Details of a multimillionaire in Kivu will be given in Chapter 6; information on one of three that I know of in Lower Zaire is relevant here and comparable in several ways to histories of Kisangani businessmen.[6]

Mr T. was raised in the the port of Matadi; his father was a sailor and he had a good Catholic secondary education. He worked for a Belgian company from 1950–72 in the meat business, maintaining his own enterprise on the side. He built up his own business in food stores and became a big importer. His businesses were large enough to be radicalized; by the time they were returned to him he had lost Z4,000,000. Thereafter he called his stores by a name which, being interpreted, means: 'I have been in this business longer than you have.'

At the beginning of 1979 Mr T. bought up part of a big Belgian cattle ranching concern, obtaining two ranches with 5,000 and 2,000 head of cattle of a tsetse resistant breed, also a slaughterhouse. He grows corn extensively, experimenting with new strains; other foodstuffs, such as manioc, peanuts and vegetables; and in 1980 was starting a pig farm, using his corn for feed. He believes that moving into production is crucial: 'the time is past for setting up stores and bakeries'. He also owns another ranch and a slaughterhouse in Lubumbashi and is starting a bottle factory in Kinshasa. When not

107

overseeing his businesses in Lower Zaire, he lives in a luxurious house in Kinshasa. He also owns an apartment building in Brussels. He has received Belgian development aid, visited the United States twice and also Mexico and China. In 1979 he had a turnover of Z64,000,000 and paid Z2,000,000 in taxes.

He has organized the infrastructure he needs for himself: he has an airstrip and a seven-passenger plane, a radio-telephone communication network, has put Z10,000 into maintenance of public roads and runs transportation for his workers daily to and from the local town. To save on expensive fuel he acquired horses for range work.

He believes that personal qualities, training and involvement in, and knowledge of, all aspects of business and decision making are the basis of business success, and has contempt for those who do not keep track of everything for themselves and who waste money by employing foreigners.[7] One of his sons manages one of his ranches, another is in charge of wine imports and chemical products. He employs a Belgian-trained vet from Kivu, who experiments with new pasture and oversees weekly cattle dipping. Mr T. has raised wages and improved conditions for his workers, setting up a new store with low prices and providing a well-supplied infirmary.

Mr T.'s case history includes features typical of entrepreneurs in Kisangani and of particular significance in the process of formation of the new commercial middle class. His holdings include productive as well as distributive enterprise and he himself stresses the need to move into production; he concerns himself with effective management and invests his profits in expanding his enterprises in true rational capitalist fashion; and he is building a stable workforce by regular wage payment and provision of benefits. His business is on a sufficient scale that he can afford to cope with the deterioration of infrastructure by creating and maintaining his own, and with the uncertainty of the political climate by investment overseas on which to fall back if disaster overtakes him. Some of the larger entrepreneurs in Kisangani and Kivu do likewise; one has bought ranch land in the United States.

SOME AFRICAN COMPARISONS

The indigenous capitalism developing in Zaire shows features observable in other parts of Africa, because entrepreneurs are facing broadly similar political and economic conditions throughout the continent.

Sheer entrepreneurial talent and innovative flair are a significant factor in the success of local businessmen and women in Kisangani. A study of Zambian businessmen showed that innovation, though not necessary, was the most significant factor for success in both rural and urban settings, and that both schooling and experience had a positive impact (Beveridge and Oberschall 1979: 226). In Nigeria a high degree of pure personal qualities of entrepreneurship of Nigerian business owners is notable, also their response to possible gain, their vigorous pursuit of economic advantage and their flexible and venturesome behaviour (Schatz 1971: 95). In

Ghana the capacity to innovate seemed to be related to businesses success, particularly among manufacturers and traders (Kennedy. 1980: 123).

Merchant capital moved into agricultural production, then into manu-facturing, and thereafter forged links to foreign capital in Kisangani as in Kenya (Swainson 1980: 207–8). Just as the initial concentration of capital in the agricultural sector in Kenya involved primary processing for the local market, in Kisangani plantations and ranches feature prominently among the holdings of local capitalists and so do rice, manioc and coffee mills and processing plants. Some of the case histories show that Zairian business-men are seeking new sources of capital overseas.

As Kisangani entrepreneurs became successful they increased their scale of operation by moving into new lines of business rather than by expanding the original one. Sayre Schatz reports the same characteristic for Nigerian entrepreneurs and ascribes it to conditions that we also find in Zaire: limited market opportunities, the flood of competitors that enter any new and successful line of business and problems in the economic environment making enlargement of any one line of business difficult (Schatz 1977: 94). Typically in Nigeria as in Kisangani, the most frequent combinations of business concerns were trading with transport, manufacturing and/or construction and investment in real estate. In his study of wholesale and retail traders in Accra and Kumasi in Ghana, Peter Garlick sought to explain the lack of expansion of their businesses between 1957 and 1962. He interviewed ninety-nine traders with permanent premises and found that, given the stagnation of the economy after independence and the uncertainty of the business climate, it made more sense for these men to invest in cocoa farms and real estate than to expand their businesses by ploughing back capital into a single enterprise and employing large numbers of people (Garlick 1971: 145).

A tendency to invest in speculative concerns that reproduced capital quickly, rather than in manufacturing enterprise requiring large amounts of capital is apparent in Kenya as in Zaire (Swainson 1980: 50–1). In Nigeria Schatz reasons that entrepreneurs cannot be expected to pass up lucrative and safe investment in real estate (in which annual returns are frequently 20–5 per cent), or forgo investment in trading activities with large returns, to sink limited capital into riskier, lower yielding, long-term industrial projects with smaller chances of evading taxes (Schatz 1977: 93). This reasoning applies equally in Kisangani.

The problems for the development of business found in Zaire are paralleled elsewhere. Schatz lists them for Nigeria as: the difficulty and high cost of getting goods and materials; massive theft and inordinate delays, and therefore deterioration, in transit; the expense of imported equipment and its installation, and maintenance difficulties because of the shortage of spares; the shortage of skilled labour and expense of foreign personnel; lack of advice and information; the competition of foreign

*Entrepreneurs and parasites*

firms; and inadequate infrastructure (Schatz 1977: 98–114). Kisangani entrepreneurs confront all these difficulties.

In this chapter we have described the opportunities for entering and expanding business careers that arose because of the direct and indirect effects of the indigenization of foreign capital, and because of the articulation of non-capitalist and capitalist modes of production. This accumulation of capital, its investment in inheritable, productive property, and the rational management of enterprise indicate the emergence of the new indigenous capitalist class. We will now proceed to examine the part the second economy plays in this process.

# 5

# Opportunities for capital accumulation: fending for oneself in the second economy

For an African...*magendo* is nothing wrong. It is a perfectly permissible form of economic activity, which simply gets around regulations perceived as meddling, interfering and created by the state bourgeoisie to levy their tithes willy nilly...[it] represents, across the artificiality of official frontiers, a form of social solidarity...a valuable means of preserving threatened commercial exchange. (Prunier 1983: 53)

It is simultaneously a popular economy of survival for the many and a means of enrichment for the few, and its oddness lies in the combination of these two contradictory aspects. (Morice 1985: 110)

Smuggling appears as an act of rebellion against the political and economic systems and the dominant groups. (Vwakyanakazi 1982: 339–40)

From official figures on wages, prices and the decline of real income, it would seem to be impossible for the majority of people to stay alive in Zaire. Living there, however, it is soon apparent that people somehow not only feed themselves but pay for housing and utilities, clothing, school fees and beer and cigarettes, and that they not only survive but some do very well as they 'fend for themselves' (*on se débrouille*) in a highly organized system of income-generating activities that are unrecorded in official figures and left out of official reports. The scale and extensiveness of these activities have profound implications for determining the real power of the state, for understanding the processes of class formation and class struggle and for assessing Zaire's degree of economic development.

The activities of the second economy deprive the state of enormous amounts of revenue and significantly decrease foreign exchange earnings from primary export commodities. The huge scale on which these activities take place and their pervasiveness at all levels of society are evidence of the weakness of the state's administrative capacities and its ability to control the structures of production and distribution. This situation affects the process of class formation and class struggle: the opportunities for capital accumulation provided by the more lucrative activities of the second economy have been instrumental in the emergence of the commercial middle class outside the state that we have been documenting; rural and

111

urban workers find not only a means for survival but also alternatives to proletarianization and in so doing find means to rebel against oppression; the political aristocracy consolidates its position with enormous accumulation of wealth and, in addition, seeks to control and monopolize the most profitable of irregular activities in order to close its class boundary against mobility from below, a process that Chapters 6 and 8 will document further.

In addition to its role in class formation, the second economy has become so extensive that it forces a re-evaluation of the usual criteria for economic development. Its recent rapid expansion means that an increasingly large fraction of the total economy is unrepresented in official figures and is thus left out of assessments of Zaire's development, generally measured by the GNP. In consequence such assessments seriously misrepresent reality.

The second economy's principal activities can be categorized as productive or distributive. Productive activities consist of illegal production in clandestine gold or diamond mining, production for illegal distribution of food and export crops,[1] for barter and private channels of distribution, poaching of ivory and rare game for skins, and production in small-scale craft or manufacturing enterprises for non-licensed trade. The principal distributive activities are smuggling and fraudulent export; theft; usury; barter; speculation, hoarding and middleman activity; and bribery, corruption and embezzlement. People from all levels of society, who can by some means get access to them, participate in these activities. The personnel of the state use their position as a means of access to resources for smuggling and speculation, and for corruption and embezzlement. Rural and urban workers struggle to survive on inadequate, seldom paid or no wages by means of illegal production, smuggling, barter and private channels of trade, theft or middlemen activity. Petty producers seek higher returns for their labour in unofficial marketing channels.

We will begin with details of the size of the second economy and of the means by which it is possible to assess its huge scale and pervasiveness.

## THE EXTENT OF THE SECOND ECONOMY

Since the second economy is by definition unrecorded, it is impossible to quantify its exact size relative to the official economy. An estimate for 1971 was that the equivalent of 60 per cent of the state's ordinary revenues were lost or at least diverted to other purposes than the official ones, so as to deprive the state of revenue (Peemans 1975c: 162). It is possible to come up with quantitative estimates for some of the sectors of this economy and to find specific indicators of its magnitude and pervasiveness. Firstly, a few official estimates exist on the loss of revenues to the state from some of its activities; losses on others can be calculated by putting together information from different sources; and newspapers occasionally report specific values of large-scale transactions. Secondly, population figures provide means to estimate the approximate number of urban dwellers involved in this economy. Thirdly, surprising manifestation of affluence among those who, according to all official criteria, are grossly disadvantaged in society, furnish evidence that lucrative second economy activities are available to some extent for even the socially disadvantaged.

Revenue losses to the state from smuggling and fraudulent export of primary export products are enormous. In 1961, Dupriez estimated the total value of unofficial exports of commodities for which he could obtain figures to be 1,045,052,000 CF (Dupriez 1962: 86). This figure, considerably less than the actual total of such exports, amounted to 18 per cent of the value of all official exports of 5,783,775,000 CF. This percentage had certainly not declined by 1980; to the contrary there is every reason to believe it had very considerably increased.

In the seventies coffee replaced palm oil as Zaire's primary agricultural export, yet as much as 40 per cent or more of this crop is smuggled out of the country annually, representing a significant reduction in foreign exchange earnings. From 1975–9, coffee smuggling was estimated to have cost Zaire 350 million (*Quarterly Economic Review, Ruanda and Burundi* 1980). In 1976 the Bank of Zaire cited coffee exports of 108.5 thousand tonnes, representing $315 million at prevailing world market prices. Customs data, however, showed exports amounting to only 40.6 per cent of this value, of $128 million (World Bank 1980: 95), a difference of $187 million. In 1977 the loss to Zaire in foreign exchange from illegal export of coffee was estimated at upwards of $280 million (*L'Entrepreneur* 1979: 6). One assessment of the loss of the bumper $500 million crop of 1977 was that not more than one-third returned as foreign exchange to the state (D. Gould 1980: 145). One report asserted that in 1978 the official export of coffee was 90,000 tonnes, but that an estimated additional 60,000 tonnes were fraudulently exported (*L'Entrepreneur* 1979: 6). At this time even more coffee was smuggled out of Zaire than out of Uganda: in 1979–80 up to 70,000 tonnes of the 200,000 tonnes Ugandan crop were smuggled (Green 1981: 55), that is 35 per cent of the total crop compared to 40 per cent in Zaire in 1978. In 1979 Zaire suffered an estimated loss of $70 million from coffee smuggling, with an additional loss of state revenues from evaded taxes of Z14,925,500 (*Conjoncture Economique* 1979: 64).

Coffee production statistics from Kivu, when compared with figures on acreage under cultivation, provide additional evidence of production for illegal export. Figures on arabica and robusta coffee acreage show that the hectares of arabica have increased from 28,197 in 1970 to 33,514 in 1977. Production figures for the same period, however, have more than halved! They drop from 24,433 tonnes in 1970 to 11,930 in 1977. Robusta coffee shows an increase in both acreage under cultivation and production figures; it is relatively much less valuable than arabica (Bianga 1982: 221–2). This state of affairs suggests heavy smuggling activity.

Ivory smuggling also deprives the state of huge amounts of revenue. It commands high prices in the urban or world market but is bought for a low price from hunters who subsist in non-capitalist modes of production. A 1973 decree established the National Ivory Bureau (NBI), allowing elephant hunting only under licence and ivory sale only to the agency at a fixed price. Emizet Kisangani comments that 'the NBI bureaucrats became involved in smuggling activities and the agency became the instrument of those in power'; it simply functioned to increase illegal trade. By 1976 90 per cent of Zaire's ivory was smuggled, the agency was abolished and regulation of ivory hunting left to the discretion of local authorities (Kisangani forthcoming). Exports of ivory were banned in 1978 and sale prohibited in April 1979, except through the Institution Zairoise de Conservation de la Nature, but in 1979–80 it was selling clandestinely in Kisangani for Z200 a kilogram. Each tusk weighs 20–5 kilograms, so a 20-kilogram tusk brings Z4,000.

Ivory poachers are decimating Zaire's elephant herds. Rangers in Virunga National Park, and also the newspapers, report extensive poaching by officials and military officers. They use powerful carbines or hang poisoned fruit on trees. A few reported incidents indicate just how large their operations can be. A zone commissioner in Kisangani was temporarily removed from his post in 1979 after allowing passage across the river of a truck containing 3 tonnes of ivory. At current Kisangani prices the value of this was Z600,000 (about $100,000). The commissioner was said to be acting for someone much more powerful. In March 1980 officials in Athens intercepted four cases containing 1,200 kilograms of ivory exported undeclared from Zaire, and a further 3.5 tonnes were seized from a large truck in Zaire, both belonging to a woman apparently acting as agent for an influential politician in Kinshasa (*Boyoma* 27 March 1980). In 1979 the authorities arrested four West Africans in Kisangani with a total of 200 kilograms of ivory (*Elima* 21 April 1979).[2] It should be noted here, however, that it is not only the politically powerful who participate in these activities: any gun owner can lend his gun to a local hunter and commission him to kill an elephant.

The state thus suffers enormous losses from coffee and ivory smuggling. In addition it is defrauded of huge amounts of revenues from its principal exports of copper, cobalt and other minerals. In 1977, GECAMINES, the mining consortium which produces 90 per cent of Zaire's copper, earned $677 million, but in 1978 only $542 million, despite a rise in copper and cobalt prices; the difference was pocketed by high government officials (Bézy *et al.*, 1981: 186). Figures on GECAMINES' production show that it declined in 1977–8 but only by 11 per cent (World Bank 1980: 188). Even if 1978 earnings were only as much as those of 1977, the difference was $135 million. This amount was equal to a loss of 25 per cent of GECAMINES' official earnings, Zaire's primary source of foreign exchange and source of 90 per cent of taxes on the mining industry (Bézy *et al.*, 1981: 82). These are losses on the principal products produced; they give some idea of just how large and how significant the second economy is relative to the official economy.

Zaire is the world's largest producer of industrial diamonds. In 1979, they constituted the country's fourth most valuable export, after cobalt, copper and coffee (Bézy *et al.*, 1981: 223). However, 5.5 million carats of diamonds were smuggled out, primarily by government personnel, and exported from Brazzaville and Bujumbura. Official diamond production in Zaire was only 8.06 million carats (World Bank 1980: 172), so that the amount smuggled equalled 68 per cent of official exports, a loss of nearly $59 million.

We can make a rough calculation of the amount lost for the year 1978. Assuming diamond smuggling to be on the same scale as 1979 and including $87.5 million as the average yearly loss of coffee, the total amounts to $282.5 million. Had the state realized these revenues, plus those for smuggled gold, ivory, tea, papain,[3] palm oil etc., it could have avoided entirely the $332 million of new borrowing necessary in that year. These estimates refer to only a few products; the total loss of revenue from all underground activity was of course very much larger.

Estimates of the number of urban dwellers depending on the second economy provide further means by which to assess its extent. Two-thirds of Zaire's population are estimated to exist outside the modern exchange economy in the subsistence economy; they mostly practise traditional agriculture (Huybrechts and Van der Steen 1981: 205). The total population in 1980 was estimated to be over twenty-four million (Vanderlinden 1981: 58) of which one-third, approximately six million people, was urbanized (Huybrechts and Van der Steen 1981: 189). Unemployment in the cities, however, was very high: in Kinshasa, which has half the country's wage earners, the rate was over 40 per cent for males over eighteen; in Kananga and Mbuji Mayi it was worse, about 80 per cent; and in Kisangani it was 72 per cent. Mining centres, such as Lubumbashi and Kolwezi, were relatively unaffected by this problem (*ibid.*: 207).

In assessing dependence on second economy activities, however, the absolute inadequacy of the wages of those who are employed must also be taken into account. By 1977 the index of real salaries was only 16 per cent and by 1979 only 6 per cent of what it was in 1960 (*ibid.*: 241). In terms of purchasing power: in 1979 an unskilled labourer needed to work for 5 days to buy a kilogram of rice, 116 days for a sack of manioc, 7 for a kilogram of dried beans and 3 for a loaf of bread (Mubake 1984: 268).[4] In Lubumbashi in 1982, to purchase basic necessities a worker needed an average monthly salary of Z1,000, but a clerk earned only Z115.21 and even high administrators, such as regional directors or divisional heads, earned only Z832.12 a month (Nsaman 1983: 27). In 1980 not even the Secretary of State (a junior minister immediately below cabinet rank) could feed a family of six on his monthly salary. His total income was Z855.80; a twice

115

daily snack (of tea with sugar and bread) and a daily meal (of only cassava, corn, pigs' feet twice a week, vegetables, oil, onions, salt and tomatoes) for himself and his family cost Z923 a month (*Lettre Ouverte . . .* 1981).

Given such grossly inadequate wages how do people stay alive? In answer people say: 'on se débrouille' (one fends for oneself) or 'nous vivons mystérieusement'. Both these things mean participation in the second economy. This means that the six million urbanites in Zaire, both the employed and the unemployed, in the absence of unemployment compensation, must find total or supplementary sources of income or subsistence outside the official economy's wages and salaries. In 1978 one estimate was that these supplementary sources were equal to 40–80 per cent of a household's budget (Bézy *et al.*, 1981: 79).

In fact people not only survive but can rouse up considerable amounts of cash when necessary. An event I observed in Kisangani in 1979, which the figures on wages and salaries just cited make astonishing, reveals the degree to which very ordinary and poor people may have money at their disposal.

In 1979 the Partriarch of Alexandria visited the Kimbanguist Church in Kisangani. The Kimbanguist congregation for the whole city is approximately 5,000; it is subdivided into congregations in the different city zones, who all meet once a month at the main church. Members are not drawn from the affluent classes; the large majority are very poor and simple people. Influential members include only one people's commissioner and a few businessmen. Nevertheless this congregation raised among themselves sufficient money to build an entire house, with four complete bathrooms, and furnish it quite luxuriously to house the Patriarch and his retinue for one night. Furthermore, they provided food for a lavish meal for over a hundred people, dozens of costly gifts and new green and white uniforms (the Kimbanguist colours) for most of the faithful. Various groups within the church, such as the chorale, the theatrical group, the watchmen and the congregations of the different zones, presented gifts in addition to their contributions to general expenses. These gifts included whole elephant tusks, ivory and wood carvings, ebony, a carved throne and table, a 15 foot python skin and other rare skins, including an okapi skin[5] from the congregation of the zone of Kabondo, one of the poorer areas of the city, who had collected Z2,000 among themselves to pay for it.

Such lavish generosity indicates a greater prosperity among the general population than the gloomy official figures allow. This prosperity certainly cannot be derived from Zaire's meagre wages and small-scale, self-employed enterprise; it can come only from participation in the second economy. Young and Turner point out that figures on increasing beer consumption between 1960 and 1973 are startling, given the wage and price structure; per capita consumption doubled in this period and was much higher in the towns than the villages, 'suggestive of the supplementary resources entering households beyond wages' (Young and Turner

1985: 88). Access to this economy, however, is highly uneven and intensely competitive; the redistribution of resources taking place in its activities is not at all fair. Clearly opportunities for participation in its trade and in smuggling of commodities vary from one region of the country to another and depend on access to land and its fertility, proximity to mineral or other natural resources, and location with regard to truck routes or frontiers. Conditions of appalling hardship exist, because the possibility of fending for oneself is not equally available to everyone. Between 1979 and 1980 kwashiorkor and malnutrition were fifth in the number of cases treated in Kinshasa hospitals, and accounted for 10.6 per cent of deaths (Mbumba 1982: 75).

## HISTORICAL DEVELOPMENT

The second economy is not a new phenomenon. Details of its development since independence show the part it has played in class formation. The upheavals and chaos that followed independence seriously weakened the government's capacity to maintain effective administration and public services; commercial regulations were not enforced and in some areas border control became almost non-existent. Trade networks for smuggling commodities in and out of the country sprang up rapidly. These commercial circuits, outside the control of the state, provided competing markets and resulted in an increase in producer prices. The outcome of the class struggle thus shifted in favour of the direct producers and also of traders. Another shift occurred when the foreign commercial class was displaced with the indigenization of foreign capital; as foreigners left the country, and their enterprises were taken over, nationals replaced them in lucrative smuggling ventures. These and other opportunities for capital accumulation outside the state in second economy activities were instrumental in the formation of the indigenous capitalist class.

Antecedents for the modern activities of the second economy existed in the colonial period and earlier. Commodities were smuggled in this period also, and patterns for illicit trade back and forth across Zaire's borders were established when people fled temporarily into neighbouring countries to take refuge from taxes and forced labour (Monnier and Willame 1964: 30); presumably older pre-colonial trade routes were reactivated. African retailers evaded colonial restrictions on African business by forming informal and illegal alliances with European wholesalers and selling goods on commission in African urban areas, the only areas in which they could operate and in which European trade was forbidden. Europeans thus evaded price controls and extended their business operations, while Africans ensured a supply of goods, charged high prices and expanded their enterprises (Mukenge 1974: 363).

After independence political chaos weakened the administrative capacity of the state and the second economy expanded rapidly. The unreal value of the Congo franc (FC) at this time created 'an almost institutional-

117

ised smuggling business' (Young 1965: 355); illicit trade with the Sudan and Uganda had reached disturbing proportions by 1963 (Willame 1972: 47).

A remarkably extensive set of figures on the extent of the illegal trade of this period is furnished by Pierre Dupriez (1962). He provides a detailed account of three different types of export fraud, showing the mechanisms by which each one primarily furthered the interests of a different class sector.

After independence the rapid development of export fraud resulted from the difference in the official rate of exchange of the Congo franc and the parallel market rate. For example, a kilogram of coffee selling at 30 FB in Antwerp realized 90 FC[6] for the producer selling for legal export at the official rate of exchange, but 210 FC if illegally exported at the parallel market rate (Dupriez 1968: 674). Numerous traders took up a profitable illegal commerce, organizing trade networks throughout the country and across its borders and easily evading the weakened administrative and border controls.

The first type of fraudulent export described by Dupriez is that of palm oil from Mayombe and Lower Zaire. Production was largely dependent on purchase of palm fruits from petty producers, and, in some areas, of palm kernels for palm kernel oil also. When a difference existed between the official rate of exchange, which determined the prices paid by the oil exporting firms, and the rate on the parallel market, which determined the price paid by traders, the producer had a choice between selling palm fruits to the companies or of making oil himself and selling it, and palm kernels, to traders. Generally palm kernels were fraudulently exported and palm oil sold in the domestic market.

Demand in the domestic market increased because of a fall in the production of high acidity oil in many areas. High acidity oil of lower quality than that exported was used locally. Exported oils, with an acidity of only 5 per cent were produced by the big companies, but they were obliged by law to keep back a part for internal markets. If they were unable to supply the local demand additional oil came from independent producers. Thus increased domestic demand from urban centres resulted in competition in purchasing palm fruit between the big oil companies and traders and broke the monopsony previously held by the companies. In this competition the big companies were at a disadvantage because their prices were tied to the official rate of exchange, while the traders, selling in the towns where demand exceeded supply, could easily offer higher prices to the producers. Kasai, in particular in areas wealthy from diamond smuggling, could support high prices. By 1965, the price of oil per kilogram paid to petty producers was 30 CF, up from 17 CF in 1963.

With two competing markets available, the producers could gear their activities to yield and income. Hand methods of oil extraction produced only 10 per cent of oil, in contrast to the 17 per cent extracted by machinery, but the difference in price between the two markets compen-

Table 5.1 *Value of 120 kilograms of palm fruit in 1958, 1963 and 1965 (in FC)*

|  | 1958 | 1963 | 1965 | |
|---|---|---|---|---|
|  |  |  | To producer | To intermediary |
| Exchange value of fruit sold to oil export companies (a) | 120 | 160 | 380 | 380 |
| Value of oil and kernels on uncontrolled market (b) | 132 | 434 | 619 | 900 |
| (b)/(a) | 1.1 | 2.7 | 1.6 | 2.6 |

*Source:* Dupriez 1968: 676.

sated for the difference in yield, as shown in Table 5.1. In 1958 it was not worth the labour for the farmer to produce oil; by 1963 many of them were doing so. However, the producers always kept some fruit to sell to the palm oil companies, because, so long as they kept up a regular supply, the companies recognized them as cutters and gave them the right to buy goods at the much lower prices of the company stores.[7] Furthermore, the companies maintained the roads which enabled the traders to get out to the villages (*ibid.*: 674–7). The producers were thus dependent on capitalism for goods and for the necessary infrastructure of roads, and therefore, by these means, were still constrained to supply capitalist enterprise.

Thus, two buying circuits developed: the official one in which palm fruits were collected by the companies for processing in factories, and the unofficial one in which oil, processed in the villages, and palm kernels, were bought by traders to be sold on the internal market or fraudulently exported. In 1962 about 15 per cent of the production of North Mayombe was so exported (Dupriez 1962: 78). Dupriez shows how each circuit also distributed consumer goods at different prices. In the official circuit consumers goods were sold cheaply in company stores at prices related to those of palm fruit bought from the petty producers and set by the official rate of exchange. In the unofficial circuit the prices of consumer good were higher. They were sold by traders who bought them from the countries to which they smuggled palm kernels; prices were dependent on the parallel market currency rate.

Whichever of these circuits was most advantageous at a particular time took a larger share of production. The devaluation of November 1963 doubled the prices offered in the official circuit, giving it an advantage over the unofficial circuit; this advantage disappeared after March 1965, when the difference between official and parallel rates of exchange increased rapidly. Thereafter the oil companies began to cut back on the sale of consumer goods, previously a source of advantage. There was great elasticity in this situation because producers could shift from one circuit to the other to maximize their income (*ibid.*: 677–9).

Breaking of the monopsony with the growth of unofficial commercial circuits led to an increase in the quantities of palm fruit harvested and to increased income of rural producers. The growth of unofficial commercial circuits led to an increase of production because zones outside the official circuits, for example near the Angolan border, began commercial production in response to increase in demand (*ibid.*: 679). The quantities were not very large but, nevertheless, petty producers clearly benefited from the creation of unofficial circuits, while the state was deprived of important export income. One might add that, although Dupriez refers to it as a 'distortion of the system', the wealth from diamond smuggling in Kasai led to increasing demand for palm oil in that region and hence expansion of production in Lower Zaire.

The significance of this fraudulent export trade in palm oil, in terms of class control of the accumulation process, was the decreased control of capitalism over petty producers. This was manifested in the relaxation of the price squeeze described by Bernstein (discussed on p. 26), because of competing buyers, and in the rise in producer incomes and the incomes of local traders.

The second type of fraud identified by Dupriez mostly benefited the foreign planter class in the sixties, but in the seventies a shift occurred in the process of class struggle as foreigners were dispossessed of their assets and nationals displaced them in profitable illegal trade.

The troubled political situation in Oriental and Kivu Provinces in 1960–1 meant that coffee and tea, important export crops of these regions, could not be exported in the usual way. The political isolation and distance from the control of the central government of the foreign planters who grew these crops allowed them to organize an export system of their own through smuggling, principally to the east. Intermediaries organized export through Uganda and Tanzania, sometimes under cover of licence from local authorities, but usually by crossing frontiers illegally with the collusion of customs officials, or if necessary by armed force (*ibid.*: 679).

Details of the scale and organization of such trade are given in one account from North Kivu, a principal route of illegal export of agricultural products to Uganda. In 1963 a European customs expert filmed a caravan of 500 men with armed guards, exporting products bought by 'les trafiquants Ismaéliens'. These Asians, in cooperation with local chiefs, organized the trade in coffee, tea, papain, foodstuffs and imported consumer goods. It was estimated in January 1962 that official exports represented only 25 per cent of local agricultural production in the region (Willame 1964: 28).

Robusta coffee and palm oil were exported to the north in this way; Arabica coffee and tea to the south. The statistics of East African railways allow some estimates of this illegal export, since smuggled coffee and tea

Table 5.2 *Products sent by rail from Beni and Kasese to Mombasa, 1961–4*

|      | Robusta | Arabica | Tea   | Palm oil   |
|------|---------|---------|-------|------------|
| 1961 | 15,000  | 8,000   | 4,000 | 5,762[*]   |
| 1962 | 20,000  | 5,000   |       |            |
| 1963 | 3,000   |         |       |            |
| 1964 | 3,500   |         | 2,100 |            |

[*] Calculated from the tonnage of East African Railways and official imports and customs records of Central African Republic.

*Source:* DUPRIEZ 1968: 680; 1962: 76–8 .

were sent by rail from Beni and Kasese to Mombasa, as Table 5.2 shows. The table shows minimum amounts. Cinchona, papain, gold and casseterite were also part of this trade.

The positive effects of this illegal trade were that plantation production was maintained when it might have otherwise collapsed with the breakdown of the official export system. Negative effects were again the loss of state revenues. This type of fraud originally benefited foreign planters and intermediaries who made little contribution to expanding the local economy but repatriated profits to their countries of origin (Dupriez 1968: 680–1).

We see a change after the mid-seventies in those who were able to accumulate wealth from this type of illegal export. In Zairianization nationals took over the profitable coffee sector from foreigners. Those with political connections acquired large plantations, but so did some business-men and women without state position. In addition, many small-scale producers took to growing plots of coffee, often smuggling out their crop or selling it to traders for illegal export for good prices after the price rise of 1976. Rapid accumulation in this and in other forms of illegal trade was a factor in a shift in the pattern of class formation and the emergence of the commercial middle class.

The third type of fraudulent export that developed in the early sixties, and the most profitable, was of diamonds from Kasai. The diamond mining companies reduced and even ceased production for a time, putting many people out of work who were experienced in the extraction and sorting of diamonds. They found it easy to continue their work in the river beds in the dry season; traders then bought the stones from the villagers and organized networks to smuggle them out of the country. This trade initially went through Brazzaville, a country with no diamond deposits. Its figures on diamond exports therefore allow calculation of the quantity of diamonds smuggled out of Zaire. In 1964, it became difficult to export through Brazzaville, so the trade went through Lubumbashi and Bujumbura; when

Table 5.3 *Extent of losses in diamond revenues through smuggling to Congo Brazzaville*

| | Diamond production of Zaire (in carats)* | Diamond revenue as % of total mineral export revenue** | Diamond exports of Congo Brazzaville (in carats)*** | Brazzaville exports as % of Zaire's production |
|---|---|---|---|---|
| 1961 | 18,011,000 | — | 89,500 | 0.5 |
| 1962 | 14,656,000 | 10.4 | 2,629,000 | 17.8 |
| 1963 | 14,784,000 | 11.5 | 5,683,600 | 38.5 |
| 1964 | 14,752,000 | 11.2 | 5,264,900 | 35.6 |
| 1965 | 12,490,000 | 8.3 | 5,303,700 | 42.4 |
| 1966 | 12,418,000 | 6.3 | 4,251,500 | 34.2 |

*Sources:* *Bézy *et al.*, 1981: 217;  ***ibid.*: 223;  ****Dupriez 1962: 682.

this outlet was threatened it was rerouted to Nairobi (Dupriez 1968: 681–2). Table 5.3 gives the unofficial export of diamonds from Zaire through Brazzaville and shows the enormous losses this smuggling represented to the state, especially considering these figures only apply to one destination of this illegal trade. Dupriez is able to estimate the *total* amount of all diamond smuggling for 1964, which he gives as 10–12 million carats (*ibid.*: 682). This means that as much as 81 per cent again of Zaire's official diamond production was fraudulently exported. At that time diamonds were the country's third most valuable export and the loss in revenue could have amounted to as much as 11.5 million zaires.[8] By 1967 mining executives estimated clandestine production in the diamond mining areas of Kasai Oriental to *equal* official annual production (Young and Turner 1985: 92). Thereafter this scandalous state of affairs somewhat improved as the authorities succeeded to some degree in enforcing anti-smuggling measures.

Dupriez emphasizes that such losses impoverished the economy. He considers that the profits made in this trade distorted rather than stimulated the economy because the diamond trade incited petty producers to abandon cultivation. The decreased production of food crops, such as rice or maize, forced the country to import food, while at the same time diamond smuggling reduced its foreign exchange earnings. He notes that high retail prices in the diamond areas could have stimulated food production in neighbouring regions, but only did so in Gandajika, Kasai, because of lack of transport and organization elsewhere. Demand was mostly met by costly alternatives, such as imports by the diamond traders themselves or imports of fish from Kivu by air from Goma, or palm oil from Lower Zaire (*ibid.*: 683). It is not quite clear why Dupriez chooses to consider this as a distortion of the economy rather than as stimulus for the expansion of production in Kivu and Lower Zaire. Nor, since it is women who cultivate food crops, is it necessarily the case that the pre-occupation of men with clandestine diamond production should result in a decline in local food production, though export crops such as cotton declined considerably (*ibid.*: 704). The reported decline in rice and maize may only reflect low producer prices, deterioration of market facilities and an increase in unofficial channels of trade.

Illicit diamond digging and trade at this period resulted in enormous accumulation of wealth for some of those who participated in it. It was widely reported at the time that one reason smuggling was so difficult to prevent was because the biggest smugglers were the authorities themselves. We do not know very much about the traders and intermediaries. Some of them were the *Sénégalais* who established efficient, illicit export networks for diamonds, gold and other commodities. But the diamond miners, intermediaries and traders from the local population also profited. The trade raised their incomes and stimulated production of palm oil in Lower Zaire and fish in Kivu.

RESISTANCE TO THE PREDATORS AND
OPPORTUNITIES TO ACCUMULATE

An enormous expansion of the second economy took place in the seventies. As the economic crisis deepened, conditions worsened and the pillaging activities of the political aristocracy increased, people took advantage of the weakening of the administrative apparatus to organize an independent system of production and distribution outside state control. They obtained foreign exchange by smuggling, appropriated commodities from capitalist enterprise, and made their own arrangements to compensate for the deterioration of infrastructure. They not only managed to survive but found alternatives to wage labour and thus the means to avoid proletarianization and to resist the excessive appropriation and predatory activities of the dominant class. Furthermore some even accumulated considerable wealth.

We will now turn to details of the organization of the second economy's productive and distributive activities and infrastructure, taken primarily from northeastern Zaire. The principal commodities involved are coffee, gold, ivory, papain, tea, cotton, palm oil, foodstuffs (both local and imported), imported manufactured goods and fuel.

*Production*

Three distinct forms of production are identifiable: small-scale independent production by individuals or small groups who have access to the means of production in either non-capitalist or capitalist systems; production in organized enclaves in rural areas, which are developing their own relations of production; and production in the capitalist system from

123

which commodities are appropriated and distributed in the second economy.

There are three ways for petty producers to gain access to the means of production. The first is through non-capitalist systems which afford access to land and participation in relations of production for growing food or export crops or for hunting. Urban dwellers may be able to go to their rural area of origin and get use of land for cultivation, or access to hunting and fishing grounds, to which they are entitled by ties of kinship (J. MacGaffey 1983). Farmers in these systems grow foodcrops some of which they sell but some of which they send to kin in town for consumption and sale; in return they get kerosene, salt, soap, cooking oil and other items that are unobtainable or unaffordable in rural areas.

Several sources indicate that this production in non-capitalist systems provides an alternative to wage labour. Government reports from early in the seventies onwards complain that workers were deserting plantations because they could make better money from their own cultivations or by fishing or hunting. In 1977, for example, many workers were deserting Lever Plantations (PLZ) because their salaries, at Z28 a month, were too low. The Bambole rubber plantations, in the zones of Opala and Yanonge, north of Kisangani, part of CELZA, the plantation empire owned by the president and his late wife (for details of this empire see Young and Turner 1985: 180), had similar troubles: local Bambole were unwilling to work because wages were so low and work conditions so poor; they could make more money by cultivating their own rice, bananas and manioc than by working on the plantations (Mitoro Litekya 1976: 24–33). In 1979 an official in Kisangani with coffee and citrus plantations outside the city complained that his workers from the local Bakumu people only showed up irregularly because they could make more than their Z2 a day wage by fishing and working their own gardens. Foodcrops may be distributed through private channels of trade; they are also smuggled out of the country. In 1979–80 the average amount smuggled daily to Burundi from Uvira zone in eastern Kivu was 70 bags of potatoes, 60 bags of beans, 50 piles of tobacco, plus other basketfuls (Bianga 1982: 230).

Farming is not the only alternative to working for low wages. Business owners in Kisangani in 1979–80 complained that workers in their commercial agricultural ventures were deserting to dig gold, at which they were said to make as much as Z200 a month instead of their Z40–60 wages. One said that the number of her workers had dropped from 200 to 40. Individuals can dig for gold or pan for it in rivers; permission from local land owners is not necessary everywhere, though local experts are sought out for locating the best places to try. In town and on plantations, wages are so low that the only reason many people continue in wage employment is for the health and housing benefits that come with it; these double the cost of wages employers pay.

Petty producers also grow export crops such as coffee, tea, palm oil, cotton, papain, and export some of them through illicit channels. Hunters from hunter-gatherer or lineage-based societies sell meat, fish, rare skins and, most profitably, ivory to villagers, dealers or middlemen for the powerful. Coffee is a particularly profitable crop. Upper Zaire and Kivu are the two principle coffee-growing regions of Zaire and in 1980 coffee was the country's third most valuable export. It is profitable because of the low wages paid to plantation workers, the low prices paid to peasant producers and the high prices realized by sale at world market prices. It is grown in plantations but also in small patches by peasant cultivators, who can get higher prices by selling it though unofficial channels or smuggling it out of the country themselves.

Such wealth accumulated by small-scale producers may be invested in the official economy. Details will be given in the next chapter of the Nande in North Kivu, some of whom derived starting capital for businesses from smuggling gold or growing small patches of coffee on lineage land and taking the harvest across the border for sale where prices were higher. A nice illustration in Upper Zaire of the accumulation of starting capital from coffee growing and the ivory trade is given in a recent account by a traveller through the Ituri forest: two Balese farmers planted coffee; with the Z300 they made from its sale they bought soap, shirt and pants to pay an Efe hunter to kill an elephant with spears; they sold the ivory to a local smuggler for Z2,000 with which they were going to start a store (Shoumatoff 1984: 111).

The second form of access for petty producers to the means of production is through ownership of tools or a sewing machine for small-scale craft and manufacturing enterprises in rural areas or cities. In Kisangani, people produce basketry, raffia shopping bags and mats, and pottery; carved ebony and ivory for the tourist market; pestles and mortars, furniture and made-to-order clothing. They may operate in the official economy under licence but the government charges Z150 for a trading licence for a market stall, Z100 for petty commerce, and many people, especially in the outlying urban zones, operate without one or under the licence of a friend, or else regularly bribe the market police.

Finally, theft is the third way of acquiring means of production, when it provides equipment and raw materials with which to set up small-scale production. A striking example is the fishing industry of Lake Mobutu. In 1974 it supported thirteen industrial fisheries; by 1979, only two continued to function because of lack of fuel and theft of fishing nets and spare parts. But the number of independent small fishing businesses (*artisanat*) had increased from 237 in 1974 to 1,470 in 1975 and 1,658 in 1976 (*Rapport Economique Régional Haut Zaire* 1974 and 1976); the stolen nets and spares must surely have been a factor in this increase. Production declined for the industrial fisheries but increased for the independent producers and also overall, in this period, as shown in Table 5.4.

Table 5.4 *Production of fishing industry of Lake Mobutu 1976–7*

|      | Industrial fisheries | Independent producers | Total |
| ---- | -------------------- | --------------------- | ----- |
| 1976 | 1,636,572  kg | 3,506,665  kg | 5,143,237 |
| 1977 | 980,466  kg | 6,396,234  kg | 7,376,700 |

*Source: Rapport Annuel du Service Sous-Régional de l'Economie Nationale et l'Industrie Ituri/Bunia 1977.*

These figures, like all others in Zaire, must be treated with circumspection; they are highly unreliable and can only indicate a rough approximation rather than the precise state of affairs. This reported increase of overall production of 30 per cent, under the expansion of small-scale independent producers is, however, highly significant; we will return to it later.

Another example of theft furnishing the means to set up in independent production comes from the palm oil industry. In 1978, the third largest palm oil producer reported a drop in production resulting from lack of palm fruit cutters, shortage of spare parts and theft of palm fruit. It also reported that oil from developing local independent (*artisanale*) production (presumably connected to theft of palm fruit) was being smuggled out for sale at the higher prices offered in Brazzaville (*Conjoncture Economique* 1979: 233, 237).

Small-scale independent production by individuals is one form of undocumented production; another is production in organized enclaves, which generate their own relations of production. Gold and diamonds are both produced in this way.

Upper Zaire and Kivu are the sites of Zaire's most important gold deposits. Gold is mined by the Kilo-moto and SOMINKI mining companies and panned in rivers in Kivu. After 1974 the deposits became depleted: production dropped from 6,100 kilograms in 1974 to 1,300 kilograms in 1978 (*Conjoncture Economique* 1979: 87) and the deposits were no longer considered worth exploiting. But with the spectacular rise in the price of gold in 1978–9, from $147.7 an ounce to $380 on the London Metal Exchange, unauthorized gold digging developed on a large scale and the illegal gold trade expanded rapidly.

Vwakyanakazi gives an account of the semi-permanent villages set up by illegal gold miners in Kivu, with their own power and authority structure and economic relations. The miners are under the protection of the local headman, who receives a share of the mining profits. These mining camps exist outside the local government administration, often in remote areas inaccessible to local authorities and police, but they also organize armed forces to deal with any interference. These camps average about sixty diggers, all young and mostly single and without families, operating in teams of six to ten. The founders of the camps are their leaders, if they are enterprising enough. The miners grow some of their food and the camps provide a market for salt, soap, cigarettes, clothes and beer brought by men and women from local rural centres. This trade also supplies small villages, formerly unable to obtain such commodities, and has resulted in some increase in the size of a number of rural centres (Vwakyanakazi 1982: 332–5). Miners may spend their money in consumption but they also invest it in small stores, thus moving into the official economy. Clandestine gold production, therefore, brings about some expansion of the local economy.

Informants give similar accounts of gold mining in Upper Zaire, with formation of private armed militias in some areas to protect the digging areas against soldiers and the government, or highly organized systems of payoffs to local authorities. Near Bafwasende, east of Kisangani, a newly constructed road leads into the forest to the gold trenches. Businessmen, officials, police, the military and others come openly to buy or to barter goods directly for gold. At every stage of the journey payoffs are made: to local officials, to the guide, to the gold digger. In 1977 a government report attributed the increase of population in Djugu zone to a massive influx of gold diggers and traders (*Rapport Annuel, Région de Haut Zaire* 1977).

Illicit diamond mining in Kasai is similarly organized. Willame quotes an account, from the 1980 inquiry into the Kasai massacre, of the details of the organization of clandestine diamond mining in a village near Mbuji Mayi. Diamond-bearing gravels were dug out of a hill outside the village, taken to the river and panned. The miners were boys and young men aged between twelve and thirty. To obtain digging rights in an area, they had to pay the local chief; the amount could be as much as Z100 a day, depending on the richness of the diamond beds, plus a percentage of the profit. He performed a ceremony to the ancestors to ensure success. The miners also paid Z5 a day to the gendarmes and Z20 to the local diamond dealers, for which they received numbered tickets as receipts. The diamond miners, like gold miners, provided a market for the sale of foodstuffs. Women and girls aged between twelve and twenty, mostly from Mbuji Mayi, formed a little market on the path to the river; some of them sold their sexual services and also traded in diamonds on a small scale as they tried to supplement their husband's meagre wages or support the family if he was unemployed (Willame 1984: 85–6).

These enclaves establish their own systems of relations of production. They have their own political authority outside the official system, backed by armed force and by an ideological superstructure manifested in the ceremonies performed by the traditional chief and believed by the miners to be essential for their success.[9]

In some instances enclave production results from the withdrawal of whole groups to live autonomously from society deep in the forest. Government administrators in Kisangani report the existence of the

127

religious sects of Kitawala, Monama, Lulwa and Idome, living in the bush out of reach of the authorities in the zones of Bafwasende and Irumu and in the sub-region of Tshopo. These groups refuse to carry out public works (*Salongo*) or to pay taxes; they hunt elephants, selling the ivory to poachers, and dig gold (*Rapport Annuel, Affaires Politiques, Haut Zaire 1973, 1976; Rapport Annuel, Administration du Territoire, Haut Zaire 1977*). Kitawalists are estimated to number 15,000 in Equateur. A report of a visit to one of their camps estimated its population at 800, housed in 165 huts, and described them as very active in fishing and hunting. They ran their own schools and dispensaries. They specifically gave the reason for their retreat to the forest as avoidance of taxes (for these and other details of the Kitawalists and their 'militant apathy', see Schatzberg: forthcoming, ch. 7).

Finally, an account of production for the second economy must take into account commodities produced in the capitalist mode of production and appropriated for distribution in the second economy. They include imported manufactured goods, foodstuffs, fuel, construction materials, beer from Zaire's breweries, coffee from plantations, diamonds from the operations of MIBA (the big mining company), cobalt and other minerals.

## Distribution

Distributive activities of the second economy are more extensive and more lucrative than its productive activities. Some commodities produced in non-capitalist modes, such as food and export crops, fish and game, enter private channels of trade and are sold locally or bartered, or sent to the cities to relatives or to others connected by ethnic or other ties, for consumption or for sale which is unlicensed and therefore untaxed. Other commodities produced in the capitalist system are appropriated for the second economy to be distributed by speculation and middleman activity, smuggling and other forms of fraudulent export, theft and barter.

Gold, coffee, ivory, diamonds, tea, cotton, palm oil, papain and other commodities, most recently cobalt, are exported in this economy through smuggling and various forms of fraudulent export, such as underinvoicing and false declaration. Gold, diamonds, ivory, cobalt and coffee are the major earners of foreign exchange by this means.

The gold trade provides a lucrative alternative to wage labour for those with the opportunity to enter it. In 1980 soldiers were reported to have sold their uniforms and arms and abandoned the military camp at Watsa completely to enter the gold trade (Willame 1984: 86). One gold dealer in Kisangani had left a job in a hotel because of the poor pay and long hours. He made high profits: he bought gold in 1979 at Z30 the *likuta* (weight of a small coin) in Bunia, a town northeast of Kisangani, and sold it in Kisangani for Z50–65 the *likuta* (from which he had to deduct transportation costs and payoffs to the police). Such payments were quite regular and predictable: he declared what he carried and paid a standard amount each time to be allowed to pass the roadblocks on the road to Kisangani. The same dealer bought ivory for Z80 a kilogram and sold it in Kisangani for Z120.

In North Kivu it is widely recognized that the illegal gold trade is the basis for the founding and expansion of many businesses: 'You get gold, take it to Nairobi and sell it for dollars or Kenyan shillings, which you put in the bank. Then you buy merchandise and take it back to Zaire, having all the necessary purchase documents to cross the border.' In Upper Zaire gold and diamonds move rapidly along person to person trade networks for which certain Greeks, Asians and *Sénégalais* are notorious.

Regional economic reports in Upper Zaire from 1970 onwards repeatedly include complaints that the government marketing boards for cotton and coffee lack sufficient vehicles and funds to collect harvests and, simultaneously, deplore the smuggling of these commodities to neighbouring countries, where prices were higher. In 1970 and 1971, for example, the price of seed cotton in Zaire was 4.31 K per kilogram; in the Central African Republic it was 5.40 in 1970, 6.00 in 1971; in Uganda it was 7.72–8.40 in 1970 (Tollens 1975: 67). In 1978 the price offered for cotton in Kivu was raised from 45 K to 90 K per kilogram; but in neighbouring Burundi it was the equivalent of Z1.50 (Bianga 1982: 225). Table 5.5 shows that from 1971–6 coffee prices were as much as two to four times higher in all Zaire's neighbouring countries, except in Uganda between 1974 and 1976.

Coffee smuggling became extremely profitable and many people made fortunes after the sudden rise in the world price of coffee in 1976. Very large profits could be made smuggling coffee across the borders. In 1978, for example, traders were buying coffee at Z1.05 a kilogram in Isiro, the centre of the coffee growing area of Upper Zaire, and selling for Z10 a kilogram in the Sudan (*Conjoncture Economique* 1978: 44). Coffee is smuggled out by truck (a big truck of coffee is worth as much as Z250,000), or by bicycle or headload along forest paths. Once across the border it is sold or bartered directly for cars, trucks, motorbikes, spare parts or manufactured goods. In Kivu one big coffee dealer owns two Brittania aircraft for exporting his coffee. He is licensed to export second grade coffee but in fact exports first grade coffee which he underinvoices as second, paying less tax, then selling it at the higher price of the superior grade. Individuals at all levels of society, politicians and officials, plantation owners and businessmen, and small farmers, participate in the illegal export which results in such enormous losses of state revenues.

Table 5.6 summarizes the modes of production and distribution, in both the second and the official economies, of the commodities discussed so far. For the first five locally produced commodities, it is production in a non-capitalist mode and sale in the urban markets or for export at world market prices that makes them profitable.

Table 5.5 *Producer prices for coffee in Zaire and neighbouring countries, 1971–6 (in US cents per pound green equivalent)*

| Country | 1971 | 1972 | 1973 | 1974 | 1975 | 1976 |
|---|---|---|---|---|---|---|
| Tanzania | 41.20 | 45.09 | 42.63 | 38.76 | 31.75 | 59.31 |
| Kenya | 34.55 | 42.93 | 54.16 | 62.90 | 59.69 | 121.40 |
| Uganda | 15.12 | 15.12 | 19.32 | 15.24 | 15.87 | 15.24 |
| Rwanda | 20.00 | 21.66 | 23.77 | 21.99 | 21.99 | 31.76 |
| Burundi | 22.84 | 23.90 | 26.61 | 30.06 | 29.52 | 37.25 |
| Zaire | 9.98 | 9.98 | 10.98 | 16.33 | 16.33 | 34.62 |

*Source*: M. Michael Msuya, *Coffee in the Economy of Tanzania and the Implications of Membership in the International Coffee Agreement*. Ph.D. Dissertation, Univ. of Wisconsin, 1979, p. 238, given in Bianga 1982: 153.

Some of the other distributive activities of the second economy include middleman activity and speculation, theft, barter and usury.

Middlemen and women obtain goods by voucher at official, controlled prices; these vouchers are then sold, often several times and each time for a higher price; by the time the goods are collected and sold to the consumer, they cost many times the official price.[10] In 1978–9 in Kinshasa, there was a 258 per cent difference between the official price of consumer goods and their actual market price (Mubake 1984: 266–7).

In Kisangani I sometimes witnessed transactions involving these vouchers. On one occasion a Greek offered another Z700,000 worth of miscellaneous goods coming off a boat from Kinshasa, at 20 per cent above the official price. The deal was accepted with satisfaction as a good one. Another time a man owning a market stall was beckoned over by a passing soldier on a scooter. He returned with a bundle of money. The soldier had a connection to the manager of SEDEC who sold him a voucher for some cases of matches; he in turn sold it to the market man. Before delivering it, however, the soldier had found someone else willing to pay a higher price so had come to return the money. The stall owner was left lamenting 'that's what business is like here'.

*Boyoma* reported other such activities. In Isiro in 1976:

> The representative of SEDEC gets 600 sacks of flour from Kisangani of which the two bakeries get only 30 sacks each for a varying period of two, three or four months, paralysing their activities. The SEDEC manager keeps the rest...to sell on his own account at a price 'Isirois,' that is to say, not regulated. (*Boyoma* 20 May 1976)

In December it was reported that Kisangani bakers accused SEDEC of being the cause of speculation by selling flour to retailers rather than direct to the bakers, forcing them to buy at high retail prices. In addition the SEDEC manager preferred to sell flour in Bunia, Isiro or Butembo for

Table 5.6 *Production and distribution of commodities in the second economy in northeast Zaire*

| Commodity | Imported or local | Mode of production | Mode of distribution (official economy upper case) |
|---|---|---|---|
| Coffee | Local | Non-capitalist | Barter |
| | | | Smuggling |
| | | | Fraudulent export |
| | | Capitalist | MARKET SALE |
| | | | EXPORT |
| Gold | Local | Non-capitalist. Organized illegal production. | Barter |
| | | | Smuggling |
| | | | Private sale |
| | | Capitalist ——— | EXPORT |
| Ivory | Local | Non-capitalist (also poaching) | Barter |
| | | | Smuggling |
| | | | Private sale |
| Papain | Local | Non-capitalist | Smuggling |
| | | Capitalist | EXPORT |
| Foodstuffs | Local and imported (legally or smuggled) | Non-capitalist | —— Through kin networks |
| | | | Barter |
| | | | Theft |
| | | | Hoarding and speculation |
| | | Capitalist | MARKET SALE |
| Manufactured goods | Imported (legally or smuggled) local | Capitalist | Barter |
| | | | Hoarding and speculation |
| | | | Theft |
| | | | MARKET SALE |
| Beer | Kisangani breweries | Capitalist | Speculation |
| | | | MARKET SALE |
| Fuel | Imported (legally or smuggled) | Capitalist | Hoarding and speculation |
| | | | MARKET SALE |

three times the price he could get in Kisangani, thus creating shortages (*Boyoma* 31 December 1976).

Those who have control of merchandise, fuel or beer are in very strategic positions. One man referred to the managers of the big wholesale houses as 'les grands seigneurs' of Kisangani, pointing out the opulence of their villas and their high-spending lifestyle. Besides putting up prices, middleman activities greatly increase the difficulty of supply for licensed traders, store and market stall owners who have to seek out these illicit suppliers. These *vendeurs du papier* are more to blame for high prices than traders who have to bear high risks because of transportation difficulties.

Shortages of manufactured goods, foodstuffs and fuel allow for large-scale profit making not only in middleman activity but also through speculation. Enormous price mark-ups are imposed as goods are shipped from one part of the country to another, where they are in short supply, or as they are smuggled in across the borders. During periods of gasoline shortage in Kisangani in 1980, petrol stations were only occasionally open to sell petrol at the official price, but black market sellers offered it for sale at all hours at three to four times the controlled price. By April 1980 there were no petrol stations at all selling diesel fuel at the controlled price of Z140 a 200-litre drum: all truckers had to buy it from those who had quotas or some other means of obtaining it, who were selling it at Z1,000 a drum. Likewise beer production was nowhere near adequate to fill the demand. Anyone with a beer quota from the breweries or with connections to their managers could obtain beer at the official price of Z13.39 a case and sell it wholesale with the huge mark-up of up to Z50 the case. Buyers by the case would sell it by the bottle with another mark-up in price.

In the situation of acute scarcity, theft on a massive and all-pervasive scale has become a major form of redistribution. As one man said, despairingly, 'What can you do in an economy in which it is worthwhile to steal nails?' Wholesalers reckon to increase their prices by 10 per cent to recoup losses incurred from theft in transit. This means that an amount equivalent to 10 per cent of total wholesale sales in Zaire equals the value of transactions of the second economy taking place through theft on boats, from trucks and trains, at the docks and customs and in airports. There are also, of course, many other kinds of theft.

Barter deprives the state of the taxes due to it if exchange of the items bartered took place using money; it is therefore part of the second economy. In addition to direct exchange, various kinds of barter have developed to counteract the spiralling prices resulting from scarcity or to deal with the shortage of foreign exchange. For example, an auto assembly plant 'sells' its scarce trucks at the low controlled price to a rice or cloth importer, who in turn 'sells' rice or cloth at controlled prices for sale in the company's commissary. The money paid in this sale is insignificant; what is really going on is the barter of one scarce good for another. Big firms take coffee in exchange for their products because they need the foreign exchange realized by coffee, rather than zaires. One large company in Kinshasa supplies its product only to those who will deal in coffee.

Barter is so common that values for exchange become standardized. In 1980 16 tonnes of coffee bought a Land Rover in Kinshasa; in the trade across the Sudan border, 2 tonnes of coffee were worth a light truck, 5 sacks, a motorcycle (Vwakyanakazi 1982: 286). In 1981 1 tonne of ivory bought a large Fiat truck; its official import price at the port would have been $40,000 (Kisangani: forthcoming). Willame quotes a government report of a visit by officials to a village on the Sudanese frontier, for other equivalences in this trade: a four-wheel drive Toyota or a pickup was worth 6 tonnes of coffee, a 7-ton Toyota truck 15 tonnes. On this occasion, thirty such new vehicles from Saudi Arabia via the Sudan were available for exchange against coffee or tea.[11] Other items imported in this trade included TV sets, radios and auto spares (Willame 1984: 86). Traders in Kivu go to Nairobi, buy goods on credit, sell them in Kivu and buy coffee with the proceeds; the coffee is then shipped to the Nairobi creditor under cover of somebody's export quota, often through the underinvoicing procedure described above. Barter is extensive within Zaire for commodities produced and circulating internally, as well as for imports; many rural producers prefer it to sale (Schoepf and Schoepf 1984: 90).

People who cannot find some profitable hustle or means of getting by in the second economy have to find loans for occasional cash outlays, such as medical bills or school fees or initial capital to try to enter commerce to make a living. The unemployed and those with few resources who lack the guarantees for loans from the official financial institutions in the form of collateral or personal backing, commonly resort to what is popularly known as 'Banque Lambert', private loans at usurious rates. Usury, or interest charges over the normal rate, is prohibited by law (Decree of 26 August 1959, Bk III of the Civil Code) and punishable by fine and/or imprisonment. The normal rate, however, is not defined by law but left up to the judge in any case brought to court. Banks charge 18–40 per cent interest a year. 'Banque Lambert' charges interest rates of 20–50 per cent a month. At the end of the month, if the loan is not paid off, the unpaid interest is added to the capital to calculate interest for the next month (Ntambwe 1983).

We will turn now to consider how all these distributive activities of the second economy are organized and how people cope with the decline of the economic infrastructure so clearly in evidence.

*Infrastructure*

Zaire's transportation system is in serious straits for lack of government investment in the road, rail and river-boat system. Roads have deteriorated steadily since independence, for lack of maintenance, and many rural areas have become completely inaccessible to vehicles. In 1980 the parastatal *Office des Routes*, or *Office des Trous* as it is popularly known, barely functioned for lack of road-mending vehicles, spare parts and fuel. Stretches of some major roads become impassable for days because of mud from heavy rains. Bogholes develop that can swallow up an entire truck; bridges are unmaintained and become unusable; ferries stop functioning for lack of spare parts or fuel. The trip from Kivu to Kisangani, a distance of 717 kilometres, which used to take two to three days, now takes up to two weeks or more. Trucks and spare parts are in short supply; in Kisangani in 1980, diesel fuel for trucks was available only at black market prices. Economic reports repeatedly cite the deterioration of roads as the reason harvests of rice, cotton and coffee remain unsold and deplore the impossibility of increasing production in the absence of access roads (*Rapport Economique Régional* 1970, 1971, 1974, *Sous-Régional* 1976).

133

*Entrepreneurs and parasites*

Government reports show that ONATRA, the parastatal river service and port agency, began to cut back boat services up the river from Kinshasa in 1970; the decline has continued. By 1979, goods could take two and a half to three months to arrive and services were so erratic, infrequent and plagued by theft that wholesalers preferred private boat services, despite their high costs. Air Zaire, the national airline, was referred to as Air Peut-Etre in 1980, for good reason: it was sometimes necessary to wait two weeks for space; flights were often cancelled without notice or delayed for hours or days; many a cargo of perishable foodstuffs rotted while waiting. Rail services have suffered from shortage of rolling stock and the deterioration of the track, since SNCZ, the rail parastatal, has been inadequately financed and subjected to mismanagement. The telephone and telegraph system is likewise erratic and undependable.

Nevertheless, as we have shown, enormous quantities of commodities are shifted around the country, fraudulently exported and smuggled, illegally imported, and exchanged between rural and urban areas. How is this possible, given the collapse of infrastructure described above?

People have solved the problem of deterioration of the official infrastructure by organizing their own or by participating in arrangements made by others. Large-scale concerns, such as the religious missions, multinational companies and large national companies run their own transportation systems, owning aircraft, river barges and fleets of trucks. Others import their own trucks, spare parts and fuel in the second economy, or make arrangements to buy from those who do so. Big businessmen and plantation companies repair the roads they use themselves. In one village north of Aru, on a road heavily used by trucks for the illegal ivory and coffee trade, the villagers make a living repairing the bridges for the truckers. Smaller enterprises and individuals use kin and ethnic ties to form networks of mutual assistance for transportation problems or to provide the necessary connections to ship goods or travel by participating in the organizations set up by larger concerns. People pay a fee or offer some favour in return for room on a company truck; 'arrangements' are made with the personnel of official transport services. The big companies forbid their drivers to take on passengers or freight but such rules are routinely broken. The second economy thus organizes this part of its infrastructure by being parasitic on the private capitalist sector, which must bear all capital, running and depreciation costs.

Prices are high for illegally imported trucks, spare parts and fuel. Spares are smuggled from Burundi, Rwanda, Tanzania and Kenya for the eastern regions (Bianga 1982: 229). A trader who needs to buy a truck, but cannot get foreign exchange officially, can obtain it on the parallel market, though the truck will then cost him almost twice as much. The cost of maintenance and repairs for a 10-ton Mercedes truck in zaires per kilometre was Z1.48 at the official exchange rate, Z2.91 at the parallel market rate in 1980 (*Société de Développement International Desjardins* 1981: 247–51).

The political and economic situation after independence made a large contribution to the weakening of the administrative capacity of the state and resulted in the development of extensive second economy activities outside state control. But another major reason for the expansion of this economy was the widespread participation of the personnel of the state in its activities and the consequent decline of state revenue and efficiency. The self-interest of the officials involved prevented any efforts at reform.

## PARTICIPATION OF STATE PERSONNEL

By the late sixties, as we have seen, state personnel were smuggling diamonds on a large scale. By the mid-seventies, they were using their position in the state apparatus to accumulate wealth on a massive scale in a widespread range of activities that deprived the state of its revenues and seriously interfered with effective administration. Foreign business interests are also involved in these activities but little documentation exists (see Lemarchand 1987). Lemarchand points out that foreigners offer the skills and contacts that facilitate African access to corporate bribes and illicit foreign exchange transactions, in return for personal favours, rip-offs and kickbacks.

Bribery, corruption and embezzlement have become rampant (Mukenge 1973; D. Gould 1980; Schatzberg 1980a). A survey of government personnel in Lubumbashi in 1982 revealed the principal ways in which officials regularly supplement their inadequate salaries: corruption, embezzlement, pay-offs, forgeries of official signatures and seals, sale of false documents of certification, illegal taxation, use of spouses for commerce and other unauthorized practices, overcharging on document fees, usury, second jobs and cultivation and sale of foodstuffs (Nsaman 1983: 276). David Gould gives several more: false bills and profit-margin cheating on the allowed rate of profit by business; import, export and excise stamp fraud; distribution of merchandise quotas; postal and judicial fraud; and extortion at military barricades (D. Gould 1980: 138–49). Embezzlement includes direct payroll theft, often by means of payrolls padded with fictitious names.

By virtue of their office in the state, the political aristocracy control the allocation of scarce resources. In so doing they are able to maintain relationships of patronage necessary to sustain their class position. Sally Falk Moore emphasizes the element of exchange in this use of state position:

> All these extra-legal givings can be called 'bribery' if one chooses to emphasize their extra-legal qualities. One could instead use the classical anthropological opposition of moral to legal obligations and call these 'moral' obligations, since they are obligations of relationship that are not legally enforceable, but which depend for their enforcement on the values of the relationship itself. They are all gifts or attentions calculated to induce or ease the allocation of scarce resources... The flow of prestations, attention and

135

favors in the direction of persons who have it in their power to allocate labor, capital, or business deals, may be thought of as the 'price of allocation'. (Moore 1978:62–3)

She points out that it is official position that gives individuals who hold it something to exchange; were it not for their position they would not be in control of scarce resources (*ibid.*: 64). Vwakyanakazi calls this a 'new form of trade'. He describes the sale of administrative equipment and symbols of authority as a whole sector of trade parallel to that of goods and commodities (Vwakyanakazi 1982: 305). The process is made quite overt in a November 1977 speech by President Mobutu:

> To sum it up, everything is for sale, everything is bought in our country. And in this traffic, holding any slice of public power constitutes a veritable exchange instrument, convertible into illicit acquisition of money or other goods, or the evasion of all sorts of obligations. Worse, even the use, by an individual, of his most legitimate right is subjected to an invisible tax, openly pocketed by individuals. Thus, an audience with an official, enrolling children in school, obtaining school certificates, access to medical care, a seat on a plane, an import licence, a diploma, among other things, are all subject to this tax which is invisible, yet known to the whole world. (Quoted in Callaghy 1984: 190)

Officials make use of their position to obtain the vouchers used for speculation and middleman activity. In Kisangani in 1976, an annual government report complained of the massive entry of state personnel into these activities:

> It is necessary to point out the appearance in commerce of a class of intermediaries, extremely powerful and rapacious, who dangerously restrict the distribution circuits. There are magistrates, directors of the JMPR,[12] managers of the wholesale houses, state functionaries but especially political and administrative officials (sub-regional and zone commissioners). These intermediaries use their power to seize for themselves all the merchandise to the detriment of the real merchants who must content themselves with the crumbs although they have money, shops, taxes to pay, and, especially, personnel in their care. The scandal is that it is with money taken from the real merchants that vouchers are paid for and then resold to these same merchants at higher prices. The complicity between these intermediaries and the managers of the wholesale houses means that the latter become, in the long run, untouchable and uncontrollable. Merchandise is thus sold at triple, quadruple or more than its original price.

The report continues, describing the dwindling power of the economic affairs office in the face of the collaboration of higher authorities in these activities.

> The inspectors of the economic affairs have become the errand boys of the sub-regional commissioners... their powers date from laws of 1960–61 when magistrates and state functionaries could not engage in commerce. Now these inspectors must control all the authorities (political, people's, state, regional and sub-regional commissioners) who have become businessmen. In

our humble opinion new laws are needed to reinforce their power otherwise all instructions concerning price control are doomed to defeat. (*Rapport Economique Régional Haut Zaire* 1976)

Position in the state apparatus is also advantageous for acquiring commodities such as cobalt, gold, diamonds, ivory and coffee for smuggling and fraudulent export.

Government personnel, military officers and others with official position, however, generally attempt to avoid participating in the second economy in their public official capacity. They frequently use intermediaries, have a spouse or relative act as a front for their operations, or are careful to use words or gestures that in popular usage refer to the second economy, in order to avoid openly defrauding the state. Examples of such expressions are *l'économie de débrouillardise* or *système D*. Participation is referred to as *article 15* (after a legendary last article in the Congolese Constitution), *débrouillements personels* or more blandly as *affaires personelles*, or as *on se débrouille*. In Kisangani, unrecorded business deals, speculative transactions and other such illegal practices are known as 'bizniz'. A euphemistic vocabulary for bribes exists in various local languages as well as in French: *madesu ya bana* (beans for the children) or *tia ngai mbeli* (stab me) in Lingala; *kulowanish a ndebu* (moisten the beard) or *kupoza koo* (refresh the throat) in Swahili.[13] Certain words are understood as indication that a bribe is appropriate: *comprendre, s'arranger, coopérer. Achat par commission* on an invoice gives the charge made over and above the price (Mubake 1984: 271–2). Particular gestures, such as stroking under the chin, also indicate the need for a bribe.

This conceptualization in people's minds of a distinct system of activities that need a special vocabulary to differentiate them from the transactions of the official economy and from a normal, socially acceptable mode of operations is significant. Although in this patrimonial state the distinction between the public and private capacity of officials is blurred and officials may not bother to disguise the ways in which they deprive the state of revenue and misuse state position, the fact that it is more often thought politic to do so reflects an ideology of public morality still retained in Zaire, albeit in increasingly hollow form, for its necessary part in upholding the authority of the state.[14] In fact, despite great bitterness and cynicism among people in general and the extraordinary difficulty in a system of such venality for a public servant to maintain any integrity, an appreciable number of office-holders strive against impossible odds to do a good job and remain honest.

The expansion of the second economy has thus enabled the political aristocracy to consolidate their position with sometimes enormous accumulation of wealth with which to maintain the patronage on which their position depends. It has offered alternatives and supplements to wage labour and enabled rural and urban workers to avoid proletarianization, as well as the means to survive conditions of sometimes extraordinary hardship. The opportunities it has presented for some individuals, despite and, in some instances, because of the economic crisis, have allowed considerable capital accumulation, which has been a factor in the emergence of a small true indigenous capitalist class. We will now conclude by considering the implications of second economy activities for economic development.

## IMPLICATIONS FOR ECONOMIC DEVELOPMENT

Reginald Green, discussing the World Bank's 1981 report, *Accelerated Development in Sub-Saharan Africa: an Agenda for Action*, comments on 'the oddity of saying that low official prices to the growers lead to wholesale parallel marketing AND serve to reduce output, or that crop movement restrictions are serious deterrents to food production AND that the whole of a 400,000 tonnes peasant paddy crop is black marketed, much of it over several 100 miles' (Green 1984: 21). It is indeed odd, but not unusual: it is generally the case that the production and distribution in the second economy are ignored in discussions of development because they do not appear in figures on the GNP, GDP or per capita output.

Given the size of the second economy in Zaire and other countries of Africa, these official figures are a long way from reflecting the reality of the situation. James Paul, in a symposium on the World Bank report, asserts that the statistical base on which the report rests is weak, with the result that the problems and their prescriptions are oversimplified (Paul 1984: 4). Polly Hill, in a slashing critique of economic statistics from third word countries, goes so far as to assert that

> Lacking evidence to the contrary, it should be *assumed* that all statistics covering whole countries or large states, which relate to such matters as agricultural yields, crop values and production, are bound to include a large element of estimation—to the point that they may not indicate the right trends...It should be generally recognized that the fact that statistical series show consistent trends is no indication of reliability since so much statistical 'cooking' (much of it unavoidable) is partly designed to provide such assurance. (Hill 1985: 12)

She considers that efforts should be directed towards producing far fewer figures of far higher quality and that basic conditions should be analysed both qualitatively and statistically (*ibid.*: 11).

Dupriez has pointed out that a decline in export figures does not necessarily mean a decline in production; in certain cases production can actually have increased but a larger part of it is being fraudulently exported (Dupriez 1968: 674). In his view, in Zaire in the sixties fraud offered increased incomes, pushing cultivators to increase production. It is this modification of real income that determines the behaviour of producers, so that the disappearance of administrative organization in the early sixties, although it reduced some crop yields such as cotton, also allowed monetary stimulants to operate more freely in some instances.

Official figures show a decline in Zaire's food production (World Bank 1980: 11; Bézy *et al.*, 1981: 221) but, as we have shown above, much of the food produced never enters official channels of distribution and is thus unrecorded. Bézy *et al.* comment that two-thirds of peasant production is non-commercialized and escapes statistics, so that total production is difficult to ascertain; also food production has increased in response to increasing demand from urban centres (Bézy *et al.*, 1981: 131). There are plenty of indications that food production is much greater than it appears to be. The figures on the expansion of fish production of 30 per cent by a growing number of small independent producers, given earlier, are significant here. Although Kinshasa suffers food shortages, one of the reasons is not a shortage of production but the deflection of foodstuffs produced along the river, from Mai Ndombe to Equateur and Upper Zaire, and their fraudulent export to Brazzaville, with the connivance of the personnel of ONATRA (Mbumba 1982: 47). Food produced in Manianga is similarly smuggled out and border guards bribed; sacks of manioc wait by the roadside for trucks from Brazzaville. One writer even speculates whether unrecorded production of palm oil by petty producers for direct sale to consumers, may not make up for the drop in production for the internal market that is shown in official statistics: the imports of palm oil forecast as necessary since 1974 to supply domestic consumption have never occurred, despite the continued drop in official production and despite the fact that palm oil is a necessary ingredient for two dishes consumed regularly by the population (M'Bela 1982: 77).

Food production and distribution outside official circuits is reported in other countries besides Zaire. Bates gives sources for Tanzania indicating that the cause of the decline in food purchases by the marketing agencies was not a decline in production but rather a flight from the government controlled market and a massive diversion into private channels of trade (Bates 1981: 85). Chazan writes of a similar phenomenon in Ghana: farmers marketed their produce through their own channels with a 'substitute marketing system which took full advantage of the inadequacies of formal mechanisms' and the creation of 'self-propelled enclosures autonomous of the state and as self-sufficient as possible' (Chazan 1982: 119, 22). Beckman's view of Nigeria is that the picture of economic stagnation and decline

> conceals one of the major, dynamic changes in the development of Nigerian capitalism: a dramatic increase in the commercialization of agriculture oriented toward the domestic food market and the consequent radical broadening of the rural market for manufactured goods. (Beckman 1985: 88)

However, Beckman points out that although increasing food imports in Nigeria reflect changing consumption patterns, the increase in food production nevertheless cannot keep up with population growth. In Zaire, Peemans has shown that a spontaneous mobilization of a food surplus arose in response to trade opportunities to supply the cities, following the collapse of export agriculture (Peemans 1986: 75).

Thus food production by small-scale independent producers in Zaire has increased in response to rising demand as the formal production and distribution system becomes increasingly irrational, disorganized and unpredictable. The second economy offers higher producer prices and greater profit opportunities for traders with its more reliable and efficient organization; as the formal system becomes increasingly unrewarding and oppressive people turn to the second economy for survival and for profit.

From this perspective, it can be shown that in Zaire some of the steps advocated by the World Bank as remedies for resolving the crisis in food production are already in effect through the second economy. Paul summarizes these policy remedies as including a reduction of import and export duties, marketing costs and subsidies to consumers; realistic valuation of the currency; raising of farmgate prices to reflect actual market conditions; developing alternatives to the monopoly exercised by parastatals over input supply and marketing services (Paul 1984: 2). Smuggling is importing and exporting without duty. The parallel exchange rate of the zaire reflects its real value. In the proliferation of second economy trading activities, private firms and traders compete with parastatals; as a result, some producer prices reflect actual market conditions. As Please and Amoako writing for the Bank note, 'Smallholders in both pre- and post-independent Africa have demonstrated a very great responsiveness to changes in price signals and to changing market opportunities' (Please and Amoako 1984: 54).

Taking these considerations into account, it is becoming increasingly necessary to find some means of incorporating the activities of the second economy into assessments of Zaire's development. If, instead of taking economic development to be reflected in figures on the GNP or GDP, we take the approach proposed by M. G. Smith, we can take into consideration total economic activity in both the official and the second economy.

> Development is that process by which the capacity of a given unit to act more efficiently and appropriately in differing situations and conditions improves and increases... Development involves enhancement of [the organic or other unit's] adjustive and performance capacities... through increasing differentiation and interdependence of the unit's activities, components, and their relations, and typically finds expression in more efficient, complex and comprehensive networks of interaction and communication that multiply the variety, number and range of linkages between members of a given society. (Smith 1983: 349–50)

I am not suggesting that in these terms Zaire will, after all, appear to be undergoing satisfactory development; merely that such an approach, because it can include the second economy, can open lines of inquiry that will result in a more realistic assessment of the economic situation in Zaire, or in other countries, than do official figures on the rate of growth of the official economy.

Taking this perspective, the organization of production, distribution and infrastructure in Zaire's second economy, described above, show the capacity of groups and individuals to act efficiently. Jan Vansina points out that people in Zaire use networks to mobilize solidarity and organize themselves when faced with the breakdown of official structures. Men and women learned to cope by acquiring all sorts of skills that would have been wasted in a better regulated environment because of such breakdowns of the system generally (Vansina 1982: 55). As Portes has put it,

> Contrary to the usual image, the response of the exploited to conditions created for them by the capitalist system is seldom passive acquiescence. Their effort to manipulate, in turn, these conditions is based on the two resources left in the absence of capital: one's own labor and social bonds of solidarity and mutual support within the working class. (Portes and Walton 1981: 64)

In Latin America people 'organise their relationships as a social capital that also substitutes for the credentials and organised careers of the official economy' (Machado da Silva, quoted in Roberts 1976: 114). And Roberts points out that 'normative procedures, economic opportunities and administrative regulation are not simply means by which populations are organized but are themselves used by people to reinterpret or even subvert existing organization' (Roberts 1976: 118–25). He sees small-scale activities as active agents in economic development. From this perspective we can see the use of social bonds of solidarity and mutual support in Zaire as social capital, a usage which fulfils Smith's development criteria of enhanced adjustive and performance capacities.

Another significant aspect of second economy activities for economic development is that illicit production and production for illicit distribution of some commodities are generating considerable wealth for some individuals at all levels of the population, thus expanding markets. Robert Bates has said that 'in Africa the market is the setting for the struggle between the peasant and the state' (1981: 6). In Zaire the market is less in the control of the state and less susceptible to state intervention because so much is bought and sold in the second economy. Bates considers that only Nigeria offers a market of sufficient size and wealth to engender competitive struggles between a large number of firms (*ibid.*: 73). But Zaire's natural resources offer comparable potential for wealth to Nigeria's; although much of this wealth in Zaire escapes the control of the state and circulates in the second economy, it is still in existence and offers enormous market potential.

Zaire thus seems to fulfil some of Smith's criteria for development: the expansion of second economy activities certainly shows the organization of more efficient, complex and comprehensive networks of interaction and communication, and an increase in the variety, number and range of linkages between people. These forms of organization indicate that some kind of economic development is taking place.

Economic development and the emergence of nascent capitalists imply rationality: the calculability and predictability in the social, economic, technical and attitudinal context suggested by Weber, referred to in Chapter 1. In the profound irrationality and unpredictability of Zaire's present situation, the organizations and enterprises which function are those which have created their own rational environment; for many, the second economy offers greater possibilities for rational, predictable operation than does the official economy. Tension arises over the preservation and protection of such autonomy from the banditry of the political aristocracy.

The question then arises whether the second economy would diminish if the decline of the state were to be reversed and the efficiency of the administrative apparatus restored. This, however, is an extremely complex question to which there is no simple answer; in the United States and Europe, where administration is much more effective than in Zaire, the second economy is expanding rapidy (see Tanzi 1982; Mattera 1985). It will be very interesting to see the effects of the various reforms made in Zaire in 1983 (see Young and Turner 1985: 384–5).

The next two chapters give details of people who have particularly made use of the second economy for upward mobility: the Nande of Kivu and women in Kisangani. Both are politically and economically disadvantaged in Zairian society.

# 6

# Long-distance trade, smuggling and the new commercial class: the Nande of North Kivu

The government never comes here, we have to fend for ourselves. (The Bishop of Butembo)

A particularly striking example of the emergence of local capitalism in Zaire is evident among the Nande of North Kivu. Nande traders dominate the trade of dried beans and vegetables between Kivu, Kisangani and Kinshasa and form a distinct group in Kisangani's commercial community, renowned for their success in business, the extensiveness of their real estate construction in the city and the cohesiveness and cooperation among them in their business affairs.[1] Located in the country's easternmost region, the Nande are outside the national political scene, have very little political influence or connections and are neglected in government development programmes. Yet they have managed to develop themselves without benefit of political position and connections, and are intensely proud of having done so. A commercial middle class is emerging among them which is investing in productive enterprise producing for the local market.

Various factors have contributed to this process. North Kivu's fertile soils and temperate climate produce a variety of crops, including vegetables and beans,[2] in demand in other parts of the country. The region produces export crops of coffee and tea, is highly suitable for cattle ranching and its natural resources include gold. This abundance of resources and location on the frontier to East Africa have resulted in the development of various forms of trade, both legal and illegal. Nande wealth and prosperity are based not only on their long-distance trade to Kisangani and Kinshasa, but also on the illegal gold trade and coffee smuggling. The rise of a commercial middle class among the Nande thus furnishes a particularly striking example of class formation outside the state and of the significance of the second economy in this process.

Beni and Butembo, the two principal Nande towns, situated within 50 kilometres of one another (see Map 3 p. 83), are described as 'a veritable pole of development' with over 300 dynamic, enterprising and effective traders (SDID 1981: 114). There is little capital investment by large companies or the government in these Nande towns but a great deal of private investment and commercial development. This local enterprise is evident in the number of stores and the greater variety of merchandise in them, far surpassing that in most other regions of Zaire; in the hotels, bus services, banks and coffee factories; and in the number of trucks and Land Rovers in the streets, rather than the luxury Mercedes and Range Rovers that are common in Kisangani and Kinshasa.

An account of the pre-colonial society of the Nande and of their particular colonial experience shows why they are marginal, why so few have attained position in the dominant class and why they lack political position and influence in post-independence Zaire. The conduct of the Nande long-distance trade in vegetables from Kivu to Kisangani and Kinshasa constitutes a trading diaspora similar to that of Asians between African countries and cities and reminiscent of the historical trading diasporas of West Africa. Present political and economic features in Zaire provide interesting parallels to the conditions generating these earlier diasporas. Histories of some of the large businesses of the Nande show that the emergence of indigenous capitalism in Kivu shares features described above for Kisangani: opportunity for starting in business and access to the previously foreign-dominated coffee sector came as foreigners left in the troubles following independence; profits for merchant capital result from the articulation between capitalist and non-capitalist modes of production; and capital is accumulated in the second economy.

HISTORICAL BACKGROUND

The Nande are a Bantu-speaking people, related historically, linguistically and culturally to the Bakonjo of Uganda and one of the four ethnic groups making up three-quarters of the population of Kivu (Kasay 1982: 347). They live in the zones of Beni and Lubero, the most densely populated part of North Kivu. To the east of Beni zone the Ruwenzori mountains rise to over 3,000 metres, causing altitude to modify the equatorial climate. The population concentrates in the high plateau lands of 15,000–25,000 metres. In 1982 it averaged 45.4 per square kilometre, with over 77 per square kilometre in the rich volcanic soils of the market gardening area, and only 1–2 per square kilometre in the forest zone to the west (Sivirihauma 1984: 215; Kahavo 1980: 8–9). The abandonment of colonial anti-erosion meausres since independence, however, and the 43.8 per cent rate of population growth have resulted in severe erosion in some heavily populated areas and consequent severe malnutrition (Vwakyanakazi 1982: 329).

The Nande migrated to this area from the Rift Valley grasslands in the seventeenth and early eighteenth centuries, probably for reasons of drought, disease and famine (Packard 1981: 58–63). In pre-colonial times they practised agriculture, growing beans, plantain bananas, yams and sweet potatoes, and they traded in salt to Uganda. At the end of the nineteenth century, the upper Semliki valley and mountains were an important source of ivory, and the valley a major route for its trade. Chiefs imposed a tax of one tusk per elephant and the ivory trade increased their political authority. This trade remained important for the first two decades of the twentieth century. During this period a significant agricultural surplus was produced and used for tribute to chiefs and ritual leaders, for insurance against famine and for the salt trade (*ibid.*: 88–90, 134–75).

The Nande had a stratified society with a tributary mode of production. Powerful ritual chiefs (*bwami*, sing. *mwami*) ruled territories which were divided into regions ruled by *vasoki* (sing. *musoki*). The *musoki* paid an annual tribute to his *mwami*, consisting of goats, part of the harvest, and beer, or the equivalent in money. The amount depended on the area cultivated, its fertility, the cordiality of the relationship and the economic situation. Regions are divided into 'hills', or mountain ridges. Heads of the groups living on these ridges (*vaghundu*, sing. *mughundu*) collected tribute in cattle and poultry and were dependants of a *musoki*. Land use could also be individually paid for by a chicken and part of the harvest, which equalled a rental contract. The amount was calculated according to the quantity of the harvest. For perennial crops, such as coffee or plantains, the right to land use tended to become perpetual and inherited (Sivirihauma 1984: 213; Kahavo 1980: 12–14; Bergmans 1970: 7, 28).

Belgian colonial rule undermined this tributary mode of production. The region's fertile soils, moderate temperatures and abundant rainfall were highly suitable for cattle-raising and the cultivation of a variety of crops. The colonists introduced coffee, tea, papain, cinchona,[3] wheat and vegetables. Kivu also has abundant mineral resources, of which gold and tin were the most important in the colonial period. The development of mining, plantations and cash crops introduced wage labour, taxation and the development of commerce, disrupting the Nande economic system. Forced labour and taxation used up the resources that had gone to trade and reduced labour available for production. New political and judicial authorities challenged traditional ones. The Nande put up a prolonged resistance to conquest; the area was not pacified until 1925, and hostility revived in World War II in the form of objections to social and economic exploitation and reluctance to fulfil labour obligations. Such antagonism brought the Nande into disfavour with the Belgians and they were not part of the African colonial elite (Willame 1964: 35).

Kivu was disadvantaged educationally as well as politically in the colonial period. Schools in North Kivu were mainly provided by the Assumptionist Fathers, whose standards were lower than those of the Jesuits and Marist Brothers in other regions. Until 1968, secondary education, with the exception of seminaries, consisted of only three years of post-primary education; 90 per cent of educated Nande were school teachers (Luhindi Fataki 1979).

After independence, therefore, very few Nande moved into the new dominant class, which was drawn primarily from the ranks of the colonial bureaucracy and made up of members of ethnic groups which had achieved advantageous positions under the Belgians. The Nande found themselves underrepresented in the national political scene and unable to participate in national decision-making, nor could they advance through the bureau-cracy and professions because of their lack of education. Since they were also at a distance from Kinshasa, the centre of national affairs, their region was neglected by the government in all development programmes and allocation of resources. After independence, when foreign exchange was allocated by quotas, the East was passed by. An ex-minister of the provincial government recalled bitterly how he tried in vain to get quotas but 'the only way to get goods or fuel was in exchange for coffee or gold in Uganda or Ruanda'.

However, this distance from the central government also meant that the Nande were to some extent beyond its control. It gave them a certain degree of autonomy, making it easier to organize their own affairs in response to government neglect. From the early sixties on, many Nande began growing, buying and selling coffee, and Butembo also became the centre of a flourishing illegal gold trade to which the government in Bukavu turned a blind eye. In exchange for coffee and gold, the Nande imported gasoline, diesel fuel, manufactured goods and medicines from Kenya and Uganda.

Coffee growing and export has only been a means for the Nande to acquire wealth since Europeans were displaced from this sector of the economy. European planters began coffee cultivation in the 1920s and it remained exclusively a European crop in Kivu until after World War II (Bianga 1982: 130). In 1935–6 the colonial government had attempted to promote African coffee growing in Kivu but had met with strong opposition from European planters. African cultivation did not begin until 1954 (Tshibanda 1974). At the end of the colonial period coffee growing was mandatory so that people could acquire money to pay taxes and purchase goods. They were supposed to plant at first 50, then, in the better areas, 200–500 bushes a head (Bianga 1982: 133). But it was difficult and expensive to maintain plantations of any size and white planters had significant advantages. Their labour costs were almost nothing; the government helped them financially; and they had more capital than Africans or else could get credit at the bank. Europeans continued to dominate plantation growing of coffee after independence; many Belgian planters left in the political troubles of the sixties, but were replaced by Greeks. Nande villagers did, however, plant small fields, gradually increasing their size. Proximity to Zaire's eastern frontier and the higher

146

producer prices offered in neighbouring countries in East Africa gave rise to the heavy coffee smuggling described in Chapter 5. In 1976 after the world increase in the price of coffee Nande coffee buyers who had bought at low prices and could sell at the new high ones made fortunes.

Coffee has been an important source of wealth for the Nande, but it was general knowledge in the town of Butembo in 1980 that the basis for the prosperity of many Nande businesses was the illegal gold trade, which brought plentiful supplies of otherwise unobtainable imports. The Nande emphasized that their earnings from smuggling and illegal gold trading were brought home and invested in their local economy: 'There's a great outcry against fraud but at least we bring back manufactured goods and medicines that are needed and sell them, instead of putting foreign currency into Swiss bank accounts and living in Europe, as do the rich and powerful in Kinshasa.' The gold that is smuggled out is brought back into the economy in the form of imported goods and equipment so that increased purchasing power diffuses throughout the population (SDID 1981: 115). Vwakyanakazi points out also that as soon as those involved acquire capital they tend to withdraw from these second economy activities into more legal forms of commerce (Vwakyanakazi 1981: 340).

As the Nande accumulated capital they invested in trucks sometimes imported from East Africa in exchange for coffee or gold, and moved into the trade in vegetables between Kivu, Kisangani and Kinshasa.

DEVELOPMENT AND CONDUCT OF THE LONG-DISTANCE TRADE

Meillassoux defines long-distance trade not by distance or by the nature of the goods but according to the 'notion of complementary geographical zones producing rare or non-existent goods for export' (Meillassoux 1971: 67). Nande country is particularly suitable for producing beans and other vegetables in demand elsewhere in Zaire; in return the Nande import goods unavailable in Kivu. The colonists introduced food and cash crops: coffee, tea, pyrethrum, cinchona, rice, manioc, maize, peanuts and vegetables. Africans, however, were not allowed to grow the profitable export crops till late in the colonial period and were unable to enter commerce on any scale; wages were too low for them to accumulate starting capital and they were ineligible for loans till 1956. By 1960 they had only received 12 per cent of total loans and 1.3 per cent of the capital of loan institutions, the rest going to settlers. A proposal of the provincial administration in 1957 to let Africans handle retail trade and service stations in urban areas met with fierce settler opposition (Vwakyanakazi 1982: 149). After independence in 1960 the Nande began to develop market gardening themselves, growing a range of European vegetables, chiefly potatoes, onions, leeks, cabbages, carrots and salad greens.

At first the markets for this produce were to the south, but in 1963, during the government's attempts to reunite North and Central Kivu into a single province, road access in this direction was cut off. The Nande were forced to seek markets in Kisangani and other towns of Upper Zaire (Willame 1964: 28). The removal to Goma of the Belgian company TMK (*Transport et Messageries de Kivu*), a principal buyer of produce,[4] forced the Nande to establish their own distribution system, and the devastation and breakdown of food production in Kisangani after the rebellion of 1964 opened up new market opportunities.

By 1979 the Nande had a near monopoly in the shipping of vegetables by road from Kivu to Kisangani and they were the principal shippers of beans down river to Kinshasa. This trade is conducted by Nande living in these cities and organized through a network of kin and ethnic ties. They make up a trade diaspora: an 'interrelated net of commercial communities forming a trade network' (Curtin 1984: 2).

Writing of historical trading diasporas in West Africa, Abner Cohen states that:

> under pre-industrial social conditions—characterised by ethnic heterogeneity of the communities involved in the trade, the absence of regular services for communication and transportation, and of effective central institutions to ensure the respect of contract, etc.—these technical problems have often been overcome when men from one ethnic group control all or most of the stages of the trade in specific commodities. (Cohen 1971: 266)

He implies a contrast between pre-industrial and modern states but the social conditions he specifies as pre-industrial exist today in the modern state of Zaire. The problems arising from such conditions have here also been overcome by organization of a trade diaspora, in which one ethnic group controls all stages of the trade in certain commodities.

In the well-known trading diasporas of West Africa the guarantees and regulations necessary for the conduct of the trade 'come from the assimilation of business relationships to the obligations of kinship, affinity or clientage' (Meillassoux 1971: 72). Such use of kin ties has ancient historical precedents in the family businesses of the trans-Saharan trade of the fourteenth century (Johnson 1976: 110–11), of which a good example were the

> five brothers of the Macqquari family settled in Tlensen, Sijilmasa and Walata, from which places they could control the Trans-Saharan trade in all its stages by responding to the fluctuations of supply and demand at both ends of the route. (Levtzion 1968: 226)

Communities of traders living among strangers in associated networks are to be found throughout the world and date back to the beginnings of urban life (Curtin 1984: 3). A variety of extensive trading diasporas based on kinship and ethnicity developed in West Africa from the fourteenth century onwards (Baier 1980: 57ff.; Curtin 1984 ch. 2 and 3, 1975 ch. 2; Meillassoux 1971). The classic case is that of the Hausa, who monopolize the long-distance cattle and kola trade betwen forest and savanna in

Nigeria, handling large sums of money and extensive credit. Abner Cohen's account shows how an ethnic group manipulates the idiom of religion and custom, values and symbols, as a weapon in the struggle for power and privilege (Cohen 1969).

Unlike these extensive West African diasporas, the Nande trade network is on a small not a large scale and it is not supported by a religious ideology. Nande connected by close ties of kinship or friendship conduct the trade, living in the cities strategic to its operation. They organize the shipping and purchase of goods, transmit information and arrange credit. This control of all stages of the trade by trusted agents helps the Nande to overcome problems caused by the social conditions of modern Zaire that are similar to those described by Cohen above: degeneration of the transport and communication systems; scarcity of goods; restricted access to capital; and the suspicion and mistrust that prevail between people from different regions and from different ethnic groups in Zaire. It is not, however, competition and rivalry with other ethnic groups that have given rise to this trade diaspora, but rather the efforts of some Nande to make use of ethnic ties to advance themselves and improve their position in the new nationwide class structure in process of formation since independence.

Nande communities exist in Kisangani and Kinshasa. They do not always live in close-knit neighbourhoods but they know each other, maintain contact and offer mutual assistance through their ethnic association. In Kabondo, one of Kisangani's poorer zones, they form a neighbourhood that dates from their earliest arrival in the colonial period. These early migrants worked as masons, carpenters and plantation workers; today the Nande who live in this neighbourhood mostly work as watchmen and houseboys or cultivating farms out of town. Middle-class Nande are scattered throughout the city but know and interact with each other. Newcomers to town stay with a fellow Nande who takes them around and introduces them to others to find contacts for jobs. Class divisions have emerged among the Nande since independence but Willame suggests that they may have retained a strong feeling of solidarity which has translated into an ability to work together, because they are more numerous than other groups in northeast Zaire (1964: 32–3). In 1960 their number was estimated at 70,000.[5] Cooperation depends on trust and therefore on a common ethic. As one Nande put it

> We are used to working together: we have the same kind of mentality, way of thinking and methods of working: it is therefore easier for us to work with each other, find empathy and affinity and have trust because we can predict one another's actions and reactions.

People in Kisangani frequently commented that the Nande work well together compared to other peoples in Zaire, but that they are closed to outsiders.

Family members cooperate in owning and running Nande businesses.

149

This cooperation, reflecting mutual confidence and trust, is not restricted to the family, but can extend to friends. In the pre-colonial period the family was the basis of the economic unit. The Nande system of land tenure is based on patron-client relations between the clan section of the first occupants and clearers of land, and later settlers making up the groups resident on mountain ridges. Descent is of minimal importance and clans have very little corporate identity (Packard 1981: 66–9). Cooperation has always been strong within these localized units: 'the family and the group were very individualistic, living closed in upon themselves and keeping a distance from the families of neighbouring groups' (Bergmans 1970: 30).

Nande help each other in various ways to start out in trade. One way is for a father to give his son a small capital sum or a second-hand truck. The history of a storekeeper illustrates such a beginning:

> Mr F.'s father gave him Z200 with which he bought cigarettes and set up as a roadside vendor. He gradually expanded to include soap and biscuits, moved into a shop and built up a stock worth Z20,000. He bought a bicycle with his first profits to make it easier to get around and obtain the cheapest goods. His store prospered and finally he had Z40,000 to invest. He decided to go into coffee buying and selling rather than expanding his retail business because coffee is profitable and the turnover is quicker.

A second way of starting out is when a group of young men from the same village work together growing coffee, then smuggle the coffee into Uganda, sell it and with the proceeds build and stock a vending booth. A third way is through a loan: a successful trader will lend money to one who is starting out. A fourth route into business is apprenticeship or sponsorship, described by Vwakyanakazi. Apprenticeship to a trader is considered to be a relation of *musoki*, the dependence expressed through the payment of tribute in traditional Nande society. A sponsor is a substantial businessman who trains a group of three to five young traders; he is called their 'father', they his 'sons'. He uses them to work under his supervision in some of his enterprises, thus gaining extra workers while passing on his knowledge, skills and contacts. Those under the sponsorship of the same father have an obligation to give each other mutual aid and material support. After a year or two, a 'father' will transfer some goods and capital to a 'son', who will be set up on his own, acquiring a trading licence in his own name (Vwakyanakazi 1982: 265–8).

In times of crisis Nande businessmen may lend each other money without interest. Failing this, if loans cannot be obtained from the banks, there are unofficial lending institutions which charge usurious rates for very short-term loans. Defaulting on such loans is taken up in informal courts set up to deal with business problems; these courts have no legal status and are ignored by the local administration. Sanctions imposed by them range from fines to beatings to confiscation of goods (*ibid.*: 261–3).

Nande overcome transportation problems by helping each other in truck breakdowns on the roads. They also use their local agent to ship goods from Kisangani; another in Kinshasa goes down to the docks every day, with all the necessary papers, to take immediate charge of shipments. Since mail and telegraph services are unreliable, the information necessary to conduct trade is communicated mostly by word of mouth or hand-carried letter, in which again mutual trust and cooperation are essential.

In sum, the conduct of the trade by the Nande solves problems in the manner specified by Cohen for trading diasporas elsewhere (Cohen 1971: 266). The close ties of the managers of the different depots and branches of businesses provide for the regular exchange of information about the conditions of supply and demand; speedy despatch and reception of goods, if not their speedy transportation, is ensured by Nande agents, and mutual assistance is provided between Nande on the roads; relations of trust are created and maintained between the Nande involved in the chain of the trade; and they arrange the necessary credit among themselves to ensure that trade will flow.

As Nande traders accumulated capital in the vegetable trade, or in illegal gold trading and coffee smuggling, they acquired wholesale and retail businesses, ranches and plantations, and real estate, and began to enjoy a middle-class lifestyle. We will look now at the details of this Nande commerce and at the histories of some substantial Nande businesses to show how these traders are becoming part of the new indigenous capitalist class.

## NANDE ENTREPRENEURS: THEIR LEGAL AND ILLEGAL TRADE AND INVESTMENTS

Nande informants estimated the number of large-scale businessmen, owning several trucks and engaged in the export of vegetables to Kisangani and Kinshasa, at about fifty, with many more operating on a smaller scale. The Butembo Chamber of Commerce (ANEZA) provided a list of the thirty-five of its members trading to Kisangani, all of whom owned several trucks. In her 1979 study of Nande trade between Kivu and Kisangani, Kahavo found over fifty traders, some not large enough to belong to ANEZA.

Beans are the most important commodity in this trade. The centre of production for coloured beans is in the higher areas of Lubero zone which commercializes 5,000 tonnes a year; white beans are primarily produced at lower altitudes, particularly around Bunia but also near Beni. The trade is on a large scale: in 1979–80 over 11,000 tonnes of beans were shipped to Kinshasa, 8,720 from North Kivu, 2,900 from Bunia, making up 84 per cent of the city's supply. In the same year Kinshasa imported 1,300–1,600 tonnes of potatoes from North Kivu, also leeks and onions. The zones of Beni and Lubero commercialize about 600 tonnes of leeks a year. (SDID 1981: 73–7). Table 6.1 gives details of the volume of this trade.

151

Table 6.1 *Volume of products traded from North Kivu 1979–80 (in tonnes)*

| | | | |
|---|---|---|---|
| Beans | 549 ⟶ Isiro | | |
| | 11073 ⟶ Kisangani (local consumption 982) | | |
| | 9170 | ONATRA | |
| | 21 | Air Zaire | ⟶ Kinshasa |
| | 900* | private boat | |
| | 283 | Goma ⟶ Kinshasa | |
| Potatoes | 230 ⟶ Isiro | | |
| | 1105 ⟶ Kisangani (local consumption 188) | | |
| | 600 | ONATRA | |
| | 17 | Air Zaire | ⟶ Kinshasa |
| | 300* | private boat | |
| | 700 | Goma ⟶ Kinshasa (local 1,000)[†] | |
| Onions | 42 ⟶ Isiro | | |
| | 200 ⟶ Kisangani (local consumption 153) | | |
| | 22 | ONATRA | |
| | 25 | Air Zaire | ⟶ Kinshasa |
| | 438 | Goma ⟶ Kinshasa | |
| Leeks | 42 ⟶ Isiro | | |
| | 201 ⟶ Kisangani | | |
| | 100 | ONATRA*+ | |
| | 5 | Air Zaire | ⟶ Kinshasa |
| | 273 | Goma ⟶ Kinshasa | |

* estimate
+ accompanied by travelling merchants
† large because Goma is a tourist centre

*Source:* SDID 1981: 67–80.

Fish and beef are also part of the trade from the northeast. Fish from the fisheries, industrial and artisanal, of Lake Mobutu and from Lake Amin are shipped to Kinshasa. In 1979–80 1,708 tonnes went through Kisangani, to be shipped by ONATRA (452 tonnes) and Air Zaire (762 tonnes); and 87 tonnes were flown from Goma. Masisi, west of Goma, exported 35 tonnes by air to Kinshasa; only 14 tonnes were sent from the Bunia region through Kisangani. But these shipments made up only 370 of the 6,000 tonnes consumed that year in Kinshasa (*ibid.*: 83–5).

In addition of this legal, recorded trade, Nande participate heavily in unrecorded trade, particularly coffee smuggling and the illegal gold trade. 'From Nairobi, Kenya, Butembo is supplied with general retail commodities including clothing, hardware, laundry and toilet material, jewelry, perfumes, medical products ... These are entirely paid for in gold,' to the amount of four to five truckloads of goods every month (Vwakyanakazi 1982: 282–3). As mentioned above in Chapter 5, coffee is fraudulently

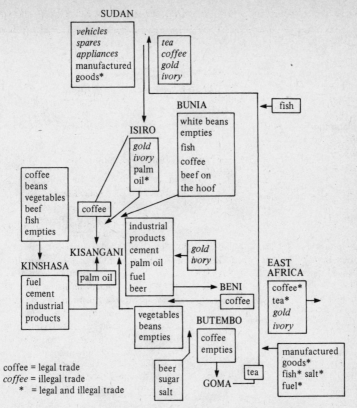

SUDAN

vehicles
spares
appliances
manufactured
goods*

tea
coffee
gold
ivory

BUNIA

white beans
empties
fish
coffee
beef on
the hoof

fish

ISIRO

gold
ivory
palm
oil*

coffee
beans
vegetables
beef
fish
empties

coffee

KINSANGANI

industrial
products
cement
palm oil
fuel
beer

gold
ivory

EAST
AFRICA

coffee*
tea*
gold
ivory

KINSHASA

fuel
cement
industrial
products

palm oil

BENI

coffee

vegetables
beans
empties

BUTEMBO

coffee
empties

coffee = legal trade
*coffee* = illegal trade
* = legal and illegal trade

beer
sugar
salt

GOMA

tea

manufactured
goods*
fish* salt*
fuel*

Fig. 6.1. Flow chart of commodities traded in northeast Zaire

exported to East Africa; to the north, Nande tea is exchanged for trucks, spares and electrical appliances in direct barter across the Sudanese frontier. The imports from Isiro, Fig. 6.1, must include goods brought in from the Sudan to Kisangani. Asians owning stores in the city said that they were largely supplied from the Sudan.

Fig. 6.1, a flow chart of the commodities traded, both legally and illegally, up river from Kinshasa, through Kisangani to Upper Zaire and North Kivu, across the northern border to the Sudan and across the eastern border to Uganda, Ruanda, Burundi and Kenya puts Nande trade into the context of the total commerce carried out in the northeast region.

Interviews with managers or owners of some of the larger Nande concerns showed that besides engaging in trade these entrepreneurs also own plantations, livestock ranches and wholesale and retail stores. Their buinesses are substantial, as indicated by their membership in ANEZA, by their ownership of multiple enterprises, the number of workers they employ (over one hundred in several instances), and the number of vehicles they own. Another significant indicator of the prosperity and scale

Table 6.2 *Examples of Nande businesses represented in Kisangani*

| Businesses | No. of workers | Vehicles | Goods |
|---|---|---|---|
| 1. wholesaler<br>3 pharmacies<br>3 ranches<br>2 plantations<br>coffee export<br>papain<br>cinchona | 150 | 2 trucks<br>4 cars<br>2 pickups | beer from Kisangani<br>medicines from Nairobi<br>soap, palm oil from<br>  Kinshasa |
| 2. wholesaler<br>coffee export<br>tea planta-<br>  tion, ranch | 140 | 5 trucks | vegetables to Kisangani<br>  and Kinshasa<br>cement, palm oil, fuel<br>cloth from Kinshasa<br>beer from Kisangani |
| 3. wholesaler<br>coffee plant-<br>  ation, ranch<br>buys coffee | 30+ | 2 trucks | beans, leeks, onions,<br>  cabbage to Kisangani<br>beer, palm oil from Kisangani<br>beans, potatoes to Kinshasa |
| 4. wholesaler<br>plantations<br>  coffee<br>  cinchona<br>buys coffee | 27 | 5 trucks<br>2 pickups<br>2 cars<br>1 bus | beans, potatoes to Kinshasa<br>beer from Kisangani<br>oil, tyres, fuel, construction<br>  materials, roofing iron<br>  from Kinshasa |
| 5. retail-Beni<br>  Butembo<br>pharmacy<br>3 coffee<br>  plantations<br>2 ranches | 37* | 5 trucks | beans, onions, maize<br>  to Kinshasa<br>palm oil, clothes, household<br>  goods from Kinshasa<br>medicines from Kinshasa<br>beer from Kisangani |
| 6. wholesaler<br>2 coffee<br>  plantations,<br>ranch, pharmacy | 115 | 3 trucks<br>4 pickups<br>1 car | beans, potatotes, onions,<br>  leeks to Kisangani<br>beer, cloth from Kisangani<br>cement from Kinshasa |
| 7. wholesaler<br>retail<br>plantations<br>coffee export | 360 | ? | clothes, household goods<br>cloth, shoes from Kinshasa |
| 8. ranch<br>(400 cattle)<br>wholesaler | 50 | ? | beans, potatoes, onions,<br>  leeks to Kisangani,<br>beer depot, milk,<br>butter, meat to Butembo |

\* plus 'lots' on the plantations

of operations of these Nande businessmen is that in 1980 the Nande were carrying out 30–50 per cent of the construction in Kisangani, chiefly in building warehouses and houses. Details of examples of larger businesses are summarized in Table 6.2. Six are based in Butembo, one in Beni and one in Kisangani. This table shows how profits in trade of all kinds are invested in productive enterprises, principally ranches and plantations.

Histories of these business owners show that they mostly started in the sixties as coffee buyers or producers or in trade and gradually accumulated capital. Vwakyanakazi says that many businessmen got their starting capital in the illegal gold trade, organized as early as 1937 by Asians (Vwakyanakazi 1982: 160, 237). Those in wage employment combined their salaries with the earnings from trade on the side to save money. The histories also reveal the details of cooperation between family members in running businesses: in all but one, managers of branches are related to the owners.

> No. 6 bought coffee in the early sixties and acquired a plantation in 1966. He had enough money to buy a truck by 1975; he sent out buyers with sacks and money, then sent out the truck to pick them up. By 1979 he had started trading vegetables to Kisangani and owned three large trucks, four pickups and a Peugeot car. His shipments are mostly bought by women traders coming up to Kisangani from Kinshasa; anything left over he ships down himself. His Kisangani manager is his brother-in-law.

> No. 2 began with trade from Butembo to Kisangani in 1966 and expanded to trade with Kinshasa in 1977. In 1980 he was buying up coffee from peasant producers and exporting it by selling to OZACAF. He planned to buy spare parts, trucks and construction materials with the foreign exchange he earned. His ranch has fifty cows and will produce cheese, butter and sausage. He intended to open stores in Goma and Butembo, and to raise beef cattle and export meat by air to Kinshasa. His cousin manages the Kisangani branch of the business.

> No. 4 began by trading on a small scale to Isiro and by working for a local coffee factory. He bought his first truck in 1967 and went into transport. By 1970 he had two trucks and he bought three more in 1974. He sells to women traders from Kinshasa in Kisangani. He plans to invest in construction and a hotel.

> No. 3 began by buying and selling coffee in 1968, invested his profits in a truck and began transporting vegetables to Kisangani and Isiro, and soap from Isiro to Butembo. In 1977 he had a depot in Kisangani for shipping potatoes and beans to Kinshasa, importing palm oil and beer to Butembo in return. He sells to traders from Kinshasa, often making a direct exchange of a whole truck of beans for the equivalent value in cement, palm oil or fuel. He works with three friends and they help each other in finding goods. His brother-in-law manages his Kisangani branch.

The histories in Table 6.2 are all of men. Some Nande women also own substantial businesses:[6] in Butembo five have trade licences, many more trade without. One of the five owns a bakery, another a transport business, the others deal in general commerce, especially *wax* prints. One owned three trucks and a car, another two stores and a fifty-room hotel (Vwakyanakazi 1982: 226–7).

The scale of Nande business expanded rapidly in the late seventies. Kahavo lists the total tonnage exported to Kisangani by six of the

155

large-scale businesses in 1978 as 348.9, 329.7, 251.8, 231.8, 217.7 and 141 respectively (Kahavo 1980: 30,44). The tonnages I collected for some of the businesses in Table 6.2 indicate an increase in scale: two were shipping about 576 tonnes each to Kinshasa per year; another 720 tonnes to Kisangani and 360 to Kinshasa. The expansion of trade was the result of the sudden escalation of coffee and gold prices and of the smuggling and illegal trade in these commodities. After the world price increase in coffee in 1976 those Nande who had bought at low prices and sold at the new high prices made fortunes. A good example is Number 5 in Table 6.2.

> No. 5 went to Uganda and attended secondary school during the years of the rebellion. His father was a trader and gave him starting money and a small van to start as a coffee buyer in 1976. He bought coffee at 20K per kilo and sold it at Z3 because of the sudden price rise. The profits he made enabled him to buy a house and two trucks and to start a transport business. He bought three more trucks in the next two years and also three coffee plantations. By 1980 he also had two stores, a pharmacy and two cattle ranches with 100–50 head of cattle. He ships 48 tonnes of produce every month to Kinshasa and goes there himself twice a month. He imports palm oil, medicines, clothes, household goods, cement and beer. He wants to become a coffee exporter and to start a roofing-iron factory in Butembo with the hard currency that he earns by exporting. His brothers manage his affairs in Kivu. He runs the business from Kisangani.

This is a remarkable expansion in only four years; presumably gold trading or smuggling coffee across the border played some part in it. Another trader who was using the gold trade to finance his business expansion made this involvement clear by trying to make a gold deal in the course of an interview.[7]

> This gold dealer had been in business since 1950. His parents and his paternal uncle had been in trade and helped to provide his starting capital. He has a wholesale business and owned two trucks, which in 1980 made three trips a month to Kisangani and Goma to sell beans and other vegetables. He imported beer, cement, flour and palm oil, which he sold wholesale. He also owned eight dispensaries in Beni, Lubero and Butembo, and a pharmacy in another small town. He supplied his dispensaries from Bukavu, Goma (with imports from Kinshasa) and Nairobi. He used to go to Nairobi himself, where he had a Nande friend who arranged the necessary currency. Another friend worked with him in Goma and his younger brother is in Kisangani, where he uses depots belonging to Nande friends.

This example gives the history of a businessman who took part in the gold trade; it also shows the help of family members for starting out in business and the cooperation of friends and kin thereafter.

The owner of the largest business enterprise in North Kivu belonging to a non-politician is a millionaire who owes his fortune to coffee. He began by working as a driver, then ran his own transport business, finally going into coffee buying and exporting. His enormous company, CAPACO, is based in Beni with branches all over Kivu, in Kisangani and other towns of Upper Zaire, and in Kinshasa. In 1980 the company had a payroll of Z50,000 a month, paid Z400,000 in taxes a year, and employed thirty Europeans. He also owns an air charter business with four planes, thirty to forty trucks, real estate, ranches and plantations. In addition CAPACO ships 25 tonnes of salt fish to Kinshasa a month.

According to Vwakyanakazi, CAPACO has ties with American capital. There are two other very large coffee exporting companies in North Kivu, one, CAFEKIT (Ets. Kitambala), belongs to a Nande businessman who has good political connections and expatriate partners; the other, RWACICO, belongs to a political commissioner. CAPACO and CAFE-KIT collected over 2,000 tonnes of coffee in 1979 (Vwakyanakazi 1982: 318). A smaller enterprise, but one that is entirely owned, managed and financed by Nande who have no political connections or foreign capital, is CUGEKI.

The history of CUGEKI, a privately owned agro-business and coffee processing plant in Butembo, reveals the problems that such enterprises face and shows how they can be surmounted. The manager who showed me around the factory emphasized with pride that it was entirely Zairian founded and run.

CUGEKI started as a fourteen-member cooperative to export vegetables to Kisangani in 1969. They owned six trucks, exporting beans, onions, leeks and potatoes and importing soap, clothing, beer and general merchandise. Bad management and the embezzlement of funds caused them to fail in 1970–1; they had to sell the trucks and give up the vegetable trade. But in 1971 an Englishman sold them a coffee factory which they began to operate the next year. They exported coffee till 1974, when all export was taken over by the coffee marketing board, but continued thereafter buying up coffee from the producers and selling it to ONC.

In 1976 the government wanted a share in the cooperative, so they changed into a private company, taking on a new member at the same time. After 1976, when restrictions were lifted, they started exporting coffee again, and invested their profits in a 340-hectare plantation, of which 70 hectares were in production by 1980.

They have expanded to own a sawmill, a pharmacy and a store. They tried papain and bought a drying machine but gave it up because of price fluctuations and problems with rotting. They continued to buy coffee from petty producers as well as producing their own and in 1978 exported 100 tonnes to Switzerland. In 1980 they employed 150 at the factory, 200 at the plantation and 300 women seasonally for sorting coffee beans, and they owned a truck and a tractor.

In 1980 they were facing considerable problems. Shortage of diesel fuel was catastrophic, causing them to run at a loss: they needed 6,000 litres a month but had a quota of only 1,000, so the rest had to be bought on the black market at Z1,000 a 200-litre barrel, instead of at the official price of Z140. The difficulty of obtaining spare parts was another serious problem and they had been unable to repair a generator that had broken down in 1977. Sacks were in short supply from the factory in Kinshasa and for three years they had had to buy higher priced imported ones. Despite these difficulties, in March 1980 they had obtained an export licence and had 48 tonnes of coffee ready for export.

CAPACO and CUGEKI compete successfully with firms owned by politicians and foreigners. ANEZA lists other firms that are coffee exporters in Butembo. In addition to those mentioned so far, one is Ets. Mulumberi, a wholesale and retail firm owned by an Asian, who also owns a garage, buys coffee and employs 147 workers (Vwakyanakazi 1982: 397); one is Number 7 in Table 6.2; another is KASEREKA SIVIRI, an affiliate of CUGEKI; and one is owned by a government minister, Paluku Mutogherwa, who employs 980 workers. For two other firms I do not have any information.

Like the entrepreneurs independent of politics in Kisangani, Nande owners of substantial businesses are heavily engaged in productive as well as distributive enterprise: ranches and plantations are productive; wholesale and retail trade and pharmacies are distributive. They are producing for the local as well as the export market and contributing to the development of the local economy. Their plans for the future continue this trend. They include farm production of cheese, butter and sausage for local consumption, and of meat to ship by air to Kinshasa; setting up a roofing-iron factory in Butembo; importing trucks, spare parts, construction materials and textiles with currency from coffee exporting; construction of houses for rent in Kisangani and Butembo; and opening an hotel.

INDIGENOUS NANDE CAPITALISM

The background of these Nande businessmen contrasts with that of the substantial business owners in Kisangani. The Nande all came from the rural agricultural background of traditional Nande society. Vwakyanakazi found that the fathers of 91.4 per cent of substantial businessmen in Butembo were agriculturalists (Vwakyanakazi 1982: 235). This situation reflects the more recent participation of the Nande in the modern economy. But not only were Nande businessmen not part of the colonial elite, neither did they come from the elite of traditional Nande society. They originated from among the cadets, or juniors, who saw little opportunity for advancement for themselves in the traditional hierarchy.

Nande businessmen are predominantly Protestant. They are poorly educated and many of them speak very little French. Protestant schools were inferior to Catholic ones and for their graduates 'with few skills from formal schooling, trade in addition to agriculture was the single avenue to improve their living' (Vwakyanakazi 1982: 244). There is no indication of a strong protestant ethic affecting their attitude to money, but it does seem that in other ways religion affected their entry into trade. Catholic education was oriented towards white collar employment and condemned the pursuit of material profit, whereas, during the colonial period,

Protestant mission communities permitted African petty trade and were neutral or positive in their teaching on wealth accumulation.[8] In 1962–3 a quarrel among the Protestant communities of Katwa, southeast of Butembo, came to a head. They disagreed on whether or not Africanization of the Gospel should be a strategy to raise Protestants from their position of social marginality. The Baptists, who favoured collaboration with foreign missionaries, withdrew from Katwa, some of them taking refuge in communities over the Ugandan border, where they became involved in trade in order to make their living. They improved their skills by contact with local merchants and facilitated their commerce by maintaining business relationships with their fellows back in Kivu, sending back goods to be retailed in Butembo market. In 1966–7, some of these Nande returned to Butembo from Uganda and found their Ugandan ties very useful in establishing successful businesses (*ibid.*: 161–4).

The recent prosperity of some Nande from trade, coffee production and gold is evident in the growth of Butembo, generally regarded as the Nande capital, and in its dynamic business community. The town grew in the colonial period from a gold mining camp to a small commercial centre for Belgians, Greeks, Portuguese and Asians. By 1958 it was a *centre extra coutumier,* or African township. Since independence, according to one estimate, the population has more than tripled to approximately 100,000 (Kasay 1982: 351), and the town has expanded as a centre of Nande commerce. In 1961 there were only five small African-owned businesses, twelve shops and a few other enterprises (Vwakyanakazi 1982:158); by 1980 Nande owned forty-eight of the fifty stores in town. Five banks had opened branches, a small airport financed entirely by local businessmen had been constructed, under the direction of the Nande bishop of Butembo, and plans were underway to built two small hydro-electric dams, also locally financed. The only electricity in the town was from private generators, but since the central government would not supply funds, a committee had formed to organize dam construction (the PDIK, *Promotion pour le Développement Industriel au Kivu*), headed by the bishop and including forty local businessmen. In 1979 the Lions International opened branches in Butembo and Beni, confirming the importance of these towns as commercial centres.

The emergence of a commercial middle class among the Nande reflects this local development. Nande businessmen interviewed in Kisangani enjoy a middle-class lifestyle, living in comfortably furnished houses complete with a range of electrical appliances. They are ensuring their reproduction as a class by investing in inheritable, productive property: plantations, ranches and other businesses, and real estate. The business on which this class is based is carried on outside the framework of politics: 'Rather it thrives on political difficulties of Zaire which provide it with a favorable environment for profitable business negotiations and transactions' (Vwakyanakazi 1982: 315).

The same factors operate in this process of class formation among the Nande as in the emergence of the commercial middle class in Kisangani. In both Kivu and Kisangani the indigenization of foreign capital, capital accumulation in the second economy and the articulation of capitalist and non-capitalist modes of production have all been significant factors in the development of local capitalism.

The post-independence political troubles and Zairianization resulted in acquisition of business plantations and the opening up of commerce to nationals in North Kivu as it did elsewhere. In 1960 there were only sixty licensed African traders in Butembo, mostly engaged in coffee collecting from rural areas and selling to exporters. After the disruption of the economy and the exodus of foreigners in the rebellion a number of foreign-owned commercial companies abandoned their activities entirely. Greek and Asian traders retreated from the rural areas into the towns and only about half the foreign planters who had fled from the rebels returned. Nationals moved into commerce and by 1970 the number of licensed African traders had increased to 118. This increase reflected acquisition of starting capital during the Mulelist period of the rebellion. In the seventies, after Zairianization, coffee plantations and forty out of fifty businesses were handed over to Nande and other nationals. As in other regions of the country the majority were local government officials and administrators without serious entrepreneurial intentions, who allowed their businesses to deteriorate (Vwakyanakazi 1982: 171–3; Bianga 1982: 137–43). However, as in Kisangani, the result of the departure of foreigners and transfer of their assets in North Kivu facilitated access of nationals to sectors of the economy that allowed capital accumulation, especially after the 1976 rise in coffee prices on the world market.

The importance of the second economy for capital accumulation is particularly evident in North Kivu. The illegal gold trade and smuggling of coffee, tea, papain and other commodities have been one source of opportunities to acquire sufficient capital for the move into production that has been the basis for the emergence of the new commercial class. Informal trade and fraudulent activities have greatly expanded since 1974; usury has been 'a valuable source of starting capital for some and a way of expanding small business for others'. In 1977–8 in particular, the Ugandan crisis and war drained considerable capital assets to North Kivu, through illegal traffic in buses, trucks and motor bikes. Coffee smuggling also intensified during this period; one dealer is reported to have obtained 200 tonnes of coffee beans from Uganda through the border post of Kasindi in just two months from August to September 1980 (Vwakyanakazi 1982: 177–9).

In Kivu, as in Kisangani, the fact that the producer can survive on such a small percentage of the cost the consumer pays, a function of the articulation of non-capitalist and capitalist modes of production, provides opportunities in some cases for traders to make profits and accumulate capital. Only in non-capitalist systems of subsistence farming and petty commodity production are such very low costs of subsistence and reproduction of the direct producers possible. Potato growers in Kivu in 1980, for example, got 4.4 per cent of the wholesale price of potatoes in Kinshasa. The high costs of distribution, however, cut down potential profits. Only those who find a favourable conjunction of circumstances make much money.

Some details of the problems that confront these Nande businessmen will make it clear why only relatively few are able to achieve the success and scale of business described above.

The decay of the transportation system since independence, detailed in Chapter 5, contributes enormously to distribution costs. The road network is particularly inadequate in Kivu (Kasay 1982: 353). The Butembo–Kisangani road is so bad that, driving ten hours a day at a speed that can only average 20 kilometres an hour, trucks average 16.67 days for the round trip, including time spent on breakdowns and searching for goods. The section of the road between Kisangani and Komande (630 kilometres) is maintained by brigade 403 of the Office des Routes. It has a workforce of 208, 160 of them road workers from the local population (*cantonniers*), and twenty-five machines (graders, bulldozers, power shovels, trucks), of which only seven were functioning in June 1980. As a result this stretch of the road is in very poor condition and is completely impassable during rain (SDID 1981: 63, 127).

Shortage of boats, spare parts, fuel and qualified personnel result in extreme variability in the number of days it takes for goods to be shipped downriver from Kisangani to Kinshasa by ONATRA: in 1979–80 it ranged from five to twenty days, making it very risky for perishable products like vegetables. In 1979–80 the journey averaged 10.46 days, with 40 per cent of trips taking over ten days. Night travel is impossible for lack of dredging. There is no cold storage at the port of Kisangani, so that it is crucial for the arrival of perishable commodities to coincide with boat departures. Such timing, given the state of the roads, is very difficult to achieve. In 1979–80 CECOPANE, a rural development project of the Canadian government, had a rate of loss for beans of 4.4 per cent, for potatoes 20.5 per cent, rice 12.6 per cent, manioc 0.6 per cent and onions 3.6 per cent (*ibid.*: 137–40).

In addition to high rates of loss because of the deterioration of road and river transport, the relatively high cost of storage and of the organization of trade itself contribute to the huge difference in wholesale prices between Kisangani and Kinshasa. In 1980 for example, 20 kilograms of potatoes cost Z4–5 from the producer in North Kivu, sold wholesale for Z7–8 in Butembo, for Z25–40 in Kisangani, and for Z90 in Kinshasa. The SDID report estimates that the fixed annual cost of construction, maintenance and depreciation of a warehouse is about equal to the 40–50K a kilogram difference in the price of beans between the harvest and three months later. The impracticality of storing more perishable products than beans is the reason they are more liable to price fluctuation (SDID 1981: 270–1). Commercialization costs are increased because each month a hundred or so traders come up from Kinshasa to Kisangani by plane to buy beans and potatoes. The role of women in this trade will be discussed in the next chapter; Nande case histories show that some Nande traders have such women traders among their primary customers. The costs of the monthly journeys amount to Z200 a tonne on transactions, generally under 10 tonnes. The traders' expenses include airfare, board and lodging in Kisangani, and, in some cases, the high interest rates from unofficial credit arrangements for the Z20,000 needed for the purchase of 10 tonnes of potatoes or beans (*ibid.*: 262–3).

Taking all these factors into account, the SDID report concludes that the cost of commercialization accounts for 85–95 per cent of the retail price but that this is the result not of excessive profit-making by the traders, but of the enormous difficulty of their task. Indeed 'the principal riches of the present system and best hope for an improved system appears to be the trader himself' (*ibid.*: 308). The case histories show the way in which successful traders solve some of these difficulties: they evade borrowing at high interest rates by direct barter of truckloads of beans for their equivalent value in palm oil, cement or other commodities; instead of travelling between Kinshasa and Kisangani, they organize their trade more efficiently with their own trusted agents on the spot. By a combination of skill, good fortune and participation in the second economy, some are able to make large enough profits to accumulate wealth and build up very substantial business enterprises. The problems besetting the Nande in their trade, however, and their response in organizing a diaspora controlling all stages of the trade themselves, need to be set in the context of class relations.

## CLASS RELATIONS

The decay of the transportation infrastructure is brought about by the administrative weakness of the state and the pillaging activities of the political aristocracy. This class sector attempts to restrict Nande enterprise in various ways and thus to close its class boundaries against mobility from below by the Nande and others. This process is particularly evident with respect to beer, palm oil and fuel, all in short supply and all essential for Nande trade. These commodities are denied to the Nande at the official price by the political aristocracy, who attempt to monopolize access to these products in order to profit by speculative sale themselves.

Beer is one of the principal commodities imported to Kivu from Kisangani by the Nande. One of their biggest grievances in 1980 was the difficulty of getting it and the high prices they are forced to pay for it. Beer is in increasingly short supply because of the cutback in production at Kisangani's two breweries for lack of foreign exchange for imported materials and spare parts. In consequence, speculation in beer is rife and it has become an extremely profitable commodity for those in a position to control its allocation. For example, according to several Nande informants, the commercial director of the brewery gets vouchers for beer which he sells at the official price to friends and relations of his; they then resell it, splitting the profit with him as part of the deal. The Nande find they cannot supply themselves with beer at the official price, so every day a crowd of them hangs about outside the brewery waiting for those with quotas and vouchers to emerge, from whom the Nande must buy what they can. As one businessman tells it,

> You have empty bottles, money, a commercial licence and a truck and arrive at the brewery to be told there is no beer or to find it closed. But people who have none of these things can get beer at the official price of Z13.39 the case because they have a voucher. If your wife has a connection to a brewery authority, for example, he gives her a voucher for thirty to fifty cases of beer. The only way for the Nande to get it is to seek out these illegal buyers and buy from them at the outrageous price of Z40–50 the case. 'The people of Kisangani are dishonest; no one tells the truth and they work through connections [*connaissances*].'

Another says bitterly:

> You take your money and your empty bottles to the brewery and the official takes it and says he'll get you the beer but next day there is no beer, nor next week nor next month—and you never see your money or the empties either.

These difficulties explain why beer cost Z70 a case in Butembo in 1980.

Palm oil, a primary import for the Nande, was likewise in short supply and equally difficult to obtain at anything but the high prices of the second economy. The sub-regional authorities allocated quotas from the factory at the official price of Z350 a barrel to particular wholesalers, who would then, according to the Nande, sell their whole allocation to a single person, a relative, friend or client, who resold it at the black market price of Z550–600 a barrel.

Fuel was also unobtainable at the official price of Z140 a barrel. The only way these traders could obtain diesel fuel was from those who had quotas or who could get vouchers, and were reselling it at Z1,000 the barrel. It takes three barrels to make the trip one way from Butembo to Kisangani. In Kisangani in 1980, the newspaper reported that lists of persons for fuel quotas were to be examined for fictitious names, a means used by government personnel to appropriate supplies for speculation (*Boyoma* 12 January 1980).

In all these cases those who are in the position to control allocation of valuable resources mobilize personal connections to restrict access to them. As the Nande put it, 'It is the authorities who do it because they can control everything.'

State restrictions and regulations also constrain Nande enterprise and initiative. In 1981, after several foreign aid allocations to build a tarred road from Kivu to Kisangani had been embezzled, the Nande offered to organize construction of the road themselves, but the government would not allow it. They were also refused permission to build a tomato canning factory.[9] As Bates has pointed out, governments seek advantageous public work projects that can be selectively apportioned to organize political support through choice of location and staff (Bates 1982: 114). The difficulty of getting coffee licences is another barrier to upward mobility. The national coffee marketing board (OZACAF) pays low prices and is always late in making payments, but obtaining a licence for coffee export is fraught with difficulties. Letters of application are not answered by Kinshasa, few Nande can afford the expense of going in person and paying for plane ticket and hotel and fewer still have the necessary personal connections in the bureaucracy to expedite their dossier. The significance of such regulations in terms of class relations will be discussed in more detail in Chapter 8.

Abner Cohen has stressed the importance of ethnic competition in the organization of trading diasporas: 'Almost invariably such an ethnic control, or monopoly, can be achieved only in the course of continued rivalry and opposition with competition from other ethnc groups' (Cohen 1971: 226). In the case of the Nande, however, it appears that, rather than the competition of other ethnic groups, it is competition and struggle in the process of class formation which provides the stimulus for their control and monopoly of the vegetable export trade from Kivu to Kisangani and Kinshasa.

# 7

# Gender and class formation: businesswomen in Kisangani

We wish to definitively end all forms of discrimination against Zairian women...to recognise rights conferring on them equal partnership with men. But it remains the case that in each household there will be a patron, and with us it is the one who wears the trousers. Our women must understand and accept this with revolutionary submission. (President Mobutu, address to the MPR Congress December 1982)

Zaire is a male dominated society, imposing social and legal disadvantages on women. They have low levels of education compared to men and in consequence are little represented in government and the professions. In the colonial period few opportunities existed in town for them to become wealthy independently of men, but since independence certain opportunities for women have opened up and some of them have become wealthy and successful in business. The Kisangani business community includes a number of prominent women, members in their own right of the emergent commercial middle class. The election of one of them to the regional committee of the Chamber of Commerce (ANEZA) in 1980 reflected this new situation.

This chapter will explore the nature of this change in the position of women and the means by which it has come about. Have men and women employed different means in the process of upward mobility? What advantages and disadvantages accrue to each of them? Do they have differential access to resources? Do women unite in opposition to male supremacy? The answers to these questions reveal that the processes of class formation are gender specific: women have found different opportunities from men for moving into the new commercial class.

Men dominate political and economic institutions and use them to attain a favourable position in society and to control women. Education has been a key factor for achieving state position, entry into the professions or wage earning; since men's education has been superior to women's men greatly outnumber women in salaried employment. Men have thus had more opportunity than women to accumulate venture capital for business, to establish useful contacts and to acquire expertise. Furthermore, men have

165

used the legal system to gain control over their wives' property and to regulate women's commercial activities through licensing and other restrictions.

In the seventies, however, the decline of the administrative apparatus of the state and the expansion of the second economy have weakened the mechanisms of male control over women. The second economy consists of unmeasured and unrecorded activities in which regulations and laws do not operate and it is particularly in such activities that women have found opportunities to become wealthy independently of men. Lack of education for women does not constitute such a disadvantage in the second economy as it does in the official system. Schooling and fluency in French are necessary to advance in the bureaucracy, the professions and official business, but the deals of the second economy can just as well be conducted in African languages as in French; education is not particularly necessary when account books, banks and licensing officials are avoided.

In addition to finding means to counteract their disadvantages as the administrative apparatus of the state weakens, women have also begun to take advantage of their social position as women. Some have acquired venture capital or Zairianized businesses or gained useful business contacts from their husbands or lovers. In this way they have had an advantage over men in gaining access to the resource constituted by foreigners, and also in establishing the connections crucial for successful business operations and for second economy activities. They have thus, to some extent, compensated for their disadvantaged position in the official political and economic system. Such processes are evident elsewhere in Africa and do not seem to be unique to Kisangani.

## THE HISTORY OF WOMEN IN KISANGANI

Women got off to a bad start in Kisangani. When they first moved into towns and cities they found themselves in a more disadvantaged position than they had been in the rural societies from which they migrated. Colonial law only allowed them to migrate to town as the dependants of a resident, and, if married, only to stay in town as long as their marriages lasted, unless they had some sort of work. They were disadvantaged for getting work because few of them had any education, so that in these early years the only occupation available to all women to enable them to legitimately remain in town was prostitution. 'Urban feminine roles inevitably came to be defined as more specifically sexual and domestic than the tribal roles to which most women had been reared in youth'(Pons 1969: 219).[1] In a study in 1952, Pons found a number of divorced or widowed women who had spent their young lives as prostitutes and who later became shopkeepers and landladies; other more fashionable women were the relatively independent mistresses of wealthy African men or were high status prostitutes with small changing sets of lovers (1969: 248, 215). Jean

LaFontaine refers to such women, more appropriately, as 'courtesans' (LaFontaine 1974: 99).

In the colonial period few women received any education. In Kisangani in 1952, only 15 per cent of women sixteen years old and over, compared to 50 per cent of the men, had received any formal schooling (Pons 1969: 37). Barbara Yates has shown how the Belgian, mission-dominated, colonial education system relegated women to a position of economic marginality, superimposing ideas on gender from a conservative, patriarchal, Christian culture. This tradition led to 'stereotyped linkages between sex differences in access to education, on the one hand, and employment in the modern sector, on the other' (Yates 1982: 128). The earliest aim of education for girls, in single sex schools, was to instil Christian virtue and domestic skills; they were given no instruction in French, the language necessary to advance in the modern economy. Post-primary vocational schooling for girls was limited to teaching, home economics and domestic agriculture, rather than the commercial agriculture in which boys were trained. Six-year secondary education was begun in 1948 for boys but not for girls; they were still taught only in the vernacular and had only three years of secondary education with an emphasis on home economics. Girls were finally admitted to six-year programmes of general secondary education in the mid-1950s. But by independence only about 1.5 per cent of girls attended any post-primary school (Yates 1982).

This system of differential education for men and women meant that wage earning opportunities for women were severely limited and stereotyped. In Kisangani in 1952, less than 2 per cent of the women, but 90 per cent of the men, were in wage-earning employment (Pons 1969: 37, 52). Out of 20, 334 women in the city, 110 were wage earners: 65 were employed in the cigarette factory, the rest as nurses or nurses' aides, teachers or maids (Xydias 1956: 287). Commerce and business were dominated by foreigners and nationals were subject to restrictions. Unlike women in West Africa,[2] few women in Kisangani were involved in trade, with the exception of the Lokele (Pons 1969: 214).

Since independence it has continued to be much more difficult for girls to complete secondary school or university than it has for boys (Schwartz 1966; T. Gould 1978) which means that women are still much less likely than men to be fluent in the French that is necessary for professional employment. It thus remains much more difficult for women to get wage employment or enter the professions than is the case for men. In Kisangani in 1979 there were no women lawyers or doctors nor any women in government. Employment figures are scanty and their accuracy is suspect. However, they are revealing for the three years for which they are available. (see Table 7.1)

Since so few women have wage earning jobs very few can accumulate savings from salaries, gain knowledge of business management or build up business connections by working in large enterprises, as can men. This

Table 7.1 *Numbers of men and women employed in office work 1976–8*

|      | Number of office employees | | Population of Kisangani | |
|------|--------|--------|--------|--------|
|      | Men    | Women  | Men    | Women  |
| 1976 | 3,563  | 176    | 67,574 | 73,119 |
| 1977 | 2,342  | 250    | 70,400 | 74,042 |
| 1978 | 3,685  | 149    | 67,213 | 71,433 |

*Source*: census figures, Town Hall, Kisangani,
*Rapports Annuels, Administration du territoire.*

privileged access to employment differentiates men and women in the process of class formation.

Although disadvantaged in employment the situation of women in general has improved since independence. In Kisangani they began to move into commerce and business in large numbers after the rebellion and the violent events of 1964–8 killed mostly men and left many women with children to support. Since this time women have outnumbered men in the city (see Appendix), reversing the trend of the colonial period. The troubles in the sixties and Zairianization in the seventies resulted in the departure of many of the foreigners who had dominated commerce, opening up opportunities for both women and men and weakening the administrative control and regulations which had particularly constrained women.

High inflation has also helped women in their move into extensive commerce. Formerly men did not want their wives to have jobs, fearing increased opportunities for infidelity (Bernard 1972: 276–7) and the undermining of their authority by the economic independence of their wives (Comhaire-Sylvain 1968: 32), although commercial activity on a small scale was always acceptable. But because of the high cost of urban life, men soon began to find it necessary for their wives to bring in an income and contribute to family support (see J. MacGaffey 1987).

Thus in Kisangani by 1980 the situation for some women had greatly improved. As stated above, nine, or 28 per cent, of the substantial business owners not connected with politics, were women. These women specialize in the retail and semi-wholesale trade, in travelling commerce and in exporting and importing goods to and from Kinshasa or to the interior by boat, plane and truck. Women also form a significant proportion of the retailers with fixed stores in the central commercial and administrative zone of the city. They numbered 24 out of 113 (21 per cent) in the rough survey that I took, and they also dominated market trade.

Some women had become big traders as early as 1965, bringing food from Kinshasa to Upper Zaire by boat and more expensive goods, such as cloth and radios, by plane. A few with larger capital resources engaged in importing food or in trade to the interior (Comhaire-Sylvain 1968: 187–8). By 1979 women were achieving renown for their success in business; some were known to be millionaires, others to have bank accounts of Z100,000–200,000. This kind of wealth must be contrasted with the incomes of those in wage employment: it must be remembered that in 1980 the monthly wage of an unskilled labourer was Z60, of a clerk Z109.80 and of a government department head Z384.

One lucrative form of trade is in *wax* print cloth; in one reported instance a woman selling *wax* prints grossed Z45,000 in a single morning (Vwakyanakazi 1982: 226). *Wax* is bought in lengths for a wrap-around skirt, blouse and a piece to be artfully knotted around the hips. It ranges from a cheap print to the highest quality imported Dutch Java, costing as much as Z1,200 a length in 1980. In Zaire's current economic crisis, supply can never meet demand and prices continually rise. Women like to show off their socio-economic levels and the wealth of their husbands by wearing the latest sensational pattern. Women merchants cause fashions in the designs of this cloth to change rapidly because they name, and themselves wear, the latest designs and colours. Patterns have names which enhance their desirability, such as the village of a popular singer or 'Super Dallas' (referring to the American television show) or names signifying particular colours or designs. '*Temba na bambanda*' threw defiance at sexual rivals (Yoka Lye Mudaba 1983: 428–9); '*MuYaka azwi le quinze*' labelled a cheaper variety and mocked those whose husbands could not make it through to payday but had to get an advance mid-month. Word of a new pattern spreads rapidly by word of mouth. This is a lucrative market operated by and for women, with its own medium of advertisement.

Another profitable form of commerce, shipping fish, rice and beans downriver to Kinshasa, is carried on by five out of the nine substantial women business owners. One of the women on the official lists of wholesalers shipped 100–200 sacks of beans down to Kinshasa every month or two. Beans in 1980 cost Z200 a 90 kilogram sack and retailed for Z300 in Kinshasa. Even after deducting river transport fees of Z24 a sack, transport to and from the docks and losses from theft, which she assessed typically as 15 sacks out of 200, net profit was around 30 per cent, higher than the 20 per cent most wholesalers and retailers hope to be able to make.

Many women who do not appear on any official lists of businesses also carry on this commerce. Such women may have commercial licences, but may not use the bank, keep accounts or report all their commerce: in so far as this is the case, they are operating in the second economy. Some of this trade is on a very large scale. The last chapter showed that a number of large-scale women traders were customers for Nande beans, often a whole truckload at a time; a Greek wholesaler said women traders regularly bought Z30,000–50,000 ($6–8,000) of smoked fish from him at a time to take down to sell in Kinshasa. But since much of this commerce is unrecorded and unmeasured, any precise assessment of the number of women engaged in it or the extent of their activities is impossible.

We see here how women can bypass male-imposed restrictions and operate independently of regulations in a very lucrative and large scale trade. Education is not necessary for entry into such commerce. One woman who was completely illiterate carried on a flourishing commerce up and down the river, making much more money than her father who worked for a regular wage. Such women are portrayed in Zabeth, the women trader in V.S. Naipaul's novel, *A Bend in the River*, a fictionalized account of Kisangani.[3] Lack of education is no longer the block that it was to successful participation in the economy. In fact, it seems possible that education or the lack of it is becoming irrelevant for at least some women in Kisangani. The Nande woman mentioned in the last chapter, who had a university degree but had abandoned a professional career to take up more lucrative commercial activities, exemplifies the situation of some women who are not seeking wage employment because they can make more money elsewhere.

Situations in which women can acquire greater wealth in independent activities than in a salaried job, or can engage in second economy activities to become wealthy and improve their class position independently of men, have been described elsewhere in Africa. In the Zambian Copper Belt women sometimes make as much profit in one illegal beer brew as their husband's monthly pay cheque (Parpart 1986: 150). In Nigeria in the 1970s in the larger towns, businesswomen, who were mostly semi-literate, conducted extensive commerce, chiefly in textiles bought wholesale from Europe, £1,000 at a time, and sold retail. Others traded in fish or palm oil, owned lorries, built European-type houses and educated their sons overseas (Little 1973: 44). In Dakar, the more profitable commercial activities have always been in the hands of women. They have always had a measure of economic independence in the city and have invested their profits in buying trucks, building houses and buying motor canoes with which their husbands fish, the women thus owning the means of production. The low level of education in Senegal limited the level of attainment of Senegalese in public affairs and they were generally employed as teachers or in hospitals. Salaried workers made less than half independent workers. Only 5 per cent of salaried workers earned over 250,000 frs. a year, whereas 60 per cent of independent women in commerce earned as much or more (Grandmaison 1969: 149–51).

In the colonial period in Kenya women were able to form an important element of an embryonic African petty bourgeoisie. Janet Bujra found that 46 per cent of the landlords in the Pumwani location of Nairobi were women. They had accumulated sufficient wealth in illicit beer brewing and prostitution to acquire property. Their ability to accumulate savings equalled or surpassed that of men in the earliest phase of Nairobi's history. They were forced into prostitution by economic necessity in the early colonial urban economy, since it was the only form of urban employment open to them, but they turned the situation into one of economic advantage. It allowed them an independence and freedom from exploitation impossible in any of the other socio-economic roles open to them. In the colonial period the petty bourgeoisie was stunted and puny, prevented from expansion by protected European and Asian control of the most profitable sectors of the economy, but women found opportunity in illicit activities 'partly because they found themselves on the credit side in the balance sheet between supply and demand and partly because institutions of male control over women were unable to develop effectively in this situation' (Bujra 1975: 234).

WOMEN IN BUSINESS

Women with substantial business concerns in Kisangani are clearly businesswomen in their own right, independently of men; they are successful by virtue of their own effort and business acumen. Some rely on men at some point in their careers, but such assistance does not necessarily imply continued dependence.[4] Of the eleven women for whom I have information, six acquired their initial capital from petty trade, one from her salary as a teacher, one by obtaining credit, and one from working as a prostitute. Only two had obtained money from their husbands. As stated in Chapter 4, women in my case histories contrast with men in the origins of their venture capital because of the difference in employment opportunities; a number of men, but only one woman, acquired venture capital through salaried employment with trading on the side. Some women save up their initial capital from their own commerce and do not marry, or else remain entirely independent of their husbands in business affairs; others marry after they have independently established themselves in business and thereafter operate in partnership with their husbands, managing their side of the business independently. Some who receive initial capital from their husbands then build up the business with no further assistance; for others the husband is clearly the subordinate partner. Some women are able to develop business connections through their lovers.

We will now look at some of the case histories on which these assertions are, in part, based. These histories are primarily of successful women. Some, however, are of those who have not done so well, since many women have tried but experienced failure. I obtained career histories and details of businesses and family background from seven of the nine women owners of substantial businesses, from seven retailers, four owners of market stalls, and two members of the Lioness Club who were involved in business but were not business owners, a total of twenty women in all.

A history of a woman owning a substantial business and working

171

completely independently of her husband is that of Madame W. given above pp. 99–100. Two other cases given in Chapter 4, Madame F. and Madame B., p. 95, are of women who established themselves in business and then married foreigners. If a woman has a foreign husband or lover, his business ties outside Zaire, holdings in foreign currency, business experience and contacts, ease of getting credit and the mutual assistance networks among members of the foreign business community all offer potential opportunities for the expansion of the enterprise of a woman. As a Greek said 'Foreigners are a resource in Zaire.' Connections to them constitute an advantage women hold over men in business affairs.

In the following history a woman's husband helped her to get started but she developed her own business thereafter.

> Madame L. had one year of university education. Her husband is a wealthy professional; through his European connections she was asked to be partner with a Greek woman in a women's dress store. The Greek went home but is still co-owner of the business. Madame L. has been running it on her own since November 1979. In early 1980, when other businesses were almost at a standstill after the demonetization of December 1979, Madame L.'s store was usually busy with plenty of customers: the changes she had made showed an eye for a good market, clearly the reason for her success. The Greek had left her unsaleable merchandise rather than money, but Madame L., with the help of her husband, put in Z1,000 and started buying dress lengths of material from Kinshasa and making it up on order into European-style, high-fashion dresses, skirts and blouses. Her dresses cost upwards of Z140. She also sells clothes, elaborate infants' outfits and other items for children, and accessories such as leather purses. She employs two tailors on the premises.
>
> Madame L. observes that she has the only shop that sells European-style women's dresses, and that wealthy women love to buy smart clothes for themselves and to dress up their children. After only a few months of operation she had a clientele of about thirty regular customers who liked her unique styles and demanded she buy costly materials for them.
>
> She has a sister in Kinshasa who buys and sends up material for her, and she also goes there herself. Her mother is an expert seamstress who supported herself and seven children by running a store after her husband, a government official, was killed by the rebels. Madame L. says she learned how to run a retail business by helping her mother.

Madame L.'s business opportunity came from retrocession. Her husband supplied the necessary initial capital and foreign connection but her own enterprise and innovative ideas were crucial factors in her success. This success is itself evidence of the wealth of some women in Kisangani today: her store caters to the expanding local market for luxury goods in the new dominant class. Her history shows, in particular, the importance of successful innovation as a factor in business success. She, like the other women discussed above, makes use of her family in business. Her mother provides an example of a woman who turned to commerce when left without means of support after her husband died in the rebellion.

Madame L. is included among the list of entrepreneurs in Table 4.1, because she was elected to the committee of the Lioness Club in 1980. Her business was new and not large, but was expanding rapidly despite the unfavourable economic situation. Her enterprise formed a contrast to a similar one that was not doing well in 1980:

> Madame Y.'s husband is a politician; she oversees his various concerns while he is in Kinshasa. She runs a store for women's and children's clothing, made by four tailors on the premises. She buys material by the yard in Kinshasa and has it made, mostly to order, into East African style machine-embroidered dresses and shirts. A dress cost Z125 and a shirt Z75. The latter were relatively expensive: imported shirts in Mr T.'s boutique cost Z45–65; her dresses cost less than Madame L.'s but were not such a fashion success. She has been in commerce since she got married in 1960. Her husband's family were already in commerce and advised her to go into it as it was more lucrative than teaching, so she did. 'It is not good to be dependent on one's husband for money for clothes, the household, children and everything.' Her husband gave her money to get her commercial licence when she started in the market. She used to go to Kinshasa once a month, but with the increase of plane fares in 1980 and the decline of business, she found it too expensive. In 1979 she was the secretary of the AFCO (the Women Merchants' Association).

Madame Y. has not been as successful as Madame L. in assessing consumer tastes and trends. She is an example of a woman unwilling to be totally dependent on her husband. Her husband's and family's reactions illustrate the gradual recognition of commercial activity and successful business as an acceptable occupation for women.

Another woman who works in partnership with her husband is clearly the dominant figure in the business.

> Madame S. had two years of secondary school, then worked two years as a teacher. She is in the retail business with two stores and two boutiques, and she also ships fish, rice and beans to Kinshasa. She began by selling doughnuts in 1974 until she had Z80 with which she started a boutique at her house for doughnuts and gradually other things as well, making enough money to start a second boutique in the market the same year and by 1975 to rent a store nearby. In 1979 her business had expanded enough to rent an additional, newly built store in a good location. She sells food, household goods, blouses, *wax* prints and cosmetics. Her suppliers are the big Kisangani wholesalers or the travelling merchants, who sell without licences. She travels by plane every three or four months to Kinshasa to buy cosmetics. She employs ten salesgirls and three watchmen. Her husband, a Zairian, is a partner in her business. They own one truck, two cars and two houses, one of which they rent out. She is on the committee of the AFCO. She complains of the lack of goods since 1976, which forces her to buy third-hand at high prices from the travelling merchants and local speculators: 'The problem is that we have the money but no means to deal directly with foreign suppliers.'

The growth of Madame S.'s business took place in the years following Zairianization, which, as we have shown, provided opportunities for those with a head for business. She was not as successful as some, but successful

173

enough to finance plane fares to Kinshasa and to expand her scale of operations to include shipping goods to Kinshasa. The profits of the business have been sufficient to buy vehicles and invest in real estate. The relative success of her business contrasts with that of women who only have one store.

> Madame D.Y. was married to a foreign merchant and worked in a foreign-owned store till the rebellion. After it her husband returned to Europe, leaving her with three children to support, so she set up in business on her own. In 1974 she rented a truck and started transporting palm oil to sell in Butembo. However, she found herself unable to compete with the Nande, so she started a retail store, gradually increasing the size of her stock. She goes to Kinshasa occasionally to get goods, but operates only the one small store. Her younger brother and sister work with her and she has no other employees. She is on the committee of the AFCO.

In this case a wrong guess as to the most profitable line of business at the start resulted in a not very successful business career, and she now suffers from the difficulty of obtaining merchandise. Her history contrasts with the success story of Madame K. on p. 98, who built up a business after the departure of her foreign lover because of Zairianization, but who had the advantage of taking over an already established business. Neither woman had much help from others.

Some women become wealthy as managers of branches of businesses. An example of a Nande woman who does so was given in the last chapter. Another is a member of the Lioness Club of Kisangani.

> Madame E.'s husband works for a parastatal company. She used to work in the central office of the Political Bureau and in Zairianization was given a petrol station concession in Kisangani. She ran this until 1978, when she gave it up because of the difficulties of getting gasoline, but had gained the experience of running a business. She took on managing the Kisangani branch of her brother-in-law's firm. He has an import/export business and plantations in Lower Zaire and Kivu. Her job is to supervise the transit of coffee, buy beans and ship them to Kinshasa, and organize the shipment to Beni, in Kivu, of a weekly beer quota of 150 cases from Kisangani's brewery. The firm gets a quota because it supplies the brewery in Boma, Lower Zaire, with materials. She buys beans from the biggest Nande wholesale firm and ships 1,000–2,000 sacks every two or three months.
>
> Madame E. gets a 5 per cent commission, not a salary. She is provided with a car and gasoline, domestic help, medical care and holidays in Europe, as well as lavish presents and favours. The opulence of her house and its furnishings testifies to her wealth.

These details of the careers of businesswomen show that both individual characteristics and socio-economics factors contribute to the successful careers of the women in the new commercial class. Individual characteristics promoting success included business acumen, hard work, and a good sense for market opportunity and timely innovation. The economic situation of scarcity made commerce difficult and risky, but also provided lucrative opportunities for those who were lucky in speculative dealings and in trade between rural and urban areas. The decline of the administrative apparatus made possible the evasion of licensing and other regulations and weakened male control over women through the institutions of the state. Some women took advantage of their social position as women and exploited their ties to men, foreigners or nationals who were their husbands or lovers, to further their commerce. Others relied on family and kin networks for assistance in gathering starting capital or in operating their enterprises.

EVASION OF MALE CONTROL

It is particularly through activities in the second economy, that women have evaded male control, because men have not been able to establish and institutionalize their control over women in the second economy as well as they have in the official one. By operating in this economy women can bypass the specific restrictions imposed on their activities by men.

The law before independence and until 1962 was that a woman must have the consent of her husband to sign a work contract. The present Labour Code says that a woman can engage her services *unless* her husband expresses opposition: if he writes to her employer and objects, her contract is voided. Although the rights of a working woman are protected by the Labour Code, in practice the law is often not applied with regard to equal pay, family allowances and housing, and women are discriminated against (Manwana 1982: 77, 81). A woman must have her husband's permission to open a bank account or obtain a commercial licence. Hence the importance for women of second economy activities which escape these restrictions because in this economy women do not need bank accounts, bank credit or commercial licences, nor do they keep records.

These operations in the second economy had started by 1965 (Comhaire–Sylvain 1968: 187). By 1979 many women were conducting large trading operations that they never reported to the authorities, taking advantage of the situation of scarcity in Zaire to engage in speculation. In Kisangani it was very difficult to obtain individual histories of careers founded on such activities or talk to many individuals who engaged in them, but it was clear that they provided widely utilized opportunities.

A precise account of women operating in the second economy came from a man who had repeatedly made his own money in '*affaires personelles*' (a euphemism for irregular activities).

> These businesswomen (*femmes d'affaires*) are different from women traders (*femmes commerçantes*): they make enormous amounts of money. There are many of them but they do not make their wealth and success as obvious as do men, although they may be richer. They are difficult to find and talk to because they distrust anyone inquiring into their business. They may have commercial licences but they usually do not keep accounts nor record

transactions because they want to avoid taxes. Some earn as much as Z100,000 a year.

These women specialize in particular kinds of goods, many of them in *wax* prints, and they are expert in women's current taste in colours and patterns. Some deal in fish, especially the Lokele in Kisangani; others, for example, in flour, if they have a relative among the big suppliers.

They are mostly older women who started in business because they found themselves in difficult circumstances, such as losing their husbands, and who achieved success because of some particular advantage, such as having a relative or connection among the authorities.

I did succeed in talking to a few women who do such business. One, for example, has a retail store run by her mother and sister while she travels and brings back merchandise for the store and for selling semi-wholesale to other retailers.

> Madame N. began in 1975 by sewing infants' dresses at home and selling them. Soon she was doing well enough to hire a tailor and they worked together. By the end of the year she had Z500 and began to travel (*faire la navette*), trading between Kinshasa and Kisangani. There was a shortage of sewing thread in Kisangani and she started out buying a lot of it in Kinshasa and selling it easily in Kisangani. Then she turned to *wax* prints and was able to open a store. In 1979 she moved to a better location and her business prospered. She sells prints, women's blouses, baby clothes, beauty products, household goods, alcohol and shoes for men, women and children.
>
> She goes to Europe three times a year, to Brussels for *wax* prints, to Bologna for shoes direct from the factory, and she is continually away on trips in Zaire or to the Sudan or Rwanda. She goes to Lubumbashi, Kivu, Isiro and Bunia in Upper Zaire, and Kinshasa. On trips to the Sudan or Ruanda she goes with a truckload of rice or palm oil to sell and buys *wax* prints. These prints supply her store but are also sold to other retailers. 'If you do not have good things to interest your customers, and plenty of them, business does not go well,' she says. Contacts are also essential to do well in business. Her husband was formerly an official in Lubumbashi and she has good connections there as a result. She also has friends in Brussels and in Italy. Otherwise she has gradually built up her own business connections in different places. She is lively, attractive and intelligent, speaks good French and also Italian, although she only had two years of secondary school because she married at sixteen. She would only say that she had 'arrangements' to get foreign currency. I learned later that she had a bank manager for her lover.

Madame N. Built up a successful business on her own from a small start and made use of her highly placed lover to expand her enterprise. Her international dealings indicate the considerable scale of her activities.

Travelling commerce and speculation start on a small scale with minute calculations and quick responses to supply and demand. Success does not always follow and many women do not achieve large-scale operations. Whether they do so or not depends on their circumstances, connections and the opportunities that come to them. The following example is of a young woman who is trying to get started.

176

> Madame H. is married to the manager of a local branch of a Kinshasa store. She has a stall in the market and carries on trade between Kinshasa and Kisangani working with her husband's brother's son in Kinshasa. One of the items she trades in is cigarettes which are always in short supply. For example, on one trip early in 1979 she bought four cases of cigarettes at a cost of Z3,400 in Kinshasa and sold them in Kisangani for Z4,000. Her plane ticket cost Z252 and air freight charges Z60, so she made a profit of Z208. But then they raised the air fare to Z500 so such a trip was longer profitable.[5] She also trades in other goods as opportunity offers. At one time there was a shortage of soap in Kinshasa, so she bought soap in Kisangani Z2 a packet, took it back to Kinshasa and sold it for Z4.20 a packet. But an attempt to repeat this success failed when the price dropped in Kinshasa and they suffered a loss. On another trip they had a loss because of theft.

This woman is an example of the way earnings in the second economy expand the market for consumer goods, since she spent some of her earnings on elaborate outfits for her baby and a frilled bassinet with mosquito net, items sold in the boutiques owned by the new commercial class. Risks in speculative trade are high, however, and success is by no means sure, but considering wage rates the profits that are sometimes made in this trade are alluring: Z208 on one trip to Kinshasa is very good money. Some, however, try it and fail on the first attempt which discourages them from trying again, as follows:

> Madame M. is a trader who sells imported second-hand clothes and kerosene from a market stall. During the drought in Lower Zaire in 1978–80, she attempted to take advantage of the reported food shortages in Kinshasa, shipping manioc and salt fish down river to sell in the city. But she could not sell at the high price she expected because a lot of other people had had the same idea, and she made a loss. She has not tried going to Kinshasa again but carries on commerce to the interior, taking her goods on a truck two days a week to two different rural markets.

It appears that women have some advantage over men in the second economy in that they can exploit their sexuality to gain access to resources. Some women obtain scarce goods for their trading through sexual liaisons; others use such connections to get purchase vouchers for goods, fuel or beer at the official price, then sell these vouchers at 20 per cent or more profit to other intermediaries or to retailers.

USES AND ABUSES OF SEXUALITY

Use of their social position by women differentiates them from men in the process of class formation. Sexuality is a resource that men, by virtue of their dominant position in society, do not generally need to use.[6] The case histories show that some women resort to sex to manipulate men to their economic advantage. Some barter sexual favours; others get capital, business connections or other assistance from their husbands or lovers. This situation results in problems for the many women who refuse to

177

exploit their sexuality in this way, because men in Kisangani assume that women only achieve success in business by sleeping with some man. Comments such as 'women prostitute themselves to further their commerce', 'a successful businesswoman must be a *femme libre*', 'a woman cannot be successful without the assistance of some man', 'if a woman is to get a good supply of merchandise she must sleep with her supplier' are frequent.[7] This equation of successful businesswoman and *femme libre* reflects the unease of men faced by the increasing economic independence of women; sexual harassment is one way they attempt to assert control.

Many women who do not wish to make their way in the world by sexual means find that they are subject to such harassment, in some cases having to give sexual favours in order to keep their jobs (Kitenge-Ya 1977: 102). One businesswoman, complaining that wholesalers wanted sexual favours in return for goods, felt that business was particularly difficult for married women like herself. Another spoke of the difficulties girls confronted while going through school: 'In order to pass exams a girl must sleep with the teacher, and the school directors are just as bad so it is no good complaining.' Facing the same trouble herself at the university, she had dropped out after one year. Another successful businesswoman, who had given radio talks on sexual harassment, described the problems:

> When a woman makes money in commerce all sorts of men will come and tell her that they love her but really they just want to get her money, which they will then spend on another woman. 'Women have to understand men's wiles.' She said she had many brothers but they had given her no assistance in her business, all they wanted was for her to work and to give them the proceeds: 'that is what it is like for women'.

The new Family Code attempts to establish a man's control over his wife's wealth. Article 45 specifies that the management of the wife's goods is presumed to be in the husband's hands, even though the marriage contract may specify separate ownerships of goods by each spouse. A woman may only take over management in cases of proven incompetence of her husband (Article 510). She may manage goods acquired in the exercise of a profession, but Article 492 specifies that her husband is allowed to take them over 'in the interests of the household' (W. MacGaffey 1982: 94).

Increased economic independence for women represents a change since the early years of independence. Initially, in the cities, their sexuality was the only resource they could command. In a study of Atu Island, off the Kenya coast, Bujra concludes that

> Without equivalent access to productive resources, and without active participation in the productive processes of their economy, women cannot gain an equal footing with men. They are forced back to utilising their sexuality as their sole resource. (Bujra 1977: 38).

Women in Kisangani found themselves in this situation at first, because prostitution was the only widely available urban occupation for single women. Benoît Verhaegen describes the way the colonial government contributed to this situation while fully exploiting it. In issuing identity cards the government made no distinction between the status of *femme libre*, or prostitute, and single woman; except for the elderly and widows, all were taxed, whether they practised prostitution or not. From 1939 to 1943, over 30 per cent of the adult women of Stanleyville (the colonial name for Kisangani) were registered as *femmes libres* and paid a tax which was the second highest source of revenue in the African urban area. Nearly 50 per cent of the men of Kisangani were unmarried, many of them must have had women as concubines or partners in temporary unions; to regard all *femmes libres* as 'prostitutes' is misleading (Verhaegen 1981: 55–7). In Lubumbashi, taxes on *femmes libres* brought in 80 per cent of revenue in the African urban area (Malira 1974: 71).

The same situation is reported elsewhere. In Kampala, Uganda, in the fifties, all single female migrants were labelled 'prostitutes', and in the seventies single women who rented rooms in rural centres, townships and towns were indiscriminately referred to as *malaya* (prostitutes) (Obbo 1980: 26, 87).

Kenneth Little points out that what in the West may be called 'prostitution' overlaps other kinds of relationships in the modern West African town. He proposes to confine the term to 'women whose livelihood over a period of time depends wholly on the sale of sexual services and whose relationship with customers does not extend beyond the sexual act'. Some women have quasi-uxorial relations with clients, or may earn money by prostitution only occasionally (Little 1973: 84–7). In Nairobi prostitutes offer various kinds of domestic services (White 1983). The term *femme libre* covers all these types of relations and is best translated literally as 'free woman'.

In a study of the free women of Kinshasa, Jean LaFontaine points out that *femme libre* refers to a new type of feminine success. It applies to women not bound by rules of wifely behaviour, who are more sophisticated and free of the stereotypes of feminine subordination to men: 'It is thus intelligible why the term *femme libre* is applied to any woman who supports herself in a job in the modern manner, be she ever so virtuous' (LaFontaine 1974: 96).

Comparison can be made here with barmaids among the Baganda of Uganda. Men stigmatize barmaids because they violate the standards of female decorum. At the same time, in comparison to married women (who are particularly hostile to them), they are independent of male authority: 'the barmaid serves to symbolise the wider society's discomfort with the major means whereby the modern woman became successful by manipulating men for economic reward' (Kilbride 1979: 252).

One businesswoman in Kisangani, important enough in the town's commerce to be on the committee of the AFCO, first worked in the city as a prostitute:

> Madame C.'s schooling was interrupted by the rebellion and she and her family fled into the forest. They returned one at a time in 1968. She was the first and worked as a prostitute to support the rest of them. She eventually married a foreigner and became a partner in his business. She carries on independent commerce, buying up goods, especially *wax* prints, as opportunity offers on her travels with her husband, and selling semi-wholesale to Kisangani retailers.

Male attitudes and actions circumscribe women's activities in many ways. One study found that men prefer their wives to work in teaching or medicine where they work with many people and are assumed to have fewer opportunities for licentiousness (Kitenge-Ya 1977: 103). Male attitudes about women working are slow to change. The members of the Lioness Club in Kisangani, founded in 1979 and including several businesswomen, have to meet in members' houses, instead of in a hotel as does the Lions Club, 'so our husbands won't object'. The club began by enrolling only wives of Lions Club members, since such husbands would not be suspicious of the club's purpose.

FEMALE SOLIDARITY VERSUS CLASS INTEREST

Do women in Kisangani organize themselves to cooperate and unite in the face of male antagonism and economic difficulties? Their attempt to do so by forming a women merchants' association, AFCO (*Asssociation des Femmes Commerçantes*), has not been very effective. This organization promotes the interests of the middle-class women who organized it; it also on occasion acts to further male control. However, the organization does in addition provide a forum in which the less successful women who make up the majority of its members can become aware of their common interests and begin to articulate them.

The AFCO was founded in 1972 to combat price rises and speculators, to represent women merchants to the authorities and to provide mutual assistance for expenses for funerals and other sudden expenses. Members must pay an initial contribution of Z50, and Z10 a month thereafter. Conditions of membership show that women in the organization are subject to men; a married woman needs her husband's consent to belong and members must have a commercial licence. The cost of such a licence was raised in 1980 to Z2,500. This high rate inevitably made it more difficult for women to engage in legal commerce. The authorities sometimes treat the association merely as a forum for traditional male opinions; Kisangani's daily newspaper, *Boyoma*, reported that in 1976 at a meeting with AFCO members, the regional commissioner urged them to combat tribalism among themselves, maintain their neighbourhoods better and pay more attention to their children (*Boyoma* 29 September 1976).

The ineffectiveness of the AFCO in serving the interests of all women in commerce is made clear by the fact that the president arranged to supply her own business from the wholesalers rather than working for a fair distribution among the members (Nzinunu 1978). Members complained that the association was useless because the authorities ignored it and it did not succeed in the vital matter of increasing the supply of goods from the wholesalers. Cooperation was lacking and 'an unpleasant atmosphere prevails among the members' (*ibid.*: 52). One woman expressed the lack of solidarity in her comment: 'Elles ne sont pas gentilles. Je reste seule' (they are not nice. I stay on my own).

Some businesswomen belong to the Lioness Club of Kisangani. Members occupy themselves with charitable concerns, providing money, food and clothing for needy cases, especially women, that are brought to the attention of the club, and also with social events, such as dances, dinners and fund-raising raffles organized with the Lions Club. But the publicity surrounding the disbursements of the club to poor individuals, which are attended and written up by a reporter from the local newspaper, and the full accounts given in this paper of social events, with the listing of names of important officials and others who attend, suggest that an important function of the club's activities is to make evident the class position of its members.

This latent function for some women's associations is suggested by Patricia Caplan in her study of middle- and upper-class women's associations in Madras, India. She found no sense of solidarity between the dispensers of charity and their needy sisters. She suggests that a major reason for joining social welfare organizations for these Indian women was to gain prestige or to maintain prestige they already had from their class position. Women's associations provided a forum in which members could make symbolic statements about their class position relative to other women (Caplan 1982).

In Kenya likewise, the *Maendeleo ya Wanawake*, the largest women's association, which was founded to improve rural living standards, gradually changed to emphasize philanthropy. It turned into an organization serving the middle-class interests of the leadership and became indifferent to rural needs, so that its concerns had little meaning for rural women (Wipper 1975). And in Zambia, the Women's Brigade failed to represent the interests of its unskilled poor urban members and abetted in the persecution of unlicensed female traders (Schuster 1984: 25).

In Kisangani both the AFCO and the Lioness Club promote the interests of a few middle-class women. But an instance in which a large number of women have successfully united and organized to promote their interests in the face of male oppression in a rural area, is described by Catharine Newbury. Comparisons with the situation in Kisangani are revealing.

In 1982, over a hundred Tembo women in Buloho Collectivity in a rural area west of Lake Kivu, demonstrated against taxes levied on the cassava and peanuts they marketed. Dissatisfaction had grown with the consciousness among these women food producers of their exploitation by male Shi traders, and of the discrimination against them of market taxes levied exclusively on women. Their discontent with the low prices they received at the market and anger at the taxes and tolls they had to pay in cash and kind were exacerbated by the rapid rise in the price of manufactured goods. Purchase of a dress length of cloth, for example, required the sale of five times as much cassava in 1983 as in 1979.

This situation resulted in an emerging political consciousness among the women of Buloho. A large group of them succeeded in uniting and publicly voicing their complaints and confronting the authorities. In the June 1982 elections women voted for candidates sympathetic to them, who were among those elected to the collectivity council. Thereafter, the council voted to suspend the taxes and tolls (Newbury 1984a).

In Kisangani, to the contrary, the AFCO, founded in an attempt by women to organize to confront male antagonism and economic difficulties, has not been effective. These two examples are illuminating because they indicate the kinds of circumstances that promote collective solidarity among women for confronting men.

Rural Tembo women lacked formal education and had to get assistance in writing letters of protest to higher authorities after the local chief ignored them. But they were able to draw on a ready-made organization for this assistance in the Catholic church, of which they were all members. In addition, the church provided a forum for discussion of problems and local networks of communication and organization to facilitate cooperation. The women also all belonged to one ethnic group, and their very lack of education reflected the lack of other social and economic distinctions among them. However, they were also held back because lack of education prevented them from being candidates for political office themselves (*ibid.*: 49–53).

The contrast with urban women in Kisangani is marked. Pronounced ethnic and socio-economic distinctions divide these urban women and, together with the situation of intense competitiveness in the town's commerce, override the potential of women for organization to promote their common interests in opposition to men.

This situation is quite overt. Businesswomen commented to me on the absence of solidarity between them and related specific instances of lack of cooperation; they perceived their disunity as a disadvantage and contrasted it to the way foreign businessmen or the Nande worked together. Women are also divided by ethnic loyalties. In this multi-ethnic urban setting women dominant in large-scale business and in the retail trade are from the same ethnic groups that dominate the political and economic life of the town; women from disadvantaged groups do not do so well. Differing educational levels and class position further divide them. For all these reasons, city women, in contrast to the rural women of Buloho, struggle to advance in society as individuals and are not able to cooperate and organize successfully as a group. They participate in a stringent competition against each other as well as against men to acquire goods for successful commerce and to expand their enterprises.[8] They bear out Staudt's conclusion that commercialization, upward mobility, individualism and competitiveness motivate women more than female solidarity (Staudt 1982: 152).

In general women in Zaire are politically and economically disadvantaged, but a number of women in Kisangani are overcoming these problems and evading male control to achieve autonomy as successful and wealthy entrepreneurs. The women whose histories are presented here are like Ghanaian professional women, who 'partly by their own occupational skills and endeavors and partly by the skilful manipulation of their social roles and networks...are achieving a considerable level of financial and social independence' (Dinan 1977: 69). The situation for women that exists in Kisangani supports Bujra's contention that African women cannot be treated as a homogeneous category: 'gender is qualified by the places women occupy in newly emergent classes' (Bujra 1986: 118). And, as we have shown, by considerations of ethnicity and other variables.

# 8

# State, class and power: the effect of administrative decline on class formation

And on all the lips she found a weary desire for peace, the dread of officialdom with its nightmarish parody of administration without law, without security, and without justice. (Conrad *Nostromo*: 83)

'Zaire: Is there a State?' and 'Dead and Buried or Just Underground?' inquire the titles of two recent articles on the Zairian state (Young 1984; Newbury 1984b). The state performs so poorly that its very existence is questioned. Several distinct issues need to be explored here. What is the state? Whence come the expectations of its performance that seem so grossly unfulfilled in Zaire? Does it successfully carry out certain quite other purposes?

## IDEAS OF THE STATE

Crawford Young explains the development of the modern idea of the state in terms that account for common expectations of the way it should function and the consequent labelling of some states as weak or soft, others as strong. Young specifies two major universal properties of the state, territoriality and sovereignty; the state asserts its unique authority over a given territory. An important aspect of sovereignty is the 'normative derivation of its legitimacy from its constituent population'. In Europe as parliamentary institutions began to lay claim to superior legitimacy over the king as spokesmen for the people political parties structured the linkages between parliament and the populace; sovereignty no longer attached to a dynasty but to the institutions through which the authority of the state was exercised, which were presumed to embody the will of the people. More recently, the growth of Third World nationalism has elevated economic development to its present place as a central purpose of the state; the state is expected to mobilize resources and plan their rational allocation. Along with the idea of development came the rise of socialism, the link between them being the ideology of redistribution (Young 1976: 67–75).

Development has political as well as economic components. Young

184

summarizes political development as the following set of normative features: identity, or active sense of membership in the national community for the whole populace; legitimacy, or generalized acceptance of the rightness of the exercise and structure of authority by the state for obtaining willing compliance; participation, or enlargement of the number of those involved in the political arena, ideally to the entire polity; distribution, or assurance that valued resources are available on equal terms to all, with policies to inhibit excessive individual wealth; penetration, or the extension of the effective operation of the state to the farthest periphery of the system (*ibid.*: 75).

None of these features can be identified as increasing in Zaire, quite the contrary in fact; must we then regard it as de-developing politically? This question is governed by the expectation that the state has a reliable administrative apparatus, participates extensively in economic activities, and is able to enforce its policies, thanks to popular acceptance of its state's right to compel obedience. A weak state is one that is unable to collect taxes, provide social services, settle disputes or control the military, while at the same time the absence of law, order and predictable administration leads to decline in state revenues and reduces the opportunities for class formation through the state (Kasfir 1983: 9–10).

The weakness of the Zairian state in these terms is undeniable. The huge scale of the second economy is evidence of its inability to collect taxes; social services are virtually non-existent; corruption prevails instead of the rule of law; citizens have no rights; the population is subject to continual harassment from police and the military. On the other hand, however, the Zairian state has certain undeniable and obvious strengths: the longevity of the Mobutu regime, in part attributable to foreign assistance, is evidence of the effectiveness of mechanisms of political control; the state can usually monopolize the exercise of force, although it cannot adequately regulate the behaviour of the military; it operates efficient security networks and prevents the rise of organized opposition. In addition the political aristocracy uses the apparatus of the state to extract resources on a massive scale for personal gain. How should we make sense of these simultaneous strengths and weaknesses? How resolve their apparent contradiction?

Chapter 1 summarized theories explaining politics and economics in developing countries as either emphasizing external or internal factors. The approach favouring internal factors and the analysis of social classes emphasizes the political. It views the state as the locus of class struggle, separates the political from the economic and represents the state as relatively autonomous from the process of accumulation and the relations of production. This viewpoint has been called the 'class logic' approach; those who use it tend to neglect economic factors. The approach emphasizing external factors, on the other hand, focuses on capitalism from a global perspective, in which the state functions to regulate competition and labour. This view, known as the 'capital logic' approach,

185

overstresses the economic basis of political forms and neglects class factors; it fails to grasp the capitalist state as a system of structures of political domination resulting from specific historical struggles (de Janvry 1981: 185; Staniland 1985: 165; Lonsdale 1981: 167).

The drawbacks of each approach are cancelled out if they are combined and employed dialectically. Understanding of the state must be grounded in analysis of the class structure and the consequent balance of political forces in control of the state, but also in the contradictions of capitalism and resultant crises of accumulation and legitimacy. 'Class struggle is the dynamic of development, but it is mediated by past struggles and the objective functioning of the system that grew out of them; the process of capital accumulation and the crises that arise from it delimit the field of class struggle, but they do so in historically specific ways' (de Janvry 1981: 186). In addition to class struggle, we must take account of other forms of struggle: ethnic, religious, gender, etc. The combination of political, social and economic, external and internal perspectives, leads to Bernstein and Campbell's view that the inefficiency, corruption and incoherence of many states in Africa is not pathological but is simply the form and appearance of the contradictions and complexities, alliances and oppositions, of the different social forces and interests which make up the state (Bernstein and Campbell 1985: 11–12).

In Zaire, the blatant use of the state to further the interests of the political aristocracy has brought about a major crisis of state legitimacy and widespread refusal to cooperate with its policies and regulations. The huge expansion of second economy activities described in Chapter 5 has been the result. In this process different class sectors gain or lose advantage at different times and in different regions of the country. As the political aristocracy find themselves threatened by mobility from below, they engage in class actions of various kinds to protect their interests and close their boundary. We have so far been concerned with details of the emergence of a nascent indigenous capitalist class in Kisangani and North Kivu; by looking at instances of the oppressive actions of the state and the resistance they encounter in other parts of the country, we will gain a wider context in which to set this new class and make possible some assessments of its future prospects.

STATE POLICIES AND STATE REGULATIONS

Through its policies and regulations, the state dominates and extracts surplus from rural and urban workers and producers. The extremely low official wage structure, together with continually increasing prices, weighs most heavily on the subordinate classes; additional and relatively remun-erative sources of income are available to the influential and well connected. Chris Gerry has pointed out that in Senegal the institutional means of capital accumulations, such as credit facilities, contracts, licences, etc., are in the hands of the bourgeoisie, who are strongly linked to metropolitan capital, and that the continuing impoverishment of the mass of the people hampers the emergence of incipient local capitalism (Gerry 1978: 1154). We will show that in Zaire, taxes extract even such meagre resources as the poor do have, while the increasing costs of commercial licences obstruct their advancement through trade. In contrast, import licences, foreign exchange quotas and credit are allocated in ways that benefit the wealthy and powerful. We will also show how the state transfers resources from agricultural to urban sectors and from small consumers to officials by means of marketing boards and the protection of local industry.

## Wages and prices

The low wages and salaries and spiralling prices in effect in the seventies and eighties have been documented above in Chapter 5. Morice, describing the black market in Luanda, Angola, notes that goods are about thirty-five times more expensive at the parallel than at the regular market rate, proportionate to the illegal foreign exchange rate. He makes the point that such goods are not in fact overpriced, they are selling at the world market price; the problem is that work is not adequately paid. In Angola, as in Zaire, because of the level of wages compared to the cost of goods necessary for the reproduction of the worker, neither a labourer nor a high ranked official can support a family on his salary. The effects of this system weigh differently on different classes, however. Only in company stores, where prices are kept low, is purchasing power close to the minimal costs of reproduction. Officials and public sector workers are further privileged in that they get paid in kind, have direct access to factories because of official position or operate a barter system from such a base. A large part of production in this way enters the *circuits des privilégiés* and never gets to the stores. Economically speaking it is just as if these commodities were bought in government stores at low prices, but socially the effect is different because it introduces the fundamental opposition between those with official position, in control of the circulation of goods, and the rest (Morice 1985: 111–13).

In Zaire, Buakasa points out that a mere twenty years since independence saw the formation of a new social order for distribution of resources and for new control and regulation of the conditions of existence for the general population. In this time the masses have become increasingly impoverished, while holders of official positions have come to enjoy relatively good conditions of existence (Buakasa 1980: 193–5). The wage rates set by the state have been instrumental in this process.

Wages vary according to rates set for twenty-five zones across the country. In 1978 the real wage level was approximately 10–15 per cent of the 1960 level (Young and Turner 1985: 133). In April 1979 the minimum legal wage in Upper Zaire was raised by 30 per cent to 78K a day, Z20.42 a month, for the lowest paid category of manual worker; Z2.35 a day, Z60.31 a month, for highly qualified manual labour. In addition family allowances were Z2.47 a month for each child.

Verhaegen points out that few workers earn much more than this extremely low wage. A study by the National Institute of Statistics (INS) in Kisangani in 1979 on sixty-two enterprises, totalling 4,639 workers, showed that 78 per cent of these workers earned less than Z51 a month, and 98 per cent less than Z76. The gross inadequacy of wages to sustain basic needs is not new. In 1972 average monthly expenses for a household of 6.6 persons in Kisangani was Z28.7, 70 per cent of which was spent on food. Wages at that time covered only two-thirds of this amount, the remainder being acquired by independent activities in commerce or agriculture. Between 1974 and 1979 prices of staple foods, such as manioc, maize flour, rice and palm oil increased by 15–29 per cent. To maintain the same food consumption these households would thus have to spend six to ten times as much money, necessitating a salary of Z200–Z300 a month; salaries in 1979, however, were between Z15 and Z50 (Verhaegen and Kasongo 1979: 21–32).

Wages are so low that for many the major reason to keep working is the opportunities their job may offer for second economy activities, or else the fringe benefits, such as housing, company stores (*cantines*), transport subsidies and, especially, medical care. The government and large companies provide housing for their employees, relieving them of rents that range from Z200 to Z1,000 a month. Company stores sell food and other items at official prices; in 1979 this was anything from 100–500 per cent lower than the prices actually in effect in stores and markets (Mubake 1984: 267).

One way in which the state indirectly forces workers to continue working for such low wages is through the virtual disappearance of public health care. Some employers were quite explicit that the only thing that kept their workers on the job was payment of medical expenses, which they are supposed by law to provide for their employees and their families. Health care is so expensive that it is otherwise out of reach of most of the population. The university hospital in Kisangani in 1979 announced a fee scale of Z25 for a clinic visit, Z79 a day for a two-bed room. Medicines had to be bought from the pharmacies in town since they were generally unavailable at the hospital. Prices varied wildly: the same prescription cost Z25 for two packets in one pharmacy, Z36 for one in another and Z40 for two in a third. Drugs were sold for much more than the official prices. One particular course of medication, for example, cost ten times more in Kisangani pharmacies than in a mission hospital in Ituri.

One reason for this situation is the shortage of foreign exchange and the politics of its allocation. The effect on prices is illustrated by the experience of an Asian pharmacist in Kisangani. He bought drugs in Kinshasa for his pharmacy, for which the government allocated up to Z1,000 of foreign exchange per pharmacy. He was unable to obtain sufficient supplies for this amount of money, so was forced to buy additional quantities from illegal importers at much higher prices. Such drugs are often smuggled into the country by means of false invoicing. For example, he got 100 vials of penicillin a month legally from a German company at Z1.15 for 5 cc., but since he needed 1,000 vials to supply his pharmacy, he made up the difference by buying at Z2.50 per 5 cc. from illegal sources, and selling at Z5. He could get haemoglobin, from a Belgian company manufacturing in Kinshasa, at Z2.50 which he was willing to sell at Z5. But he had to wait two months for his order to be filled, so he therefore bought from illegal importers at Z5–6; after adding transportation cost and profit he sold for Z15.

Another reason medicines are expensive is that they are stolen from hospitals, by personnel who seldom receive their pay, and sold in the market. Periodically the authorities announce a crackdown on this practice and the market police round up the sellers, but the effect is short lived and the drugs are inevitably back on sale a few days later. These stolen medicines are often adulterated. In 1980 quinine for the malaria endemic in the city cost Z10 for one treatment in the pharmacies, Z6 in the market; given the wage rates, these prices are prohibitively expensive.

It is customary for employers, therefore, to pay medical costs for their employees, either directly or by paying a flat fee every month to a private clinic. A branch of a Lubumbashi-based business with two retail stores in Kisangani, for example, paid a monthly Z1,000 to such a clinic.

Health services in rural areas are almost non-existent and rural farmers have nothing to insulate them from spiralling prices for goods they must buy and the decline of prices for commodities they produce. In 1961 producer prices for foodstuffs were 42 per cent of retail prices; by September 1970 they were 24 per cent (Bézy *et al.*, 1981: 125). An example documents the extreme which this exploitation had reached. In 1979 in the Turumbu rice cooperative at Yangambi, west of Kisangani, farmers were obliged to sell rice to the cooperative at 12K a kilogram; it sold to traders at 55K and the retail price in Kisangani was around 250K. The cooperative could not even buy all that the farmers produced, so they sold some of their rice direct to the traders at 33K a kilogram. Selling to the cooperative, farmers only got 4.8 per cent of the retail price; selling direct to the traders they got 13 per cent (Mbaya 1980: 55). This difference is not attributable to transportation costs and risks since Yangambi is at a distance of only 130 kilometres from the city and rice does not rot rapidly. In Maniema sub-region, south of Kisangani, *Boyoma* reported in October 1979, that traders, with the connivance of the authorities, were actually taking rice from farmers without paying for it at all, in 'systematic pillage'.

Although wages, salaries and producer prices are derisorily low, other sources of income, to which the well-connected, moderately wealthy or politically powerful generally have access, are relatively remunerative.

189

Two examples illustrate how such people can live quite well despite inadequate salaries:

> A couple in Kisangani with four teenage children manage an apartment building owned by a government official to whom the wife is related by marriage. They owned two cars until one was wrecked in an accident, and their lifestyle evidences a comfortable income level. In addition to salaries, their prime source of income is five building plots (*parcelles*) they own in Kinshasa, which bring in monthly income from the houses built on them. In addition they have a beer business, getting a quota of thirty-two cases a week from the brewery at the official price. This quota was inherited from a restaurant which had formerly operated on the ground floor of the building they manage, but which was defunct by 1979.

> A retired government official who has a pension of only Z300 a month lives quite comfortably with his wife and family because of their real estate holdings and her money-making enterprise. She trades in *wax* prints and tourist objects. They live with one of their married children and rent out the two houses they own in Kinshasa's suburbs for high rents paid in cash; one is rented to a wealthy Asian who may pay several months in advance, making possible large investments in purchases for commerce. The wife sews her own and her children's clothes and earns some income by doing the same for friends. She also sells beer from her house; she has no quota at the official price but buys by the case at high prices and sells by the bottle at a profit.

In both these instances, connections or position in the state brought jobs, salary saving and investment in real estate. As we have seen above rents are high and good money can be earned in trade and beer selling; rentier capitalism and commerce bring relatively much higher incomes than wages and salaries. Those in the dominant class are in a favourable position to obtain supplies for commerce and to accumulate the capital to obtain real estate; the wage and price structure operates most oppressively on workers and petty producers.

## Taxation, licensing and quotas

Direct taxation is derived primarily from wages and salaries; they produced 92 per cent of Zaire's tax receipts in 1977 (World Bank 1980: 62–3). Direct taxes are also levied on corporations and on sales of all domestic business establishments and local manufacturing industry. Corporate taxes are levied on profits in commercial agriculture, construction and manufacturing. Small, unincorporated businesses and the self-employed (mostly retailers) are also taxed and revenues are low as they are difficult to collect.

The successor of the colonial head tax is the CPM (*contribution personnel minimum*); it is levied on all those not paying a wage tax earning less than a minimum amount, mostly small cultivators. The CPM is administered by the collectivity and is the principal source of its revenues. Together with other taxes and fees, the state extracts between 20 per cent and 50 per cent from the yearly income of petty producers (Callaghy 1984: 371). Schatzberg has amply documented how little the rural population receives in return. Collectivity revenue is mostly spent on salary and personnel costs, and housing and vehicles for administrators; very little is spent on maintenance of infrastructure or on any facilities for rural development. Embezzlement and extortion are widespread. The system is set up to make accumulation of capital and upward political and social mobility of village farmers extremely difficult (Schatzberg 1980a: 59–66). They are bitterly resentful. A study of a rural collectivity in Bandundu described the anger of poor farmers required to build and repair school buildings and a dispensary nurse's house for no pay, when they themselves found it very difficult to find money for school fees and medicines (Ewert 1977: 171–4). Collectivity administration, resting on the CPM, is in reality a system for rural exploitation and oppression, often including outright violence.

A report for Kisangani, requested by the central government in November 1979 for budget purposes, lists tax receipts at the sub-regional level for January–September as shown in Table 8.1. Revenues from beer, alcohol licences and school fees alone amount to 96 per cent of the total. In addition the same report lists receipts collected in September (for an unspecified period) of taxes imposed on market, commerical and transport activities. The largest amounts, 10 per cent and 5 per cent respectively, come from the sale of textiles and of food.

Taxes at the collectivity and sub-regional levels are therefore principally levied on incomes; on food, clothing (textiles) and education; and on beer, soft drinks and cigarettes. Incomes are pitifully small; food and clothing are essential items; education is necessary to improve chances of getting a job; and beer, soft drinks and cigarettes are the only widely available consumer luxuries. Given the wage and price structure, any tax at all on these items is exploitative extraction of the meagre resources of rural farmers and urban wage workers and serves to maintain their disadvantaged position.

Commerce is taxed through the licensing system, started in the colonial period with a 1951 law forbidding trade without a licence. Licences cost 250 CF for in individual, 500 CF for a business. Women had to obtain their husband's permission and minors their father's to take out a licence. Conditions for obtaining licences – knowing how to read, write, calculate and use measures of a European type – constituted an almost impassable barrier to getting them (Tshund'Olela 1976: 133). In August 1979 *Ordonnance-Loi* No. 79–021 sought to restrict the proliferation of street traders. Such petty commerce, defined as all trade in objects and goods offered for sale in streets, markets or homes, including crafts and the transportation of goods and people, was henceforth only permitted under an annual Z100 licence issued by the zone. Licences were available only to nationals who could show knowledge of accounting. They were not to be issued to magistrates, public employees or their wives or intermediaries. Penalty for infringement was a fine of Z1,000 and/or six months in jail. The

Table 8.1 *Tax receipts for the sub-region of Kisangani, January–September 1979 (in zaires)*

| | |
|---|---|
| beer consumption | 1,785,133 |
| soda | 16,460 |
| cigarettes | 28,286 |
| sale foreign ID cards | 13,195 |
| notarizations | 1,566 |
| Total | 1,844,640 |
| building permits | 14,642 |
| hearse rentals | 1,920 |
| Total | 16,562 |
| alcohol licences | 42,510 |
| land use permits | 3,070 |
| Total | 45,580 |
| *Judicial* | |
| fines | 1,389 |
| fees | 525 |
| *ad volorem* duty | 418 |
| Total | 2,332 |
| *Educational* | |
| fees—primary | 208,125 |
| —secondary | 195,600 |
| Total | 403,725 |
| Total receipts | 2,312,839 |

*Source: Rapport Circonstancié Région de Haut-Zaire, Sous-Région de Kisangani 1979.*

procedure for obtaining a commercial licence to set up a store or company is extremely complex and time-consuming. The first step is to get finger-printed at the Department of Justice, then a certificate of good behaviour must be obtained from the zone authorities and another of unemployment from the Ministry of Public Works. Finally the Department of Justice issues the licence on payment of the fee. In 1980 the cost of such a licence for an individual was Z2,500, for a company Z5,000. Licensing fees make legitimate business very difficult for small traders, who barely survive through selling a few items outside their houses or in the street.

Import licences and foreign exchange quotas are subject to political manipulations that further the interests of the political aristocracy. From 1960–7 the state monopolized transactions in foreign exchange by a system of quotas for foreign currency and import licences. Export businesses were allowed to retain 20–5 per cent of the hard currency they earned (Huybrechts and Van Der Steen 1981: 234). After the 1967 monetary reforms, the policy was liberalized; quotas were abolished and certain banks were authorized to issue import licences. In 1975 controls were re-established to counter fraud from underinvoicing; only imports characterized as basic essentials, such as food, medicines and raw materials for industry, remained free of controls (*ibid*.: 253). But allocations are in fact arbitrary rather than rational, and dependent on political influence. In September 1979, for example, the price of locally produced soap in Kinshasa increased by 100 per cent in three weeks. Amato Frères, Zaire's major soap producer since 1925, had simply been left out of the foreign exchange allocation the previous December and was unable to import caustic soda (*Elima* 22 September 1979).

## Credit restrictions

Le Brun and Gerry consider access to bank loans to be a decisive factor in the transition from petty commodity to small capitalist production (1975: 27). In Zaire restrictions on credit imposed by the big financial institutions, the agents of the state, operate to restrict this transition. Credit restrictions formed a barrier to socio-economic mobility both before and after independence.

Bank credit was forbidden to Africans by law in 1917; this law was not modified until 1938. An African savings bank was not started until 1950 (Jewsiewicki and Faradje 1974: 132–4). After independence banks continued to give credit far more readily to foreign businessmen than to Zairians. The monetary reforms of 1967 resulted in a tightening of credit: branches of banks in the interior had to issue loans by going through the head office in Kinshasa, a slow and laborious process. By the end of 1970 total bank loans to nationals amounted to only 16 per cent of total loans (Mukenge 1974: 437). In 1974 Z200,000 (64 per cent) of the Z310,658 lent out by the *Société de Crédit aux Classes Moyennes*, went to foreigners (*Rapport Economique Régional* 1974).

Government reports make it plain that difficulty in obtaining credit has been a critical obstacle for the expansion of Zairian owned business and the transition to production. The Regional Economic Report for Upper Zaire in 1970 observed that young Zairian planters generally lacked sufficient credit to take up the many abandoned foreign plantations, and that small retailers remained in a state of chronic mediocrity because they could not get credit. Another report complains in the same vein that for individuals taking up plantations

> the politics of bank credit remain generally restrictive ... The Zairian planters of our province complain that they do not receive credit from the financial institutions. They thus find great difficulty in developing their

193

plantations adequately. (*Rapport Economique Anruel. Région de Haut Zaire* 1971: 9)

No such difficulty existed for the politically powerful. Position in the state made acquisition of plantations easy in Zairianization or through other means. In November 1979 a group of top politicians toured Upper Zaire, ostensibly on a tour of inspection. In fact, according to a source in the Land Title Office they were also engaged in registering title to a number of abandoned plantations. Their purpose was to legally justify their coffee exporting activities by ownership of plantations; whether they would be properly maintained, managed and producing to capacity, as the law also demanded, was made irrelevant by virtue of the power and influence of their new owners.

The big financial institutions block the operation of cooperatives organized to combat credit difficulties, such as COOCEC (*Coopératives Centrales D'Epargne et de Crédit*), a credit union started in 1970 in Basankusu, Bukavu and Kinshasa. In 1979 their membership totalled 32,000 and their funds 5 million zaires. The Basankusu cooperative had given 47 per cent of loans for commerical ventures, 30.2 per cent for construction. But the Bank of Zaire refuses them recognition as official financial institutions and in the demonetization of 1979 they were unable to change most of their funds into the new denominations (Korse 1980).

## Marketing boards

Robert Bates shows that marketing boards operate to transfer resources from agricultural to other sectors when they purchase cash crops for export at prices set far below the prevailing market price at which they will be sold (Bates 1981: 12). Increased government revenues are not then invested in local rural development projects but in urban areas in projects that benefit the wealthy or are politically advantageous to the government.

From 1971–3 in Zaire, the government set up marketing boards for purchase and distribution to urban centres for coffee (ONC), cereals (ONACER), textiles (ONAFITEX), oils (ONO), livestock (ONDE), rubber (ONCN) and sugar (ONDS), but they paid very low prices to the producers. In 1973–4, the world market price of cotton more than doubled, but producer prices remained unchanged; and domestic lint prices were half or less than export prices (Tollens 1975: 277). In 1975 direct producers were paid 6–9K for 1 kilogram of coffee by ONC, which sold it for 40 FB[1] on the international market; in 1977, although the world market price had risen to 240 FB, the producer received only 25K (IRES 1977).

But the government proved incapable of operating these boards, which ran out of funds; by 1978 most of them had either become inactive or were grossly inadequate to their task. Government reports in Upper Zaire for this period complain that ONAFITEX and ONC had failed to collect much of the cotton and coffee harvests for lack of money and vehicles, and because of the appalling state of the roads. Large stocks of cotton remained uncollected by ONAFITEX, so discouraging the producers that recorded cotton production in Upper Zaire dropped from 18,923 tonnes in 1972–3, to 9,229 tonnes in 1973–4 and only 4,696 tonnes in 1974–5 (*Boyoma* 22 December 1976). ONC only bought up 5 per cent of the coffee harvest in 1974 in three zones of the Mongala sub-region in Equateur (Schatzberg 1980a: 75).

## Protection of local industry

Rural producers not only get low prices for their products and almost no return in government services or local development, but they must also pay high prices for the manufactured goods they need. One reason for such prices is government intervention for protection of domestic industry. The 1969 Investment Code attempted to attract foreign investors with favourable interest rates, tax exemptions and low tariffs. The actual effect of such protection, however, is to freeze patterns of competition, preventing the growth of more efficient lower-cost firms. The survival of inefficient firms results in the rise of domestic prices above those of foreign goods, for which local consumers must suffer (Bates 1981: 32–72).

Imported Michelin tyres are cheaper than Goodyear tyres made in Kinshasa from Zairian rubber. The SOTEXKI textile factory in Kisangani, set up under terms so favourable that it realized its investment in two years, produces cloth that is more expensive and of poorer quality, and thus less sought after, than imported cloth. The products of the Maluka steel mill near Kinshasa cost four times more than imported steel (Willame 1984: 84). Roofing made by SIDERNA in Kinshasa is also more expensive than the imported variety.

Quotas and favourable tariffs have eliminated competition for domestic industry with the result that products assembled in Zaire cost more than those imported fully assembled. Firms have rights of import even when they cannot fully supply the market. Thus Continental Grain has an agreement with the government whereby only American wheat can be imported,[2] it has exclusive milling rights and can approve or veto any proposals for other flour importers in the future. Import licences for steel and rubber products must receive authorization from SOSIDER, the national steel company which barely functions, or Goodyear (Bézy *et al.*, 1981: 205–6). ALUZAIRE, the aluminium factory set up in Zairian partnership by ALUSUISSE, has the advantages of one of the lowest electricity rates in the world and rights to export duty on all aluminium produced. It also has the right to veto any other aluminium project in Zaire for ten years (Willame 1984: 84–5). Inefficient firms are thus protected.

The government regularly imposes price controls on food and other essential commodities and attempts to increase the supply by importing. As Bates has pointed out, local food prices are undercut with these imports because of the overvaluation of the currency; establishing price controls fails to stop price increases because it is all too easy to divert food from official marketing channels. Such policies are responses to pressure from urban consumers whose disaffection the government fears. They in fact offer many opportunities for corruption and result in redistribution of income from consumers to officials (Bates 1981: 30–43).

Price controls mean that farmers receive lower prices for their products, but sheltering of domestic industry means they must pay more for goods.

A wage, price and tax structure thus operates to extract the maximum from petty producers and wage workers, and credit restrictions and marketing organization restrict their upward mobility should they find any independent means of acquiring wealth. However, the ineffectiveness of the state apparatus and the alternatives to wage labour of production under non-capitalist relations of production, sometimes make possible resistance to, and evasion of, some of these restrictive measures.

RESISTANCE TO STATE POWER AND CONTROL

The colonial state served the interests of metropolitan capitalism with ruthless efficiency, but since independence the state has lacked effective administrative capacity and is hampered in addition by its 'ad hoc policy formulations, incoherent policy pronouncements, and lack of attention to the concrete problems of policy implementation' (Schatzberg 1982: 348). As a result petty producers and wage workers are able to evade oppressive regulations and find alternatives to working for low wages or producing for low prices. The pervasiveness and recent enormous expansion of the second economy described in Chapter 5, is evidence of the state's inability to carry out its own policies and enforce regulations, and of its tenuous control over economic processes. Bianga Waruzi's description of Kivu comes to the same conclusion:

> Peasant agriculture under the colonial system was one of coercion. Peasants used to grow certain crops because they were forced to do so. Although in the post-independence period there has been a continuity of such policy, the growth of such agriculture depended strongly on the power of the state to enforce regulations. This has not been the case; with the breakdown of regulations peasants have recovered the choice of freedom. Peasants feel strongly today that they can now decide on what kinds of production they can carry out on the basis of their interests. Such a feeling may explain why peasants do not revolt. (Bianga 1982: 283)

Catharine Newbury has stressed that response to the depredations of the state does not consist just of passive resistance but also of a growing militancy linked to the proliferation of collectivity taxes and declining terms of trade for rural producers (Newbury 1984b: 113). We will turn now to some specific examples of resistance: evasion of compulsory cotton growing and desertion by plantation workers.

## The failure of compulsory cotton cultivation

In 1959 Zaire exported almost 53,000 tonnes of cotton fibre, representing 15 per cent of total agricultural exports (Popelier 1977: 30); by 1979 production hardly exceeded 6,000 tonnes and could not even supply the needs of domestic industry of 21,000 tonnes (Bézy *et al.*, 1981: 195). This decline is attributable to government pricing and marketing policies and to active resistance by the producers to compulsory cultivation.

Cotton is grown exclusively by petty producers. In 1917 the colonial government made cotton growing compulsory in all provinces except Leopoldville, and in the 1930s extended cotton cultivation with the introduction of farm settlement schemes (*paysannats*), organized around new or regrouped villages in which it was the principal cash crop. The eventual aim, to give the farmers individual land tenure, was not realized and the scheme, with a few exceptions, failed, primarily because price incentives were so low (Tollens 1975: 91–2, 68, 225–6). In the sixties the cotton ginning companies enjoyed a near monopoly; the Belgian company COTONCO controlled about 90 per cent of cotton marketing and the bargaining position of the producers was very weak. In comparison with some other African countries Zairian producers received the lowest price per kilogram of seed cotton, although the quality of Zairian cotton is very high (*ibid.*: 37–59, 104–5).

In 1971 ONAFITEX, the cotton marketing board, was established, with a monopoly on marketing cotton. It was responsible for the purchase, transportation and sale of cotton; the next year it took over ginning from private companies as well. By 1973, however, it was unable to supply funds to regional branches and was late in distributing seed; shortage of bags caused collecting delays and poor roads had increased transportation costs to make them higher than in neighbouring African countries (*ibid.*: 106–24, 184). In 1979 supplies for the cotton mills fell to their lowest level since 1967. ONAFITEX was dissolved in 1978 and replaced by the *Caisse de Stabilisation Cotonnière*, which contracted out some operations to private companies. Their improved marketing arrangements resulted in a rise in production (Young and Turner 1985: 321).

The evasion by petty producers of requirements for compulsory cotton cultivation is described by Lukusa Mukunayi for Gandajika, Kasai, but the same thing happens elsewhere. Cotton cultivation is enforced by the local authorities by means of imprisonment, corporal punishment and fines. The law, however, only applies to small cultivators whose farms do not exceed 5 hectares; large prodcuers whose farms exceed 20 hectares, chiefly traders and political and military authorities, may cultivate what they want. They primarily produce the more profitable corn and peanuts. Official prices are

Table 8.2 *Average yield and sale price of cotton and some food crops in Gandajika, August 1980*

| | Yield | | Price/kg. | | Average annual revenue |
|---|---|---|---|---|---|
| | Average yield/ha. | Average yield/ ha. yr | Official | Actual | |
| Cotton | 400 kg | 400 kg | 0.90 Z | 0.90 Z* | 360 Z |
| | | | 0.60 Z | 0.60 Z+ | 240 Z |
| Maize | 970 kg | 1,940 kg | 0.35 Z | 2.85 Z | 5,529 Z |
| Peanuts | 600 kg | 1,200 kg | 0.65 Z | 5.00 Z | 6,000 Z |
| Manioc | 19,000 kg | 19,000 kg | 0.35 Z | 3.00 Z | n.a. |
| Beans | 540 kg | 1,080 kg | 0.75 Z | 7.00 Z | 7,560 Z |

\* first grade cotton
+ second grade cotton

*Source: Rapport Annuel du Service de l'Agriculture de la Zone de Gandajika*, 1980, in Lukusa Mukunayi (1981:447).

set for food crops as well as for cotton, but the cotton marketing board monopolizes purchase and pays only the derisorily low official price, whereas food crops, in the absence of effective means to enforce price control, are sold on the open market at much higher prices, as shown in Table 8.2. Not only do cotton producers get low prices but, since 1974, delays in purchasing the harvest have resulted in deterioration in quality to a lower grade so that sales must often be made at lower prices than anticipated. Petty producers are not only forced to grow unremunerative cotton crops, they also suffer abuses by the marketing board agents. These agents defraud them with rigged scales or pass off first quality cotton for second or demand bribes or food and drink before they will start buying (Lukusa Mukunayi 1981: 446–8).

Lukusa's account shows how producers steadfastly refuse to cultivate more cotton than the minimum necessary to excape fines and imprisonment, and concentrate instead on producing corn, manioc and peanuts. They sabotage cotton production by diverting most of the fertilizer intended for the cotton fields to their food crops, by failing to space plants correctly, and by refusing to replant their fields as instructed. The local authorities are unable to exercise sufficient supervision to prevent these evasions of the law, which are reflected in decreasing yields – only 400 kilograms a hectare instead of a possible 500–600 kilograms – and a steady drop in production (*ibid.*: 449). A Gandajika farmer cultivating 40 hectares could buy seven goats with his annual earnings before independence; by 1977 he could not buy even one, though manioc cultivation on the same land would enable him to buy four (Popelier 1977: 33). Reports from other areas also observe that petty producers situated near main roads have abandoned the cultivation of cotton for more profitable crops, such as corn, peanuts, manioc and soy beans (*Conjoncture Economique* 1979: 262).

## Problems for the oil plantation companies

Chapter 5 suggested that palm oil production had declined less drastically than would appear from the official figures, since unrecorded production is a significant source of supply for the internal market. It is, nevertheless, the case that production for export decreased to zero. In 1959 Zaire was second only to Nigeria as a world supplier of palm oil; by 1980 it exported none. Export figures show a steady decline from 188, 593 tonnes in 1959 to 10,000 tonnes in 1979, to zero in 1980. In 1958 palm oil exports produced 13.9 per cent of foreign exchange revenues, in 1977 only 2.3 per cent (M'Bela 1982: 7).

The largest of the oil companies is Unilever. By 1961 it had invested £23 million, one-sixth of its total African investment, in its branch *Huileries du Congo Belge* (now PLZ, *Plantations Lever au Zaire*). The company's exports made up about 50 per cent of the country's total for palm products. During the troubles after independence PLZ was unable to operate profitably, suffering extensive damage to plant and stores and losing European personnel. Operations were not resumed on a large scale until 1968 (Sherrill 1973: 31).

The report of an inquiry into the causes of desertion and absenteeism by workers at PLZ Yabgimbe near Bunia, Equateur, in 1979, makes it clear that such problems were of long standing. In the colonial period, labour was often recruited at a distance to make desertion and absenteeism more difficult. Nevertheless, despite this practice, three-quarters of the recruits would desert. They would then, however, be brought back by the police (Bumba Monga Ngoy 1979). The colonial administration assisted the oil companies by forced recruitment of labour and by compulsory food cultivation to feed their workers, although before 1960 two-thirds of the supply of palm fruits came from petty producers with their own little plantations or harvest from trees in the forests (Popelier 1977: 22). Cultivation, however, was more or less obligatory in the purchase zones of the big palm oil companies. Such organized supervision backed up by force has never been exercised by the post-independence state; many small oil factories owned by Greeks and Portuguese were abandoned because they could no longer rely on the administration to ensure a regular supply of palm nuts (M'Bela 1982: 75–6). In the absence of such coercion petty producers tended to concentrate their efforts on more remunerative food crops (*Conjoncture Economique* 1979: 227). In addition, as the companies defaulted they failed to collect harvests and to pay for what had been collected; this failure also contributed to the decline in production (Ewert 1977: 176–9).

The PLZ report details conditions of work and wages for plantation workers and makes it abundantly clear why it is hard to get labour. It is extremely difficult for a worker to fulfil the demands made of him. A palm fruit cutter must produce 65–70 bunches per day to qualify for performance of a day's work; if, say, only 40–50 bunches are collected it only counts for a half day's work with the obligation of completion the day following. Weaker individuals may only succeed in earning Z4–5 in a month. This system is supposed to stimulate workers to work hard enough to get Z26 a month. Since they can get Z20 for only one sack of corn, this is hardly an incentive. Those who continue to work on the plantations do so because they want its more urban milieu, and because of the pensions they earn and the medical care for which they are eligible in the company hospital (Bumba Monga Ngoy 1979).

The proliferation of the unofficial trade and smuggling of the sixties, described in Chapter 5, resulted from the price policies of the government at that time. These factors contributed to the demise of the smaller oil companies and they have continued to be significant in the decline of palm oil exports in the seventies. From 1967–73 the price paid to the producers in Zaire was less than half that paid in Gabon and Cameroon (Peemans 1975c: 170). From 1967–72 the price of palm oil for the internal market was fixed at Z69 a tonne; on the export market it was Z130–40 a tonne but the companies were obliged to sell half their production in the interior, instead of only 20–30 per cent as before. The cost of oil varied from Z73 a tonne on the better-managed plantations to Z95 a tonne from other sources. The companies thus lost Z10–32 a tonne on half of their production. Exported oil prices barely covered this loss, allowing only a small profit margin. By 1975 the sale price was Z145, but the cost price was Z150 from plantations and Z200 from elsewhere, and high taxes were levied on exports. The result was a black market trade in this period, in which intermediaries made fabulous profits. In Goma in 1976 it was possible to get Z1,000 a tonne (Popelier 1977: 23).

Thus when petty producers did harvest palm nuts they were not necessarily for the official market. For 200 kilograms of fruit the producer could get 8 litres of oil which, in 1974, sold for Z20; the same quantity of fruit sold to the oil mill brought in only Z1. Even if he did not want to make the effort to produce oil himself, the producer could make more money selling directly to the consumer market where the profits of unofficial trade were much higher (M'Bela 1982: 76). The drop in production in 1977–8 for SCAM, one large company, was attributed to drought and to the development of small-scale production and smuggling to Congo Brazzaville (*Conjoncture Economique* 1979; 237–8).

STATE WEAKNESS AND CONSOLIDATION OF CLASS INTERESTS

'Economic inefficiency can be used for political purposes' (Bates 1981: 104): in Zaire the weakness of the state serves the interests of various class sectors. Regulations that are unenforceable have purposes other than their overt one: they provide officials with additional opportunities for harassment and extortion. Although ostensibly intended to restrict the excessive number of retailers and speculators, licences for petty commerce operate to this effect. As Huybrechts and Van Der Steen put it,

> It is the system of regulation and control itself which sustains fraud and corruption, two sources of easy and enormous profit which the political-administrative beneficiaries are not ready to give up...one could ask if [regulation] is not set up more to permit illicit profit than to clean up the situation. (1981: 285)

David Gould emphasizes that viewing mismanagement as a constraint on development misrepresents reality: it 'may be part of a conscious self-enrichment strategy on the part of those in control of the public bureaucracy' (Gould 1979: 89).

The political aristocracy use the state to extend their control over the economy but, in the process, have sometimes furthered the interests of other class sectors because of administrative ineffectiveness. The nationalization of land enables the powerful to acquire legal title to tracts of land which they take over from the local population for private exploitation. Bulu-Bobina (1984) gives an example from western Zaire in a perceptive article which makes the interplay of class forces clear. The following account is based on it.

In 1968 the state, by the so-called Bakajika law, took over sole right to allocate land; in 1973, in Law 73/021, it took over sole ownership of all land. Before this time, there had been three categories: land held under customary law, land subject to statutory law and vacant land. Since nationalization, permission for the right to use land must be obtained from the government and a yearly tax paid according to the type of use. In cities land is assessed as residential, commercial or industrial. If, after three years, at least one-fifth of the land allocated is not being developed (*mise en valeur*), use rights can be claimed by someone else.[3] Concessions are made under signed contract to the regional government for 200 hectares or less; to the Land Title Office for under 10 hectares. An inquiry into the proposed land use is held by the zone commissioners and a decision made by the sub-regional commissioner.

In Kasangulu zone in Lower Zaire, the enclosing of land for cattle raising is causing shortage of land for food production and the dispossession of small cultivators. The zone is generally dry and only some areas are suitable for cultivation. They are much in demand because of the proximity to the Kinshasa market. From 1970–83 the population increased by over 23,000 intensifying pressure on the land. Traditionally the Kongo inhabitants of the zone held the land under collective, not individual, rights of ownership based on kin relations. First the introduction of the market

201

economy and thereafter the new land legislation disrupted the functioning of this system.

Two roads into the area have made it accessible to city dwellers in search of land to follow the current trend among the wealthy for investment in cattle raising. The local population are losing land to these Kinshasa residents for their private use in two ways: one is through reallocation by the administrative authorities under the new law; the other is through sale by traditional authorities, in defiance of both the law and the traditional rights of the people.

This illegal sale and distribution of arable land by traditional authorities occurs for three reasons. It may constitute a recognition for services or favours rendered by city dwellers to a nephew, cousin or son of the clan head or other influential member. It may be done to reward those who help the local authorities to get administrative positions in the zone or collectivity. Sometimes it may result from succession quarrels, in which the division of clan land is followed by outright sale or by ownership passing to city residents who then sell it. Contracts have to be signed, so that the connivance of the authorities is necessary in these transactions, but since taxes are levied on land development it is easy to get official cooperation.

In this case the corruption and inefficiency of the administration enrich traditional authorities and assist in their transformation into a potential class of rural capitalists, at the expense of small cultivators who are prevented from farming, fishing or hunting on the alienated land. Some of this land is not in fact used, or is used only for cutting wood for charcoal, which causes deforestation and erosion. The result is a severe shortage of cultivable land in the area. As a result a process of proletarianization is taking place: some farmers who have lost their land rent plots from others; some become sharecroppers; others become agricultural wage labourers or migrate to town.

The governor of Lower Zaire, after a tour of inspection, wrote a letter advocating cessation of all concessions until the drawing up of an overall rational land-use plan. He called for the immediate return of undeveloped concessions to local cultivators. Bulu-Bobina doubts the capacity of the administration to carry out these recommendations.

A similar process of alienation is going on in the rich agricultural areas of Kivu. Businessmen and others are appropriating large estates for cattle farms and reafforestation, not all of which are well managed or even developed at all. The local population resents this developing capitalism, which threatens land-use rights held by traditional authorities (Newbury 1984b: 113; Vwakyanakazi 1982: 32). In 1975 a wealthy farmer organized successful resistance by forming a peasant union in Uvira, East Kivu. The union managed to block the process of land alienation, got rid of an agricultural agent who abused his powers and put pressure on the local sugar company to increase services to the peasants (Bianga 1982: 244).

The process of class formation and class struggle can be seen in some of these measures imposed by the state, in the successful resistance to them and in the counter-reactions that are provoked. We will now look at the details of some examples of class action undertaken by the political aristocracy to consolidate their position and close their boundaries against the upward mobility that threatens them.

## CLASS ACTIONS

Class action is collective action that has the effect of increasing or reducing social inequality and domination, or strengthening or weakening the means whereby the domination of a privileged stratum is maintained (Sklar 1979: 547). In Zaire 'the political aristocracy is a class in reality, and it is becoming increasingly conscious of its existence as a class for itself and therefore of the existence of generalized class interests' (Callaghy 1984: 193). The Zairianization measures, the demonetization of 1979, the attempts to control the profitable coffee sector, the mobilization of personal connections for closing boundaries against threatening upward mobility from below, all constitute recent instances of class action by the political aristocracy. It is not necessary to assume that the class effect of these actions is deliberate or conscious.

Zairianization in 1973–4 handed over foreign-owned commerce and plantations to Zairians. As described on pp. 47–48, implementation of these indigenization decrees was a class action in which political manipulation ensured the greatest benefits for those in the political-administrative hierarchy. The demonetization of 1979, like radicalization, was directed against those who were becoming wealthy through commerce, but this time specifically against those engaged in activities depriving the state of revenue and in transactions taking place outside the official financial institutions. Such accumulation constituted a threat to the class interests of the political aristocracy that required counter action. In December the president announced demonetization, in which all bills above the Z1 were to be replaced in the space of five days with new currency. It was, in fact, impossible for most people to get their money changed because of the short time allowed, the difficulty for most of the population of getting to a bank, the inadequate supply of the new currency and the embezzlement of much of it by bank officials and others. Announced as a measure to combat hoarding of money outside the banks, which had seriously depleted the state treasury and made it impossible to meet payrolls, the measure ruined many small businessmen and brought business in Kisangani almost to a standstill for two months. The politically powerful, of course, got by unscathed: by one estimate 20–40 per cent of the new money was appropriated by officials (Rymenam 1980: 52). The demonetization showed that the political class controlled not only the credit system of bank loans, but also the money supply itself. Some businessmen of the new commercial middle class were hit hard but recovered (one absorbed a loss of 1.5 million

203

zaires); others had difficulty (one has not been able to fully recover from a loss of Z600,000).

## The struggle to control coffee

Since coffee became the most important source of foreign exchange after copper in 1971, an intense struggle has taken place over control of its production and export. During the colonial period European planters dominated coffee growing. In Upper Zaire coffee plantations were started by Belgian planters when the railway was built in 1934. In Kivu in 1935–6 the efforts of the government to promote coffee cultivation among Africans by distributing free plants met with strong opposition from the European planters who organized into a union. Their objections were expressed as fear of increased theft and the spread of coffee disease because of peasant neglect; the real reasons were fears of the competition of African growers, of loss of labour and that insufficient land would be left into which to expand their plantations (European colonization had caused a land shortage from Beni in the north to Uvira in the south). As a result, African cultivation in this area did not begin until 1954 (Tshibanda 1974).

Plantations were mostly foreign-owned till 1973; the many Belgians who left in the 1960s were replaced by Greeks. With independence and the ensuing troubles, coffee production dropped from 68,867 tonnes in 1960 to 25,994 tonnes in 1962. It did not surpass the 1960 level until 1971 with 74,580 tonnes (IRES 1977: 5). Thereafter, the state moved to take control of this profitable commodity through its marketing board, ONC (*Office National du Café*), under the terms of *ordonnance* no. 72.030 of 27 July 1972, as follows:

> The purchasing and export of coffee will be done only by ONC; the Ministry of Agriculture will determine the prices to be paid to producers and the times and places of sale; seeds and plants can only be imported with the authorization of the Ministry under specified conditions; cultivators must report the acreage of their plantations to the territorial authorities of ONC; the Ministry can forbid cultivation in particular regions; ONC must authorize coffee purchasers.

After Zairianization in 1973 production dropped steeply; by 1975 it was down to 59,444 tonnes (IRES 1977: 5). The new owners were often city bureaucrats who neglected to pay their workers, supply company stores or invest in insecticides or fertilizers.[4] They invested their coffee profits in urban projects or conspicuous consumption, rather than in efficient management and improvement of their plantations (IRES 1977: 19). An additional problem was that ONC proved inadequate to the task it had set itself; its agents were late in making payments and had insufficient vehicles and even funds to collect all the harvests (IRES 1977: 7–8). It was estimated that in 1975 30 per cent of the national production remained unsold (Popelier 1977: 22). In February 1976, therefore, controls were liberalized to stimulate production, allowing more buyers and exporters and higher prices.

After this deregulation the spectacular rise in the world price of coffee later in the same year brought a coffee boom that offered lucrative opportunities to individuals from all levels of society, as described earlier. In the ensuing scramble to get into coffee exporting, the number of licensed exporters increased from 110 in March 1978 to 292 in June 1979[5] (*Conjoncture Economique* 1979: 63).

Class action soon followed as the political aristocracy mobilized the state apparatus to close this potential avenue for upward mobility. In 1979 the government imposed new regulations that if implemented would restrict coffee buying and export licences to the politically well connected and wealthy of the dominant class. *Ordonnance* no. 79.059 of March 1979 replaced ONC with OZACAF (*Office Zairois du Café*). Requirements for coffee buyers included ownership of a 50-hectare plantation or a coffee factory or a means of collecting and storing approved by OZACAF. Conditions for obtaining export licences included owning a 250-hectare plantation or proof of participation in production, sale or financing of plantations, or purchase of abandoned plantations. Former exporters had to have exported 750 tonnes to be relicensed (*Promoteur* no.3, July 1979). A rider was later added, including as a possible qualification for coffee buyer important investment contributing to the social and economic development of the region, in the opinion of the MPR authorities. Clearly this last provision allowed for the operation of political influence. The new regulations specified also that potential exporters must have proof of sufficient finances to export 500 tonnes of coffee (*Promoteur* no. 4, October 1979).

A Kinshasa newspaper pointed out that these measures were designed to eliminate smaller operators. For example, very few people had available the 3 million zaires required to export 500 tonnes of coffee (*Salongo*, 31 March 1980). As one informant put it, coffee export was being transformed into 'a game preserve (*chasse gardée*) for the authorities'. Many people complained that export licences were almost impossible to get without political connections to expedite the procedures.

The political aristocracy, however, find themselves in competition with planters of the foreign commercial class over coffee. Under the retrocession laws, former foreign owners can claim plantations that are mismanaged (Lukombe Nghenda 1979: 53–4) but the difficulties they have enforcing their claims are an indication of struggle between class sectors to control a very profitable commodity. One long case history and one short one illuminate the process of this struggle at the level of individual action.

Mr B. is a Greek coffee planter whose various enterprises were Zairianized. His largest coffee plantation, of 200 hectares, along with five trucks, a Land Rover, a Range Rover and a Mercedes, was taken by a former minister of the national government. This acquirer also took over several other plantations, shops and a fishery from other foreigners. He neglected Mr B.'s plantation, failing to visit for eleven months at a time, and by 1978 production was down by half to 200 tonnes. Mr B. is entited to retrocession of the plantation on grounds of its mismanagement, defined in Law 77–027, 17 November 1977, to include neglect, non-payment of workers and of taxes, debts and INSS (social security) dues. The acquirer was deficient in all these respects: he had not paid the plantation's workers for five months in March 1980; he owed Z40,000 to INSS, Z80,000 in taxes and Z130,000 to the bank. Attestation of the neglect and mismanagement of the plantation was certified in reports by the local agricultural officer and by the zone commissioner.

Fulfilling the conditions of the law, however, was not enough. The sub-regional commissioner refused to sign the reports, said he would have to see for himself and stalled the proceedings for six weeks. Mr B. appealed to the regional commissioner, who promised to help but who turned out to be a friend of a the ex-minister. Mr B. shortly received a letter saying that the documents from the file on the plantation were missing and that it would cost Z10,000 to open a new retrocession dossier. Mr B. had copies so was able to defeat this move. The last instalment of the saga that I heard from him was that another official on the retrocession committee had certified that the plantation was, after all, well maintained! The ex-minister by this time had been declared bankrupt, since all his businesses were neglected or badly run. Nevertheless, he was still too powerful to defeat because of his friends in high places.

In another case, a plantation was retroceded to the former foreign owner. The documents had all been put through when the acquirer turned up with a letter from the state commissioner assigning the plantation to him again. The state commissioner, it turned out, was a member of the acquirer's family. However, the foreign owner's brother-in-law worked for a powerful Zairian businessman, related to the president by marriage, with whose help the plantation was once again returned to its original owner. The foreigner in this case won because of powerful political connections.

## Personal connections and class formation

'What makes a class "classy" is its reproduction through coalition-building over time in order to deny resources to others' (Lonsdale 1981: 202). In his study of careers and social structure in Brazil, Anthony Leeds points out that informal groups and personal connections among the dominant class serve to allocate prerogatives to some while denying them to others. They constitute the inner organization of classes and 'sustain highly impermeable boundaries between the two major groups (the classes and the masses)' (Leeds 1965: 292, 295). In Africa, Abner Cohen has shown the significance of networks of interpersonal links to bring about closure of the Creole elite of Sierra Leone: 'Closure is most effectively attained through the operation of a network of amity which knits the members of the elite together. Such networks are developed to co-ordinate corporate action informally through mutual trust and co-operation' (Cohen 1981: 222). The dominant class in Zaire attempts to close its boundaries against perceived and threatening efforts at upward mobility by members of the subordinated class, by means of various networks of such personal connections or 'alliances within itself' (Callaghy 1983: 71). Such links are distinct from patron-client ties which involve relations between unequals. Jean-François Médard has pointed out the importance of these relationships between equals in African countries. Each person who holds an important position can exchange resources with another. Médard finds these exchanges play a leading role in the formation of the ruling class (1982: 171).

In Zaire personal connections are crucial for finding one's way through the bureaucracy or getting access to resources of all kinds. The poor and illiterate find the administration incomprehensible, alien and oppressive; they minimize contacts with it. The wealthy and influential backed by the power of office, are served by it and given whatever they want. Those in between these two categories must resort to personal relations (*circuits personelles*). Public officials give priority to their kin; others must pay money but if some sort of personal connection exists they need not pay so much (Malula 1980: 167–8, 173). Ties of kinship and ethnicity are used at all levels of society but other bases for personal connections are particular to the dominant class: alumni groups of schools and universities; the Lions International; the Rotary Club; and the particular kinds of personal connections known as *relations*. These ties are used to give the dominant class social and economic advantages which increase the difficulties confronting those achieving success in business in the subordinated classes.

The few secondary schools for Africans that existed before independence were an important source of connections between members of the elite (LaFontaine 1970: 100). After independence education became the primary means of entry to the new dominant class. Possession of a diploma became so important that the school system that dispensed it was dominated by the single aim of success in entering the university and neglected any alternative training (Buakasa 1980: 194). Ties between members of the same school classes became increasingly important. In the words of one influential businessman, 'A group becomes close at school then afterwards they all move up together and stay in touch and are useful to each other.'[6]

The Lions International is a philanthropic organization that raises money for good causes and creates a brotherhood between its members. These ties also serve other than philanthropic purposes, however. They are a source of useful connections for access to all sorts of goods and services controlled by the members. In Kisangani businessmen emphasized the importance of the club for developing business relations. In the words of one of them:

> The Lions Club is very helpful for business because people who are members are successful. To get in you can apply by asking a friend who is already a member to propose you. You are then taken as a guest several times before being proposed. The club meets and decides if it wants you. Once you belong

you get to know the others and if you have needs for your business perhaps
you know a Lion who may be able to help you or give preference to you as a
fellow Lion over someone else.

The proliferation of Clubs of the Lions International in the seventies and
the increasing number of nationals rather than foreigners in the membership indicate the usefulness of these connections.

The first Lions Club was founded in Kinshasa in 1957; by 1963 there
were nine more. None were founded during the troubled sixties, but eleven
started up in Zaire's major towns and cities between 1972 and 1979. In
1979 clubs totalled twenty-two. Twelve had from twenty to twenty-nine
members, five had thirty to thirty-nine and the three clubs in Kinshasa had
over forty. Of the clubs founded up to 1963, seven out of ten have a
majority of foreigners among their members; clubs founded after 1972 have
a majority of nationals in all but two cases.[7]

Membership lists show a roster of occupations from the ranks of the
influential and wealthy: officials of the government, the MPR and the
CND; lawyers and magistrates; professors, university administrators and
secondary school principals; businessmen, managers of big wholesale
houses and brewery officials; architects, agronomists and engineers;
directors of banks and companies; executives of railway and mining
companies, of Air Zaire and OZACAF; doctors and pharmacists; and
missionaries. The importance of connections to such people in the current
political and economic situation is obvious. The Rotary Club operates in
similar fashion. The Kisangani club had a membership list of twenty-three
Rotarians in 1980; nine of them were nationals.

Lioness Clubs founded in the last few years are also spreading: in 1980
there were four. They reflect the increasing activity of women in business,
the independence from men that this signifies and the need for women
to develop their own sets of personal connections as their position in society
improves. Lionesses in Kisangani are, as yet, mostly wives of Lions:
thirteen out of seventeen in 1979–80.

In Kisangani the activities of the Lions International in 1979 included a
dance held for a visit by the national governor of the club, and a raffle and
Ladies' Night to raise money for the city's leprosarium. Of the Z23,000
raised Z4,000 went for prizes, the remaining Z19,000 for the leprosarium.
In 1980 another raffle raised Z26,000. In earlier years they had built a
maternity clinic and presented gifts to an old people's home and to the
destitute.

In 1980 membership in ANEZA, the Chamber of Commerce, was
becoming more important as a source of useful connections, with its
increasing recognition by the government. One of the independent
businessmen was its president in Kisangani.

Another, different kind of personal connections, known as *'relations'*,
are deliberately initiated among individuals in the dominant class. Informal
groups form which include persons of expertise in different fields who can

offer one another mutual assistance in dealing with the bureaucracy or in getting access to specific resources.[8] They are maintained by visiting, buying drinks and giving money or small presents to the children and subordinates of the other party in the relationship: money is not otherwise exchanged. These ties are specifically and deliberately set up across ethnic boundaries. They are said to constitute 'the new tribalism', meaning bonds between members of the dominant class. The first items on Buakasa's list of necessary conditions for acquiring official position is 'to have "*relations*": to be known by "important" persons (have informal power), and among them to have one or more sponsors, directly or through an intermediary' (Buakasa 1980: 194). Personal connections between equals exist in all classes, but they are less effective for getting things done in the subordinate classes than they are in the dominant class.[9] Ordinary people must seek to be clients of influential and powerful patrons.

For ordinary people in town, struggling to make their way up, kin, ethnic or sexual connections to the powerful are the only way to surmount daily difficulties. One businesswoman summarized the problem of getting goods from the wholesalers:

> You have to know someone who has influence with the authorities, or you have to be a member of a wholesale manager's family, or his wife's or have a sexual relationship, or pay bribes. Otherwise the wholesaler says the goods are finished—and then you see them being given out to someone else.

One Kongo market-stall owner got part of her supply of cigarettes from a Kongo Manager of a firm supplied by BAT. On one occasion in 1979, she got five sacks of sugar from a Kongo woman who, although not a licensed trader, got them from the Kongo manager of a big wholesaler. The stall owner paid Z150 a sack and sold at Z170, a 13 per cent mark-up.

Another stall owner, who did not have good connections, spent hours of every day waiting at the wholesale warehouses. He sold soap, cooking oil, sardines, matches, corned beef and tomato paste at his stall on the edge of the market. He was on the lists of regular customers of SEDEC and MARSAVCO, but all he got from them at the official price was a carton or so, quite insufficient to supply his stall. 'It is only possible to get larger quantities if you have a "*frère*" among the managers: someone from the same ethnic group, especially the same village; a schoolfriend, or a friend from a previous place of employment.' The alternative was to supply his stall from the travelling traders who brought goods up from Kinshasa by plane and sold them at high prices. When his supplies were good, this man had a turnover of Z1,000 a day, otherwise it was a mere Z100–200.

These various kinds of connections are of critical importance in the daily life of people of all class levels. The information on them is anecdotal because, given their nature, any kind of systematic investigation is impossible. Kannyo has emphasized the close clientelistic relations necessary between politicians and businessmen (Kannyo 1979: 154). This

209

does not, however, mean that the commercial class and the political class are merged: connections of some sort to politically powerful individuals are necessary for success beyond a minimal level in all fields, but forming such connections is distinct from the massive manipulation of public office for personal interests by the political aristocracy or from partnership with them in such endeavours.

To conclude and sum up: to make sense of the combination of weakness and strength apparent in the operation of the Zairian state, we must refer to both external and internal factors, from the workings of the world capitalist system to class, gender, ethnic and other struggles within Zaire. This chapter has detailed class struggle and conflict. It has shown how the political aristocracy uses the apparatus of the state to further its interest; how the wage and price structure, and taxation and licences oppress wage workers and small farmers; how restrictions on access to foreign exchange and to bank credit favour the powerful; and how marketing boards operate to exploit petty commodity producers and transfer resources from rural to urban areas. All these instances exemplify the attempt of capital to control the productive process without directly organizing it or dispossessing the producers. The weakness of the administrative capacity of the state has allowed just the kind of successful resistance to such control that Bernstein, Cooper and Kitching describe (see Chapter 1). In the sabotage of compulsory cotton-growing programmes, the evasion of official prices for palm oil and the recourse to second economy production and distribution, we see the struggle of petty producers and wage workers against various sections of capital: the parasitic political aristocracy, the multinational plantation owners, and the new indigenous capitalists who have moved into commercial agriculture. This interplay of attempted control and successful resistance, which sometimes opens up mobility opportunities constitutes the dynamic of an ongoing class struggle in an economic system in which labour is not completely alienated from the means of production, and shows how the emergence of the new, true capitalist class is part of a much wider process.

# Conclusion

Observers of Zaire have held the view that 'no economic bourgeoisie is currently in process of formation' (Rymenam 1977; Verhaegen 1978: 377), or that 'the national bourgeois elite...have in effect absorbed the commercial bourgeoisie' (D. Gould 1978: 34). They assert that technological dependence favours Western capitalist interests and prevents local development, and that the insecure political situation prevents investment of agricultural surplus and inhibits the growth of a local bourgeoisie.

It is said that the persistence of non-capitalist modes of production in articulation with capitalism makes it unlikely that a strong indigenous entrepreneurial bourgeoisie can develop. In countries, such as Ghana suffering the same crises of shortages and high rates of inflation as Zaire, where the wealth of the military and the bureaucracy is similarly paraded in conspicuous consumption rather than being invested in production, and where scarce resources are manipulated and smuggled, 'one of the main victims of the crisis is the emergent national bourgeoisie involved in small-scale manufacture (Hutchful 1979: 54).

These assessments, however, focus only on the constraints and do not consider the opportunities inherent in prevailing economic and political circumstances. The crises into which Zaire has been plunged since independence have created problems for aspiring entrepreneurs, but also potential opportunities for those with initiative, enterprise and a measure of good fortune. The political aristocracy pillages the system but does not control it because the weakened administrative capacity of the state allows people to evade its attempts to impose commodity production and wage labour for exploitatively low returns. Nor can the political aristocracy monopolize opportunities opened up by the indigenization of foreign capital, the trading profits made possible by the articulation of modes of production, and the lucrative activities of the second economy, all of which open up the system and make possible a certain amount of socio-economic mobility.

Callaghy observes that fiscal largesse and corruption are the glue that holds the system together (Callaghy 1984: 202). But an equally significant reason the system holds together is that at all levels of society a number of individuals are doing very well for themselves in a variety of second economy activities. The significance of this fact for class formation has hitherto been ignored. This study has shown that one result of the opportunities for capital accumulation presented by these circumstances or inherent in the system itself has been that a small local capitalist class has recently begun to form, a nascent true bourgeoisie that, in its involvement with productive enterprise run in rational capitalist fashion and producing for the local market, is distinct from the parasitic aristocracy.

We have examined the processes by which this class has come into being, looking at both the political and economic factors affecting its development: the power structure, the nature of the state and its class base, the nature of the economy, the interventions of international capital and the effects of world recession. What this study emphasizes and what is generally left out of the pessimistic assessments of the developmental potential of underdeveloped countries, is the element of struggle, the on-the-ground, dynamic reality of class relations, of gender discrimination, of ethnicity. The material presented here has shown how ways have been found to circumvent oppressive regulations and to take advantage of opportunities; how class sectors have mobilized specific mechanisms, either informally or by use of the state apparatus and formal institutions, to close their boundaries against mobility from below. The data from Kisangani and Kivu presented here document the ways in which some individuals succeed, some fail; it has shown how relations between classes and between their component sectors appear in individual as well as in collective actions.

The question remains, what of the future of this small local capitalist class? Why is it not bigger than it is, what chances does it have for expansion? Schatzberg and Callaghy are pessimistic. Schatzberg dismisses the 'true' Zairian bourgeoisie as small and relatively unimportant, both politically and economically (Schatzberg 1982: 14); Callaghy, having detailed the ways in which the arbitrariness of the patrimonial state is unfavourable to capitalist investment and the rational organization of free labour (Callaghy 1984: 75–8), argues that as the indigenous capitalist class becomes more important, Mobutu and the political aristocracy will have to cut off or control its development (*ibid*.: 188). But the strongest evidence for the inability of Mobutu and the political aristocracy to exercise such control is the extent and pervasiveness of second economy activities evading state control. The administrative apparatus of the state is simply not efficient enough to impose control over political and economic processes as did the colonial state in the past. Mobutu and his cohorts strive by formal legal or institutional means, as well as by informal ones, to exert the control Callaghy envisions, but the outcome of the struggle so far allows for a reasonable doubt as to its future course. Apart from the weakness of state administration in general, as evidenced in the size of the second economy, the larger businessmen of the new commercial middle class were simply too well established and powerful to be destroyed or controlled by the measures of radicalization and demonetization, two of the most important attempts by the state to destory or exert control over this class sector so far.

In reality, the state seems willing, up to a point, to tolerate and come to arrangements with members of the new bourgeoisie. Mr T., for example, is in fact, allowed a licence to trade with China; the Kivu millionaire was once thrown in jail, but only briefly. In general, compromises of a sort are reached. Little data are available, but some entrepreneurs undoubtedly buy influence and protection, while others refuse to do so. The wealth and scale of operations of some of them seem to put them beyond the reach of government interference. So far the state has certainly not played a crucial role in assisting the formation of the local capitalist class and mediating its relationship with foreign capital, as it has in Kenya (Swainson 1980). But in Zaire, since the economy is desperately in need of the kind of rational management and expansion of productive enterprise that is evidenced in the businesses of members of this class, it is possible that the political aristocracy, under heavy pressure from the international aid organizations to reform their pillaging mode of operation, will find it in their interest to encourage the expansion of these local capitalist entrepreneurs. If the emergent bourgeoisie expands and consolidates, and comes to exert power over the state, its interests may better be served by limited government rather than by 'unstable, repressive regimes subject to revolution' (Sklar 1979: 542). In the long term, as Leys points out, the political power of domestic capital is crucial (Leys 1982: 113).

The new capitalist class has not been in process of formation for very long. Its numbers are so far small, but the reasons for this are not only the constraints of the colonial period and the difficulties of the recent political and economic situation. Many people have tried to enter business; in the shake out process that has occurred those who have lacked the necessary skills, talent and persistence have fallen by the wayside. Those who have these qualities and who have managed to surmount the problems confronting them do not yet exist in large numbers, but they are becoming established and will train others to succeed them; their numbers will increase over time.

Capitalism penetrated the African continent at a relatively late stage in its global development; in consequence it has followed a different course in African countries than it did in Europe and North America. Nevertheless, as Callaghy (1987) has pointed out, the tendency to see capitalist development in the West as having been uncontradictory or unproblematic is an exaggeration of historical reality; earlier stages of development of the advanced capitalist countries showed many of the features considered distinctive in peripheral capitalism, such as regional or urban/rural inequality, markedly dualistic labour markets and 'informal sector' activities (Kitching 1982: 163). The path of capitalist development is inevitably uneven in Africa, as it was in Europe, and contingent upon particular historical circumstances and periods, upon the fluctuations of the global economy and its changing demands for particular commodities, and upon the processes of domestic class struggle and forms of class structure.

# Appendix: Population figures

*Population growth of Kisangani 1959–79*

|  | Men | Women | Boys | Girls | Total |
|------|------|------|------|------|------|
| 1959 |  |  |  |  | 105,666* |
| 1969 | 46,698 | 63,085 | 50,778 | 44,687 | 205,248** |
| 1970 | 58,964 | 60,092 | 57,162 | 53,178 | 229,396 |
| 1971 | 56,527 | 66,223 | 59,396 | 50,379 | 232,525*** |
| 1972 | 56,344 | 69,876 | 66,639 | 65,388 | 258,247 |
| 1973 | 63,867 | 77,088 | 69,492 | 66,152 | 276,599 |
| 1974 | 71,270 | 84,262 | 77,992 | 73,449 | 306,973 |
| 1975 | 82,724 | 94,520 | 86,154 | 90,208 | 353,606 |
| 1976 | 65,629 | 71,861 | 75,294 | 72,172 | 284,956 |
| 1977 | 70,400 | 74,042 | 75,224 | 70,145 | 289,811 |
| 1978 | 67,213 | 71,433 | 80,256 | 76,876 | 295,778 |
| 1979 | 65,331 | 71,342 | 75,672 | 69,264 | 281,609 |

*Verhaegen 1979: 6 **Does not include zone of Makiso
***General census, IRS, gives 231,470, including 2,434 foreigners (Verhaegen 1979:9)

*Foreign population by zone 1972–9*

|  | Makiso | Tshopo | Mangobo | Kabondo | Kisan-gani | Lubunga | Total |
|------|------|------|------|------|------|------|------|
| 1972 | 718 | 215 | 7 | 41 | — | — | 981 |
| 1973 | 998 | 152 | 7 | 71 | — | 38 | 1266 |
| 1974 | 533 | 137 | 11 | 42 | — | 14 | 737 |
| 1975 | 726 | 1* | 5 | 35 | — | 10 | 777 |
| 1976 | 727 | 181 | 6 | 37 | — | 19 | 970 |
| 1977 | 614 | 147 | 45 | 49 | — | 18 | 873 |
| 1979 | 940 | 436** | 38 | 48 | 5 | 5 | 1472 |

* In 1975 West Africans were expelled only to return in 1976.
**Increase reflects influx of West Africans. 1978 n.a.
*Source*: Town Hall, Kisangani.

# Notes

## 1 Indigenous capitalism in peripheral economies: some theoretical considerations

1 According to Marx a commodity is profitable if its value is greater than the sum of the values of the commodities used in its production (that is, labour and the means of production). This 'surplus' value is the means by which capitalism expands:

> The only worker who is productive is one who produces surplus-value for the capitalist, or in other words contributes towards the self-valorization of capital...the concept of a productive worker therefore implies not merely a relation between the activity of work and its useful effect...but also a specifically social relation of production, a relation with a historical origin which stamps the worker as capital's direct means of valorization. (Marx 1976: 644)

Labour power is the sole commodity which 'produces' value greater than its own value.

2 By the 1970s Schatz finds Nigeria to have moved to what he terms 'Pirate Capitalism' as a result of the oil boom. The economy is inert with no power to generate growth outside the oil sector, and 'access to and manipulation of the government spending process has become the golden gateway to fortune' (Schatz 1984).

3 Jean-Loup Amselle also describes the state-based class of African countries in terms of their pillaging and clientelistic rather than productive economic activity. He refers to this class in Mali as a 'nomenklatura', the term for such a class in the USSR (Amselle 1985).

4 'A mode of production is a three-part system: an economic base, a juridico-political superstructure and an ideological superstructure' (Terray 1972: 97).

5 References are to English translations of these works where they exist.

6 Henry Bernstein prefers to talk in terms of the relations between peasant households and capital, rather than of articulation of modes of production. He argues against the concept of articulation of capitalist and non-capitalist modes on the grounds that the penetration of capitalism destroys the conditions of reproduction of these modes; they do not persist and articulation is an irrelevant concept. Therefore instead of 'modes' he talks of 'forms' of production. He himself, however, is not very happy with this formulation, noting that it cannot specify the relations of production (Bernstein 1977: 68). Another objection is that in lumping all 'peasant households' into a single category, he provides no grounds on which to distinguish them and leaves us unable to recognize the manifest empirical differences among the lineage, hunter-gatherer and tribute-based societies we find in Zaire.

7 This definition is taken from Feige's study of the underground economy in the US (Feige 1979: 5).

216

8 Grossman describes the 'illegal economy' of the USSR in terms that, as we will see, can be matched point for point in Zaire. He lists the activities of this economy as follows: theft, including theft of company time, and poaching; speculation, or the purchase and resale of goods for gain, and middleman activity; illicit production of commodities or services; and corruption. Most of the conditions he considers favourable to the development of this economy in Russia exist also in Zaire: price control with prices below equilibrium levels; high taxes; personal power in the hands of bureaucratic officials which quickly turns into the exploitation of the powers of office for personal gain; and the needs of a poor population where the sharp drop in the purchasing power of salaries increases bribe-taking by individuals (Grossman 1979: 836–42).

9 Charmes defines the 'unstructured sector' in Tunisia as activities unmeasured by official statistics and missing from national accounts (1982: 223). His definition is thus the same as the one used here, but he only actually describes small-scale enterprise. Alejandro Portes includes *all* income producing activities outside formal sector wages and social security in the informal sector (Portes and Walton 1981: 87), and thus uses a definition wider in scope than mine.

10 I have avoided using the term 'informal economy' because it usually connotes the small-scale activities of the urban poor. Of the other terms commonly used, 'parallel' is inaccurate, since this sector of the economy intersects in so many ways with the official one, while 'underground' denies the often overt characer of many of the transactions in question.

11 Marx used the concepts of the formal and real subsumption of labour to specify the process of capitalist penetration into already existing modes of production:

> Capital subsumes the labor process as it finds it, that is to say, it takes over an *existing labor process*, developed by different and more archaic modes of production... This stands in striking contrast to the development of a *specifically capitalist mode of production* (large-scale industry, etc.); the latter not only transforms the situations of the various agents of production, it also *revolutionizes* their actual mode of labor and the real nature of the labor process as a whole. It is in contradistinction to this last that we come to designate as the *formal subsumption of labor under capital*... the takeover by capital of a mode of labor developed before the emergence of capitalist relations, (Marx 1976: 1021)

Some of Geschiere's summary of the later work of Rey, in which these notions are central, is helpful here:

> Under formal subsumption of labor, the control of the dominant class remains restricted to the organization of the production, for instance in instituting wider forms of cooperation among the direct producers. Only under real subsumption of labor, when the dominant class succeeds in interfering directly with the technical aspects of the labor process, does its dominance take roots in the production process. Then it becomes to a certain extent irreversible: the direct producers can no longer continue their labor process without dependence on the dominant class. (Geschiere 1985: 87)

12 See Leys 1980; Kaplinsky 1980; Beckmans 1980; Langdon 1977. A similar debate has occurred over the Ivory Coast; it is succinctly summarized by Martin Staniland (1985: 169–75).

## 2 The political and economic context: from colonial oppression to the fend for yourself present

1 In 1950 59 per cent of the male population of working age was employed in commercial production. This degree of proletarianization was one of the highest in Africa, constituting a fundamental characteristic of the Congo economy. By 1959 manufacturing industry had

absorbed over 10 per cent of salaried workers, placing the Congo foremost in employment of industrial workers on the continent (Lacroix 1967: 25–7; see also Nzongola 1982: 69–70). These figures make Zaire's economic crisis and collapse since independence all the more striking.

2 The system was enforced with appalling ruthlessness and brutality, with the aid of African personnel not local to the area of their posting and thus strangers to the population. In addition, local 'capitas' were employed and armed with firearms, often individuals who were 'detached' in the villages; they became tyrants with parasitic followers (Buell 1928: 431). The system constituted a grim antecedent for the present one, which also ensures that government and military personnel are not local to the area, and some of whom, in the more remote areas, become brutal despots.

3 Schatzberg notes the ability of the professional magistrature to mount some institutional resistance to the political power of the regime. The judiciary has greater autonomy and independence than other branches of the state and is realtively less corrupt. Salaries of magistrates and lower level judicial administrators are relatively generous, and their career security is greater than that of political administrators (Schatzberg: forthcoming, ch. 6).

4 In 1977 Citibank estimated that the Presidential Brotherhood (the powerful clique surrounding Mobutu), the Bank of Zaire and GECAMINES each controlled about one-third of the total foreign exchange (Young 1983: 120).

5 In 1974–7 public investment in agriculture, health and education represented only 5.3 per cent of the capital expenditures of the state (Bézy *et al.*, 1981: 70).

6 The nine regions of Zaire in 1980 (see Map 1) were administered by regional commissioners and their assistants, their component sub-regions by sub-regional commissioners and assistants; all appointed by the president. Sub-regions are divided into zones, urban ones had a council of elected members who elected a zone commissioner. Zones consist of collectivities divided into localities, both headed by chiefs appointed by the State Commissioner for Political Affairs.

7 One was of the Delegate General of Air Zaire. It was revealed that the airline had not submitted accounts for several years; that in 1974 it had 3,000 employees and twenty-five planes, but in 1979, although it only had thirteen planes, it had 6,554 employees ('C'est une situation anormale'); and that it ran a chronic deficit, although in Brussels its receipts equalled 156 FB million and its expenses were only 36 million (*Boyoma* 3 January 1980).

8 Cooper points out that, although in Africa in general capital has not won the battle to make production predictable and orderly, it can, nevertheless, concentrate selectively and to its own advantage where it will make this attempt. In Zaire its interests are served so long as the copper mines keep running (Cooper 1981: 51). Palm oil plantations, on the other hand, have become a better proposition in South East Asia and investment has shifted there from Zaire.

9 This analysis focuses primarily on class sectors, a somewhat clumsy term that, for convenience, will be used interchangeably with class.

10 According to Rymenam, the first two categories constitute a 'comprador' bourgeoisie: their interests are tied to the imperialist powers and they do not invest in productive enterprise but in consumption, family and clients, real estate, commerce and transport enterprises, and overseas bank accounts (Rymenam 1980).

11 Young and Turner include all foreigners in their category of 'external estate' (1985: 106–10).

12 The foreign commercial class corresponds to Demunter's *Moyenne Bourgeoisie* of the colonial period. He specifies that their stage of development of production limited the possibilities of their development above a certain threshold, making them dependent for the commercialization of their products on the *Haute Bourgeoisie* of the multinationals and other big European companies (Demunter 1972: 83–6).

218

13 Nzongola uses the popular categories of 'intellectuals' and 'traders' to identify classes that he refers to as the national bourgeoisie, who took over the positions occupied by Europeans after independence (politicians, bureaucrats, professionals and students), and the petty bourgeoisie (including as well as traders, clerks, teachers, nurses, soldiers and police) (Nzongola 1970: 518–19). These correspond approximately to two of the 'social groups' (not classes) identified by Comeliau in Uele on the basis of degree of participation in the money economy. He, however, includes wealthy traders in his bourgeoisie, and other traders and independents form a third, separate, group from his sub-bourgeoisie (Comeliau 1965: 75–89). Young and Turner use the term 'Politico-Commercial Class' as the equivalent of Nzongola's national bourgeoisie (1985: 110–20).

## 3 Business and class in Kisangani

1 Sources included the incomplete list provided by the Town Hall, the membership rolls of the Chamber of Commerce (ANEZA), of the Lions, Lioness and Rotary clubs, and the list of acquirers of businesses in Zairianization. Dues are too large for small businesses to join ANEZA; the amount varies according to the size of the enterprise, but the minimum in 1980 was Z600. The Lions, Lioness and Rotary clubs included citizens prominent in business and other areas among their members. I confirmed the importance in the business community of the individuals on my list by further investigation and by checking with the director of ANEZA, with an official of the government's economic office and with the presidents of the Lioness Club and the Asian community.
2 I interviewed and collected life histories among these business owners and others who represented a range of class positions: administrators and officials; Asian, Greek and Belgian businessmen; managers of wholesale firms and owners of market stalls; Nande traders from Kivu. In all I interviewed a total of eighty-two people and collected thirty-eight life histories. Interviews lasted from forty minutes to an hour and a half and in some cases I returned for follow up interviews up to four or five times.
3 Nicola Swainson, in her study of corporate capital in Kenya, makes the same distinction between those individuals who occupy places in the political order and those who are primarily businessmen (Swainson 1980:204).
4 In 1971 the Congolese franc (CF) was replaced by the zaire (Z), valued at Z0.50 to the US dollar and divided into 100 makuta (K). In March 1976, the zaire was fixed at Z1.1 to the SDR (Special Drawing Rights). Devaluations in 1978, 1979 and 1980 attempted to give the zaire a realistic value, but the black market or parallel rate was more generally in use. In February 1980 Z1 = US \$0.34 and the parallel rate was Z1 = US \$0.20.
5 In Kenya too, Marris and Somerset stress that even when formal constraints were lifted after independence, African businessmen still had to succeed in a commercial network dominated by foreigners who had a great advantage in their extensive business contacts (Marris and Somerset 1972: 233).
6 Ruakabuba himself owns a huge company, RWACICO, consisting of 700 hectares of coffee, tea, vegetable, cinchona and peanut plantations, a tea factory, and general stores in four towns. The company also buys coffee, exporting 13,000 tonnes in 1976–9; it was the largest coffee exporter in Zaire in 1977–8 (*Promoteur* No. 1 1978). Nevertheless, this company, like others belonging to the political aristocracy, is not well managed. In 1978 Ruakabuba was falling behind on bank loans and was Z7.8 million in debt.

## 4 Opportunities for capital accumulation: the emergence of an indigenous bourgeoisie

1 Schatzberg points out that one of the tragedies of Zairianization is that marginal and shaky businesses were more likely to be found in rural areas and small towns. They were unlikely to recover from the ill effects of this episode and the rural population were, in consequence, likely to suffer the most from it (Schatzberg 1980a:152).

2 Since any real class system is fluid, in contrast to the rigidity of Marx's analytical model, individuals move between classes. The new commercial class in Kisangani includes two individuals who were politicians for a brief spell in the past but were unable to maintain this position; in the future some others may become politicians. In the elections of 1977 men locally prominent because of their business actvities were elected peoples' commissioners.
3 The list was not comprehensive. It showed coffee, rubber, palm and cocoa plantations, giving the name of the former foreign owner and that of the Zairian acquirer, in some cases showing payment by the new owner. It distinguished plantations assigned by the Minister of State after the decree from those simply taken up, and those which were abandoned and subsequently taken up.
4 In Ghana Kennedy found the proportion of relatives employed in the majority of firms to be quite small. His data on 168 businessmen in Accra, 1967–70, showed that 28 per cent avoided employing kinsmen and did so rarely; 30 per cent provided employment for relatives only if they were qualified and vacancies existed; 43 per cent felt it was necessary to employ relatives if they needed work; and 9 per cent preferred to employ them. Economic help was received from relatives by 42 per cent (Kennedy 1980: 109–10).
5 Since 1980, Peemans also finds a new nucleus of private capital, no longer restricted to marketing but oriented towards investment in production, mainly for the internal market, and including national as well as foreign capital. Investments in agricultural projects have represented about 60 per cent of the investments approved under the investment code. He comments: 'Of course one should not exaggerate the height and reality of this structure for the time being. But it is an emerging tendency which can take more importance with time' (Peemans 1986: 79–82).
6 I am indebted to Wyatt MacGaffey for this case history.
7 Politicians and other nationals who own large businesses often employ foreign managers because of their experience, connections and assumed reliability. Their salaries are high: an Asian working as a coffee buyer for a politician in Kisangani in 1980, for example, made Z7,000 a month, plus Z2,000 for housing, car and medical expenses. Foreigners thus cost much more than nationals. One of the breweries pays forty-nine foreigners Z4 million annually; its 12,000 Zairian labour force total wage bill is only Z1.4 million. Nationals resent the size of this pay differential; one example given to me bitterly, was from the building trade where a foreigner was paid Z5,000 a month and a Zairian with the same job and the same qualifications only Z800.

## 5 Opportunities for capital accumulation: fending for oneself in the second economy

1 I am indebted to Frederick L. Pryor for this distinction.
2 International conservation agencies report that between 1979 and 1982 the tusks of 107,000 elephants were shipped out of the Sudan where ivory trading is legal. Much of this ivory is believed to have come from Zaire and the Central African Republic.
3 Papain, made from the latex of papaya fruit, is a valuable export of the northeast. Processed into a powder, it is packed in hermetically sealed containers and exported by air to Belgium, Germany and the United States for pharmaceuticals, meat tenderizer cheese-making and the leather industry. Zaire is one of the largest producers in the world, producing 243 tonnes in 1972, 132 in 1976. Official export was monopolized in 1980 by one company but the number of small peasant producers allows for a lucrative and, I was told, large-scale, illegal export trade on which, unfortunately, no estimates exist.
4 By 1984 the situation had improved, but a worker still had to work for sixteen hours to buy a kilogram of rice, and eighty days for a sack of manioc, Kinshasa's staple food (Mubake 1984: 268).
5 The okapi is a small member of the giraffe family. It is almost extinct and is officially a protected animal.

6 The value of the Congo franc at independence in 1960 was 100 CF = 100 FB = US $2. The value of the franc declined rapidly thereafter and was subject to frequent fluctuation:
 November 1961 130 FC = 100 FB, 1 US$ = 65 FC
 November 1963 sale: 300 FC = 100 FB, US$ 1 = 150 FC
  purchase: 360 FC = 100 FB, US$1 = 180 FC
(Bézy *et al.*, 1981: 75)

7 In north Mayombe in 1963, rice cost 14 FC a kilogram in the stores of a big company, 20 FC in the stores in town and 40 FC in stores in the interior supplied by travelling traders. Salt per kilogram was 5.5 FC, 20 FC and 25 FC respectively. Dried fish was sold at 50 FC a kilogram by the company, but at 180 FC at the stores in town; cotton cloth likewise at 40 FC and 75 FC a metre (Dupriez 1968: 721 n.49).

8 Zaire's five most valuable exports in 1964, in thousands of zaires, were: copper 76,190, palm oil 17,588, diamonds 14,340, coffee 13,808, cobalt 9,333 (Bézy *et al.*, 1981: 222–4).

9 Diamond fraud decreased considerably after the industry was liberalized in 1983. The ending of the MIBA company monopoly and a 77.5 per cent devaluation of the zaire combined to produce a sharp increase in official diamond exports. In 1984, seventeen independent diamond purchasing offices bought 63 per cent of the national output as MIBA was obliged to hand over 73,000 hectares of its 78,000-hectare concession to small-scale diggers. The richest area was retained by the company but was constantly invaded by illicit diggers: during the dry season there is an estimated total of 60,000 diggers in the Mbuji Mayi area, although MIBA employs only 6,000 (*Financial Times*, 9 July 1985). One newspaper reported the operations of unlicensed buyers and continued smuggling (*Kasai*, no. 38, September 1984).

10 A similar situation is reported in Ghana where the most important medium of capital accumulation is the chit system of the state corporations: goods are supplied on credit at controlled prices and sold on the open market for much more (Hutchful 1979: 51).

11 This tea comes from Kivu. A report by a Canadian development agency operating in the area expresses puzzlement at the amount of tea exported from Butembo to Isiro to the north: 'Since the quantity exceeds any reasonable estimate for local consumption...one might ask where this tea is going to, and if it is exported, which is probable, why choose the route to Isiro which is not a frontier post and has no international airport?' (*Société de Développement International Desjardins* 1981: 114). The answer would seem to be that it is destined for illegal export to the Sudan!

12 The youth movement of the MPR.

13 David Gould lists more of such words and phrases (1980: 123).

14 I own thanks to Jane Parpart for pointing this out to me. Yves Médard observes that neo-patrimonial states differ from patrimonial states in their confusion over public and private domains: 'In neo-patrimonial societies, although the state is a facade compared to what it pretends to be, it is not only a facade, for it is able to extract and distribute resources. For legitimation it refers to public norms and universal ideologies' (Médard 1982: 180).

## 6 Long-distance trade, smuggling and the new commercial class: the Nande of North Kivu

1 I am greatly indebted to a Nande university student who acted as a voluntary research assistant and introduced me to Nande businessmen in Kisangani. I collected case histories in Kisangani, spent two weeks in Butembo and Beni and subsequently followed up some contacts to Nande in Kinshasa. The superb report on the commercialization of agricultural products in northeast Zaire, prepared for the Canadian International Development Agency, *Société de Développement International Desjardins* (henceforth SDID), in 1981, and kindly made available to me by M. Claude Miville, supplies the quantitative data on Nande trade that I had not the means to acquire.

2 Beans are also grown in quantity in Ituri around Bunia. Kivu primarily produces the coloured variety, Ituri the white.

3 A bush, the bark of which contains quinine.

4 TMK is a transportation company only and does not engage in commerce. In 1980 it owned about 100 trucks (SDID 1981: 97).

5 The Bambole, for example, in 1970 numbered only about 25,000 (Bongele Yeikolo 1975: 123); the Wagenia, who lived around Stanley Falls, only 7,000 (Droogers 1975: 153).

6 I made repeated attempts to interview some Nande businesswomen in Kisangani but was unsuccessful. One was a university graduate who had abandoned her professional career in favour of commerce. She refused my requests for an interview. Repeated efforts to contact another failed because she was so often out of town. The only Nande businesswoman I succeeded in talking to was the manager of the Kisangani branch of Number 6 in Table 6.2, the daughter of the owner. Only one man proved impossible to interview. He was the owner of one of the largest Nande businesses and though consenting to an interview he stood us up several times, so that we finally concluded that he did not in fact want to talk. The general opinion was that women were heavily involved in second economy trade and did not, therefore, want anyone, even their family members to know the details of their businesses.

7 Another informant produced a 15-kilogram chunk of onyx which he offered to me for Z35,000.

8 Kimpianga Mahania observes that one of the consequences of Protestant and Catholic evangelization was that while most of the elite was Catholic, a majority of those engaged in commerce was Protestant. The Catholics had far more post-primary education; before 1950 the Protestants only had primary or bible schools. Lacking the necessary education for employment in the colonial bureaucracy, they took up commerce as the only occupation for which their education fitted them (Kimpianga 1980: 113–14).

9 Wyatt MacGaffey cites cooperative efforts for local improvement in Lower Zaire that were likewise suppressed by the authorities (W. MacGaffey 1970: 284).

## 7 Gender and class formation: businesswomen in Kisangani

1 The increased vulnerability of women to male control in colonial as opposed to pre-colonial society is discussed by, for example, Etienne and Leacock (1982: 17–22) and by Schuster (1984).

2 A Yoruba woman's role, for example, was as much trader and producer as wife and mother, and women were widely involved in trade and business (Sudarkasa 1973: 160). Among most Zairian peoples women were not automatically expected to go into commerce and their doing so was often regarded with suspicion.

3 An abundant river trade in food and food crops on the Kasai River was observed by Anthony Oberschall in a stretch of Bandundu officially considered to have no marketed food crops (Oberschall 1981: 3).

4 Claire Robertson considers 'elite women' engaged in large-scale commerce in Accra to be merely dependent on 'superior access to influential men' (Robertson 1984: 16, 133, 242). Dinan and LaFontaine, in contrast, stress the economic potential of manipulation of women's sexual roles for achievement of economic independence, which for some can lead to economic power (Dinan 1983; LaFontaine 1974; J. MacGaffey 1987).

5 In October 1979 it increased again to Z800 and in March 1980 to Z1,176.

6 There are some exceptions. The director of an important national institution got the job solely because he was the lover of the woman who was Minister of Culture at the time, one of the few women to have held political position at the national level.

7 Women in Zambia suffer comparable problems. In a study of educated women in Lusaka, Schuster found these town women to be exploited and oppressed by men: 'male politicians, like male university students, cannot believe that women can achieve greater success than

they through merit, only through sleeping with some important man' (Schuster 1979: 101). There is a 'deep ambivalence in Zambian society towards a modernising role for women' (Schuster 1984: 21). The situation is the same in Uganda (Obbo 1980: ch. 1).

8 Schuster suggests that in Africa income-earning men are a scarce resource and that access to them is a source of competition for women and of divisiveness amongst them (Schuster 1984:19). This certainly holds true in Kisangani where men, especially foreigners, control resources to which women seek access.

## 8 State, class and power: the effect of administrative decline on class formation

1 In 1970–75 100 FB = Z1; in 1976 100 FB = Z2.36.
2 Zaire is the largest consumer of American wheat in western Africa after Nigeria (Bézy *et al.*, 1981: 201).
3 For a full discussion see W. MacGaffey 1982.
4 *Boyoma* gave an account of one, the new owner of a plantation in Isiro, who arrived by plane in Kisangani expecting to take a cab to his new property. When he discovered it was a two-day journey into the interior he returned to Kinshasa in disgust on the next plane.
5 Ivory Coast, the largest producer of coffee in Africa had only sixty coffee exporters at this time (*Conjoncture Economique* 1978: 41).
6 Reunions maintain such contacts and provide new ones: in Kisangani in 1979, Political Commissioner Zamundu Agenong'ka held the alumni reunion of the Frères Maristes at his house, with a reception afterwards (*Boyoma* 21 December 1979).
7 One is in Kinshasa which has a large foreign business population. The other is the Butembo club in Kivu, which Nande businessmen refuse to join because a number of Luba, with whom the Nande do not get along, are members.
8 They are directly comparable to the *panelinha* described by Leeds in Brazil. These relatively closed informal groups are held together by personal ties and members are selected to include a roster of key socio-economic positions (Leeds 1965: 292).
9 This point has been made by John Corbin. In Andalusia, he found that classes differ in the nature and extent of their personal networks; he shows how this difference contributes to social inequality. The Andalusian upper class has highly developed institutions of sponsorship and introduction which extend the personal influence exercised by its members well beyond the network of their own friends and relatives: 'Their social networks are better instruments than those of the lower class for getting things done in a society which depends heavily on personal relations. Lower class people are either isolated from the system of personal influence or have access to it only through an attachment to a particular member of the upper class' (Corbin 1979: 108–9).

# Bibliography

Abélès, Marc. 1976. *Anthropologie et Marxisme*. Brussels, Presses Universitaires de France

Althabe, Gérard. 1977. 'Le Quotidien en procès. *Dialectiques* 21: 67–77

Amin, Samir. 1971. 'La Politique coloniale française à l'égard de la bourgeoisie commerçante Sénégalaise (1820–1960)'. In C. Meillassoux, ed. *The Development of Indigenous Trade and Markets in West Africa*, pp. 361–76. London, Oxford University Press

  1981. 'The Development of the Senegalese Business Bourgeoisie'. In Adebayo Adedeji, ed. *Indigenization of African Economies*, pp. 309–21. New York, Africana

Amselle, Jean-Loup, 1985. 'Socialisme, capitalisme, et pré-capitalisme au Mali (1960–1982)'. In Henry Bernstein and Bonnie Campbell, eds. *Contradictions of Accumulation in Africa*, pp. 249–66. Beverly Hills, Sage

Anselin, M. 1961. 'La Classe moyenne à Elisabethville'. *Problèmes sociaux Congolais* (CEPSI), 53: 99–110

Anstey, Roger. 1970. 'Belgian Rule in the Congo and the Aspirations of the Evolué Class'. In L. H. Gann and P. Duignan, eds. *Colonialism in Africa 1870–1960*, vol.2, pp. 194–225. London, Cambridge University Press

Baier, Stephen, 1980. *An Economic History of Central Niger*. Oxford, Clarendon Press

Bates, Robert. 1981. *Markets and States in Tropical Africa: the Political Basis of Agricultural Policies*. University of California Press

Beckman, Bjorn. 1980. 'Imperialism and Capitalist Transformation: Critique of a Kenya Debate'. *Review of African Political Economy*, 19: 48–62

  1985. 'Neo-colonialism, Capitalism and the State in Nigeria'. In Henry Bernstein and Bonnie Campbell, eds. *Contradictions of Accumulation in Africa*, pp. 71–113. Beverly Hills, Sage

Bergmans, Lieven. 1970–3. *Les Wanande*, 3 vols. Butembo, Kivu: Eds. Assomption

Bernard, G. 1972. 'Conjugalité et rôle de la femme à Kinshasa'. *Canadian Journal of African Studies* 6, 2: 261–74.

Bernstein, Henry. 1977. 'Notes on Capital and Peasantry'. *Review of African Political Economy* 10: 60–73.

Bernstein, Henry, and Bonnie Campbell, eds. 1985 *Contradictions of Accumulation in Africa*. Beverly Hills, Sage

Berry, Sara. 1985. *Fathers Work for their Sons*. University of California Press

Beveridge, Andrew A., and Anthony R. Oberschall. 1979. *African Businessmen and Development in Zambia*. Princeton University Press

Bézy, Fernand, Jean-Philippe Peemans, Jean-Marie Wautelet. 1981. *Accumulation et sous-développement au Zaire, 1960–1980*. Louvain-la-Nueve, Presse Universitaire de Louvain

Bianga, Waruzi. 1982. *Peasant, State and Rural Development in Post-Independent Zaire: a*

*Case Study of 'Réforme Rurale' 1970–1980 and its Implications*. Ph.D. Dissertation, University of Wisconsin

Bibeau, Gilles, 1975. 'La Communauté musulmane de Kisangani'. In B. Verhaegen, ed. *Kisangani 1876–1976*, pp. 181–238. Kinshasa, Presses Universitaires du Zaire

Blumenthal, Erwin. 1982. 'Zaire: Report on her International Financial Credibility'. Typescript

Bongeli Yeikelo. 1975. 'Les Bambole récemment urbanisés'. In B. Verhaegen, ed. *Kisangani 1876–1976*, pp. 121–50. Kinshasa: Presses Universitaires du Zaire

Bontinck, François. 1979. 'Variations historiques sur le thème Kisangani'. *Mbegu* (Lubumbashi) 6: 23–37.

Bradby, Barbara. 1975. 'The Destruction of Natural Economy'. *Economy and Society* 4, 2: 127–61

Brenner, Robert. 1977. 'The Origins of Capitalist Development: a Critique of Neo-Smithian Marxism'. *New Left Review* 104: 25–92

Bromley, Ray, and Chris Gerry, eds. 1979. 'Who are the Casual Poor?' In *Casual Work and Poverty in Third World Cities*, pp. 3–26. New York, John Wiley

Brubaker, Rogers. 1984. *The Limits of Rationality: an Essay on the Social and Moral Thought of Max Weber*. London, Allen and Unwin

Buakasa Tulu kia Mpansu. 1980. 'L'Environnement social et cultural de christianisme. Le Zaire à l'heure du deuxième centenaire de l'Eglise Catholique'. *Cahiers des Religions Africaines* 14, 27–8: 191–8.

Buell, Raymond L. 1928. *The Native Problem in Africa*, II. New York, MacMillan

Bujra, Janet M. 1975. 'Women Entrepreneurs of Early Nairobi'. *Canadian Journal of African Studies* 9, 2: 213–34

1977. 'Sexual Politics in Atu'. *Cahier d' Études Africaines* 65, 17, 1:13–39

1978. 'Proletarianization and the "Informal Economy": a Case Study from Nairobi'. *African Urban Studies* 3: 47–66.

1986. 'Urging Women to Redouble their Efforts...: Class, Gender and Capitalist Transformation in Africa'. In Claire Robertson and Iris Berger, eds. *Women and Class in Africa*, pp. 117–40. New York, Holmes and Meier

Bulu-Bobina Bogila. 1984. 'Les Problèmes des terres cultivables en milieu rurale: cas de la zone de Kasangulu (Bas Zaire)'. *Zaire Afrique* 189: 539–52

Bumba Monga Ngoy. 1979. 'Enquête sur les causes de la desertion et de l'absentéisme du paysan salarié en milieu de travail. Analyse du cas de la main d'oeuvre des plantations/District PLZ Yabgimbe'. Ms

Callaghy, Thomas M. 1983. 'External Actors and the Relative Autonomy of the Political Aristocracy in Zaire'. *Journal of Commonwealth and Comparative Politics* 21, 3: 61–83

1984. *The State-Society Struggle: Zaire in Comparative Perspective*. New York, Columbia University Press

1987. 'The State and the Development of Capitalism in Africa: some Theoretical and Historical Reflections'. In Naomi Chazan and Donald Rothchild, eds. *The Precarious Balance: State and Society in Africa*. Boulder, Colorado, Westview Press

Caplan, Patricia. 1982. 'Women's Organizations in Madras City, India'. In Patricia Caplan and Janet Bujra, eds. *Women United, Women divided*. Bloomington, Indiana University Press

Cardoso, Fernando Henrique. 1972. 'Dependency and Development in Latin America'. *New Left Review* 74: 83–95

Charmes. Jacques. 1982. 'Méthodologie des enquêtes sur le secteur non-structuré en Tunisie'. In Ph. Hugon and I. Deblé, eds. *Vivre et survivre dans les villes Africaines*, pp. 223–39. Paris, Presses Universitaires de France

Chazan, Naomi H. 1982. Development, Underdevelopment and the State in Ghana. Working Paper no.8, Boston University African Studies Center

Clammer, John. 1978. *The New Economic Anthropology*. London, MacMillan

# Bibliography

Clément, Pierre. 1956. 'Social Patterns of Urban Life'. In UNESCO, *Social Implications of Industrialization and Urbanization in Africa South of the Sahara*, pp. 368–492. Tensions and Technology Series. London, International African Institute

Cohen, Abner. 1969. *Custom and Politics in Urban Africa: a Study of Hausa Migrants in Yoruba Towns*. London, Routledge and Kegan Paul

   1971. 'Cultural Strategies in the Organization of Trading Diasporas'. In C. Meillassoux, ed. *The Development of Indigenous Trade and Markets in West Africa*, pp. 266–81. London, Oxford University Press

   1981. *The Politics of Elite Culture*. Berkeley, University of California Press

Cohen, Ronald. 1978. 'Ethnicity: Problem and Focus in Anthropology'. *Annual Review of Anthropology* 7: 379–403

Comeliau, Christian. 1965. *Fonctions économiques et pouvoir politique: le province de l'Uele en 1963–1964*. Kinshasa, IRES

Comhaire-Sylvain, Suzanne. 1968. *Femmes de Kinshasa: hier et aujourd'hui*. Paris, Mouton

*Conjoncture Economique* 16, 1976–7. Dept de l'Economie Nationale, Industrie et Commerce, 1977

   18, 1978–9. Dept de l'Economie Nationale, Industrie et commerce, 1979

Conrad, Joseph. 1904. *Nostromo*. New York, Doubleday

Cooper, Frederick. 1981. 'Africa and the World Economy.' *African Studies Review* 24, 2–3: 1–86

   1983. 'Urban Space, Industrial Time and Wage Labor in Africa'. In ed. *The Struggle for the City: Migrant Labor, Capital and the State in Urban Africa*. Beverly Hills, Sage

Corbin, John. 1979. 'Social Class and Patron-Clientage in Andalusia: some Problems of Comparing Ethnographies'. *Anthropological Quarterly* 52, 2: 99–114

Cowen, Michael. 1981. 'Commodity Production in Kenya's Central Province'. In Judith Heyer, Pepe Roberts and Gavin Williams, eds. *Rural Development in Tropical Africa*, pp. 121–42. New York, St Martin's Press

Cruise O'Brien, Donal B. 1971. 'Co-operators and Bureaucrats: Class Formation in a Senegalese Peasant Society'. *Africa* 41, 4: 263–78

Curtin, Philip D. 1975. *Economic Change in Pre-Colonial Africa*. Madison, University of Wisconsin Press

   1984. *Cross-Cultural Trade in World History*. Cambridge University Press

de Janvry, Alain. 1981. *The Agrarian Question and Reformism in Latin America*. Baltimore: Johns Hopkins University Press

De Saint Moulin, Léon. 1975. 'La Formation de la population'. In B. Verhaegen, ed. *Kisangani 1876–1976*, pp. 31–54. Kinshasa, Presses Universitaires du Zaire

Delf, George. 1963. *Asians in East Africa*. London, Oxford University Press

Demunter, P. 1972. 'Structure de classes et lutte de classes dans le Congo colonial'. *Contradictions* 1: 67–109

Depelchin, J. 1981. 'The Transformations of the Petty Bourgeoisie and the State in Post-Colonial Zaire'. *Review of African Political Economy* 22: 20–41

Diambomba Mukanda. 1971. 'Education, Training and Other Factors Influencing Entrepreneurial Performance in Zaire'. *Cahiers Economiques et Sociaux* (Kinshasa) 9: 93–103

Dinan, C. 1977. 'Pragmatists or Feminists? The Professional Single Woman in Accra, Ghana'. *Cahiers d'Études Africaines* 65, 17, 1: 155–76.

   1983. 'Sugar Daddies and Gold-Diggers: the White Collar Single Woman in Accra'. In Christine Oppong, ed. *Female and Male in West Africa*, pp. 344–66. London, George Allen and Unwin

Droogers, André. 1975. 'Les Wagenia de Kisangani: entre le fleuve et la ville'. In B. Verhaegen, ed. *Kisangani 1876–1976*, pp. 153–77. Kinshasa: Presses Universitaires du Zaire

226

Dupré, Georges, and P. P. Rey. 1973. 'Reflections on the Pertinence of a Theory of the History of Exchange'. *Economy and Society* 2, 2: 131–63

Dupriez, Pierre. 1962. 'Eléments du commerce extérieure de la République du Congo'. *Cahiers Economiques et Sociaux* 1: 75–191.

1968. 'Les Relations économiques extérieure (du Congo)'. In *Indépendance, Inflation et Développement: l'Economie Congolaise de 1960 à 1964*, pp. 559–724. IRES. Paris, Mouton

Emmanuel, Arghiri. 1974. 'Myths of Development Versus Myths of Underdevelopment'. *New Left Review* 85: 61–82

Epée, Jacques. 1971. 'Structures et institutions politiques et administratives de la province Orientale: le cas du Haut-Congo 1960–1964'. Mémoire, Université de Kinshasa

Etienne, Mona, and Eleanor Leacock, eds. 1980. *Women and Colonization: Anthropological Perspectives*. New York, Praeger

Ewert, David M. 1977. 'Freire's Concept of Critical Consciousness and Social Structure in Rural Zaire'. Ph.D. dissertation, University of Wisconsin-Madison

Fabian, Ilona Szombati, and Johannes. 1976. 'Art, History and Society: Popular Art in Shaba, Zaire'. *Studies in the Anthropology of Visual Communication* 3: 1–21

Feige, Edgar L. 1979. 'How Big is the Irregular Economy?' *Challenge*. Nov.–Dec.

Flynn, Peter. 1974. 'Class, Clientelism and Coercion: some Mechanisms of Internal Dependency and Control'. *Journal of Commonwealth and Comparative Politics* 12, 2: 133–56

Foster-Carter, A. 1978. 'Can We Articulate "Articulation?"' In J. Clammer, ed. *The New Economic Anthropology*, pp. 210–49. New York, St Martin's Press

Frank, A. G. 1967. *Capitalism and Underdevelopment in Latin America*. New York, Monthly Review Press

Furtado, Celso. 1964. *Development and Underdevelopment*. Los Angeles, University of California Press

Gann, L. H. and Peter Duignan. 1979. *The Rulers of Belgian Africa 1884–1914*. Princeton University Press

Garlick, Peter C. 1971. *African Traders and Economic Development in Ghana*. Oxford, Clarendon Press

Gerry, Chris. 1978. 'Petty Production and Capitalist Production in Dakar: the Crisis of the Self-Employed'. *World Development* 6: 1147–60

Geschiere, Peter. 1985. 'Applications of the Lineage Mode of Production in African Studies'. *Canadian Journal of African Studies* 19, 1: 80–90

Godelier, M. 1972. *Rationality and Irrationality in Economics*. London, New Left Books.

Goodman, David, and Michael Redclift. 1982. *From Peasant to Proletarian: Capitalist Development and Agrarian Transitions*. New York, St Martin's Press

Gould, David J. 1977. 'Local Adminstration in Zaire and Underdevelopment'. *Journal of Modern African Studies* 15, 3: 349–78

1978. *From Development Administration to Underdevelopment Administration: a Study of Zairian Administration in the Light of Current Crisis*. Brussels, CEDAF, no. 6.

1979. 'The Administration of Underdevelopment'. In Guy Gran, ed. *Zaire: the Political Economy of Underdevelopment*, pp. 87–107. New York, Praeger

1980. *Bureaucratic Corruption and Underdevelopment in the Third World: the Case of Zaire*. New York: Pergamon Press

Gould, Terri F. 1978. 'Value Conflict and Development: the Struggle of the Professional Zairian Woman'. *Journal of Modern African Studies* 16, 1: 133–9

Gran, Guy, ed. 1979. *Zaire: the Political Economy of Underdevelopment*. New York, Pergamon Press

Grandmaison, Colette Le Cour. 1969. 'Activités économiques des femmes Dakaroises'. *Africa* 39: 138–52

227

## Bibliography

Green, Reginald H. 1981. '*Magendo* in the Political Economy of Uganda: Pathology, Parallel System or Dominant Sub-Mode of Production?' Discussion Paper 64, Institute of Development Studies, University of Sussex

1984. 'Consolidation and Accelerated Development of African Agriculture: What Agenda for Action?' *African Studies Review* 27, 4: 17–34

Grossman, Gregory. 1979. 'Notes on the Illegal Private Economy and Corruption'. In *Soviet Economy in a Time of Change*. A compendium of papers submitted to the Joint Economic Committee, Congress of the US. Vol. 1: 834–55. Washington, US Government Printing Office

Hart, Keith. 1973. 'Informal Income Opportunities and Urban Employment in Ghana'. *Journal of Modern African Studies* 11, 1: 61–89

Hill, Polly. 1985. 'The Gullibility of Development Economists'. *Anthropology Today* 1, 2: 10–12

Hoogvelt, Ankie. 1979. 'Indigenisation and Foreign Capital: Industrialisation in Nigeria'. *Review of African Political Economy* 14: 56–68

Hopkins, Anthony G. 1976. 'Clio-Antics: a Horoscope for African Economic History'. In Christopher Fyfe, ed. *African Studies since 1945*, pp. 31–48. London, Longman Group

Hugon, Philippe, and I. Deblé, eds. 1982. *Vivre et survivre dans les villes Africaines*. Paris, Presses Universitaires de France

Hutchful, Eboe. 1979. 'A Tale of Two Regimes: Imperialism, the Military and Class in Ghana'. *Review of African Political Economy* 14: 36–55

Huybrechts, André, and Daniel Van der Steen. 1981. 'L'Economie: structures, évolution, perspectives'. In J. Vanderlinden, ed. *Du Congo au Zaire 1960–1980*, pp. 177–289. Brussels, CRISP

Hyden, Goran. 1980. *Beyond Ujamaa in Tanzania: Underdevelopment and an Uncaptured Peasantry*. London, Heinemann

Iliffe, John. 1982. *The Emergence of African Capitalism*. University of Minnesota Press

ILO. 1972. *Employment, Incomes and Inequality: a Strategy for Increasing Public Employment in Kenya*. Geneva

IRES. 1977. 'Le Café' et l'économie zairoise'. *Lettre Mensuelle* 5: 1–35

Jeffries, Richard. 1978. *Class, Power and Ideology in Ghana: the Railwaymen of Sekoudi*. Cambridge University Press

Jewsiewicki, Bogumil. 1976. 'La Contestation sociale et la naissance du proletariat au Zaire au cours de la première moitié du XXe siècle'. *Canadian Journal of African Studies* 10, 1: 47–70

1978. *Histoire économique d'une ville coloniale: Kisangani 1877–1960*. Brussels, CEDAF, no. 5

1981. 'Capitalisme par procuration et industrialisation sans entrepreneurs; la petite entreprise au Congo Belge, 1910–1960'. In *Entreprises et entrepreneurs en Afrique XIXe et XXe siècles*, pp. 81–100. Paris: Editions l'Harmattan

1983. 'Rural Society and the Belgian Colonial Economy'. In David Birmingham and Phyllis Martin, eds. *History of Central Africa* II, pp. 95–126. New York, Longman

Jewsiewicki B., and Muhima Faradje. 1974. 'Les Planteurs individuels à Bombandana (Kivu)'. *Likondoli* (Lubumbashi), series B–Archives and Documents 2, nos. 1–2

Johnson, Marian. 1976. 'Calico Caravans: the Tripoli-Kano Trade after 1880'. *Journal of African History* 17, 1: 95–117

Kahavo-Kavyavu. 1980. 'Approvisionnement de la ville de Kisangani en produits maraichers en provenance du Nord-Kivu'. Mémoire, UNAZA, Kisangani

Kannyo, Edward. 1979. *Political Power and Class Formation in Zaire*. Ph.D. dissertation, Yale University

Kaplinsky, Raphael. 1980. 'Capitalist Accumulation in the Periphery: the Kenyan Case Re-examined'. *Review of African Political Economy* 17: 83–113

Kasay Katsuvu Lenga-Lenga. 1982. 'Le Kivu, une region éclatée: un problème de transport ou de régionalisation?' *Zaire Afrique* 166: 345–56

Kasfir, Nelson. 1984. I. 'Relating Class to State in Africa'. II. 'State, *Magendo* and Class Formation in Uganda'. In ed. *State and Class in Africa*, pp. 1–20, 84–103. London, Frank Cass

1986. 'Are African Peasants Self-Sufficient?' *Development and Change*. April

Kasongo Ngoyi Makita, Puati Abiosende M'Peti, B. Verhaegen, T. Verheust. 1977. *Les étudiants et les élèves de Kisangani (1974–5): aspirations, opinions et conditions de vie*. Brussels, CEDAF, no. 7–8

Kay, Geoffrey. 1975. *Development and Underdevelopment: a Marxist Analysis*. New York, St Martin's Press

Kennedy, Paul. 1977. 'African Businessmen and Foreign Capital: Collaboration or Conflict?' *African Affairs* 76, 303: 177–94.

1980. *Ghanaian Businessmen: from Artisan to Capitalist Entrepreneur in a Dependent Economy*. Munich, Weltforum Verlag

Kiakwama Kiziki. 1974. 'OPEZ: Instrument de politique de promotion des petites et moyennes entreprises au Zaire'. *Cahiers Zairois de la Recherche et du Développment* (Kinshasa) 18, 1: 89–114

Kilbride, Philip. 1979. 'Barmaiding as a Deviant Occupation among the Baganda of Uganda'. *Ethos* 7, 3: 232–54

Kimpianga Kia Mahaniah. 1980. 'De la Rivalité à l'oecumenisme: les relations entre les missions Catholiques et Protestantes durant le premier siècle de l'èvangelisation 1878–1980'. *Cahiers des Religions Africaines* 14, 27–8: 97–117

Kisangani, Emizet. Forthcoming. 'A Social Dilemma in a Less Developed Country: the Massacre of the African Elephant in Zaire'. National Research Council, Proceedings of the Conference on Common Property Resource Management, Annapolis, Maryland, 21–6 1985. Washington DC: National Academy Press

Kitching, Gavin. 1980. *Class and Economic Change in Kenya: the Making of an African Petite Bourgeoisie, 1905–1970*. Newhaven, Yale University Press

1982. *Development and Underdevelopment in Historical Perspective*. London, Methuen

1985. 'Politics, Method and Evidence in the "Kenya Debate"'. In Henry Bernstein and Bonnie Campbell, eds. *Contradictions of Accumulation in Africa*, pp. 115–51. Beverly Hills, Sage

Kitenge-Ya. 1977. 'Le Role de la femme zairoise dans la société contemporaine'. *Problèmes Sociaux Zairois* (Lubumbashi) 118–19: 51–114

Korse, Pierre. 1980. 'Les Cooperatives d'épargne et de crédit de Basankusu'. *Zaire Afrique* 148: 455–8

Laclau, Ernesto. 1971. 'Feudalism and Capitalism in Latin America'. *New Left Review* 67: 19–38

Lacroix, Bernadette. 1972. *Pouvoirs et structures de l'université Lovanium*. Brussels, CEDAF, no. 2–3

Lacroix, Jean-Louis. 1967. *Industrialisation au Congo: la transformation*. Paris, Mouton

LaFontaine, Jean S. 1970. *City Politics: a Study of Leopoldville 1962–63*. Cambridge University Press

1974. 'The Free Women of Kinshasa'. In J. Davis, ed. *Choice and Change: Essays in Honor of Lucy Mair*, pp. 89–113. New York, Humanities Press

Langdon, Stephen. 1975. 'Multinational Corporations, Taste Transfer and Underdevelopment: a Case Study from Kenya'. *Review of African Political Economy* 2: 12–35

1977. 'The State and Capitalism in Kenya'. *Review of African Political Economy* 8: 90–8

Le Brun, O., and C. Gerry. 1975. 'Petty Producers and Capitalism'. *Review of African Political Economy* 3: 20–32

Leeds, Anthony. 1965. 'Brazilian Careers and Social Structures: a Case History and Model'. In Dwight B. Heath, ed. *Contemporary Cultures and Societies of Latin America*, pp. 285–307. 2nd edition 1974. New York: Random House

# Bibliography

Lemarchand, René. 1964. *Political Awakening in the Belgian Congo*. University of California Press
  1981. 'Comparative Political Clientelism: Structure, Process and Optic'. In S. N. Eisenstadt and R. Lemarchand, eds. *Political Clientage, Patronage and Development*, pp. 7–32. Beverly Hills, Sage
  1987. 'The State, the Parallel Economy and the Changing Structure of Patronage Systems'. In Naomi Chazan and Donald Rothchild, eds. *The Precarious Balance: State and Society in Africa*. Boulder, Colorado, Westview Press
Lettre ouverte au citoyen Président-Fondateur du Mouvement Populaire de la Révolution, président de la République, par un groupe de parlementaires. 1981. In Jean-François Bayart, ed. 'La Fronde Parlementaire au Zaire'. *Politique Africaine* 1, 3: 90–140
Levtzion, N. 1968. 'Ibn-Hawqal, the Cheque and Awdaghost'. *Journal of African History* 9, 2: 223–33
Leys, Colin. 1974. *Underdevelopment in Kenya*. University of California Press
  1978. 'Capital Accumulation, Class Formation and Dependency – the Significance of the Kenya Case'. In Ralph Miliband and John Saville, eds. *The Socialist Register*. London, Merlin Press
  1980. Debates: 'Dependency in Kenya'. *Review of African Political Economy* 17: 83–113
  1982. 'African Economic Development in Theory and Practice'. *Daedalus* 111, 2: 99–124
Litt, Jean-Louis. 1970. *Analyse d'un procès d'acculturation*. Mémoire, Université Catholique de Louvain
Little, Kenneth. 1973. *African Women in Towns*. London, Cambridge University Press
Lokomba Baruti. 1972. *Structure et fonctionnement des institutions politiques traditionelles chez les Lokele*. Brussels, CEDAF, no. 8
  1975. 'Kisangani Centre Urbain et les Lokele'. In B. Verhaegen, ed. *Kisangani 1876–1976*, pp. 57–90. Kinshasa: Presses Universitaires du Zaire
Long, Norman. 1975. 'Structural Dependency, Modes of Production and Economic Brokerage in Rural Peru'. In Ivor Oxaal, Tony Barnett, David Booth, eds. *Beyond the Sociology of Development*, pp. 253–83. London, Routledge and Kegan Paul
Lonsdale, John. 1981. 'States and Social Process in Africa: a Historiographical Survey'. *African Studies Review* 24, 2/3: 139–225
Luhindi Seya Fataki. 1979. 'Le Legs socio-politique du mode de production précapitaliste et colonial dans la société Nande au 30 juin 1960'. Mémoire, UNAZA, Kisangani
Lukombe Nghenda. 1979. *Zairianisation, radicalisation, retrocession en République du Zaire: considerations juridiques*. Kinshasa: Presses Universitaires du Zaire
Lukusa Mukunayi. 1981. 'L' Attitude des paysans zairois face à la culture du coton: le cas des paysans de Gandajika'. *Zaire Afrique* 157: 443–50
MacGaffey, Janet. 1983. 'The Effect of Rural-Urban Ties, Kinship and Marriage on Household Structure in a Kongo Village'. *Canadian Journal of African Studies* 17, 1: 69–84
  1987. 'Evading Male Control: Women in the Second Economy in Zaire'. In Jane Parpart and Sharon Stichhter, eds. *Patriarchy and Class: African Women in the Home and Workforce*. Beverly Hills, Sage
MacGaffey, Wyatt. 1970. *Custom and Government in the Lower Congo*. University of California Press
  1982. 'The Policy of National Integration in Zaire'. *Journal of Modern African Studies* 20, 1: 87–105
  1985. 'On the Moderate Usefulness of Modes of Production'. *Canadian Journal of African Studies* 19, 1: 51–7
Malengreau, Guy. 1950. 'La Politique coloniale de la Belgique'. In *Principles and Methods of Colonial Administration*. Symposium Colston Research Society and University of Bristol. London, Butterworths Scientific Publications

230

Malira Kubuya Namulemba. 1974. 'Regard sur la situation sociale de la citoyenne Lushoise d'avant 1950'. *Likondoli* (Lubumbashi) 2, 1: 63–71

Malula Mitwensil and Kambidi Nsia-Kinguem. 1980. 'Le Public et l'administration en république du Zaire'. *Zaire Afrique* 143: 165–80

Manwana Mungongo. 1982. 'Les Droits de la femme travailleuse au Zaire'. *Zaire Afrique* 163: 73–82

Marris, Peter. 1968. 'The Social Barriers to African Entrepreneurship'. *Journal of Development Studies* 5, 1: 29–38

Marris, Peter, and Anthony Somerset. 1972. *The African Entrepreneur: a Study of Entrepreneurship and Development in Kenya*. New York, Africana

Marx, Karl. 1976. *Capital*. New York, Random House, Vintage Books

Mattera, Philip. 1985. *Off-the-Books: the Rise of the Underground Economy*. New York, St Martins Press

Mbaya Mudimba. 1980. 'Des Conditions d'interaction entre paysans, encadreurs agricoles et ingénieurs agronomes dans le processus de vulgarisation et de développement agricoles'. Ph.D. dissertation. UNAZA, Kisangani

M'bela Bole Kolaka. 1982. 'Crise de la production agricole au Zaire: le cas de l'huile de palme'. *Zaire Afrique* 162: 71–82

Mbumba Ngimbi. 1982. *Kinshasa 1881–1981. 100 ans après Stanley: problèmes et l'avenir d'une ville*. Kinshasa: Edition Centre de Recherches Pédagogiques

Médard, Jean-François. 1982. 'The Underdeveloped State in Tropical Africa: Political Clientelism or Neo-Patrimonialism?' In Chris Clapham, ed. *Private Patronage and Public Power*. New York, St Martin's Press

Meillassoux, Claude, ed. 1971. *The Development of Indigenous Trade and Markets in West Africa*. Oxford University Press

 1972. 'From Reproduction to Production'. *Economy and Society* 1, 1: 93–115

 1981. *Maidens, Meal and Money*. Cambridge University Press

Mitoro Litekya. 1976. 'L'Analyse de l'activité de la CELZA (Unité de Bamboli)'. Mémoire, UNAZA, Kisangani

Monnier, Laurent, and Jean Claude Willame. 1964. 'Les Provinces du Congo II: l'Uele'. *Cahiers Economiques et Sociaux* (IRES), Kinshasa

Moore, Sally Falk. 1978. *Law as Process*. Boston, Routledge and Kegan Paul

Morice, A. 1985. 'Commerce parallèle et troc à Luanda'. *Politique Africaine* 17: 105–20

Moser, Caroline. 1978. 'Informal Sector or Petty Commodity Production: Dualism or Dependence in Urban Development?' *World Development* 9/10: 1041–64

Mubake Mumeme. 1984. I. 'Crise, inflation et comportements individuels d'adaptation au Zaire: solution ou aggravation du problème?' II. 'Economie souterraine et secteur informal au Zaire: caractéristiques et fonctions'. *Zaire Afrique* 185: 263–72, 188: 491–2

Mudimbe, V. Y. 1981. 'La Culture'. In J. Vanderlinden *Du Congo au Zaire 1960–1980*. Brussels, CRISP, pp. 308–98

Mukenge Tshilemalema. 1973. 'Les Hommes d'affaires zairois: du travail salarié à l'entreprise personelle'. *Canadian Journal of African Studies* 7, 3: 455–75

 1974. *Businessmen of Zaire: Limited Possibilities for Capital Accumulation under Dependence*. Ph.D. dissertation, McGill University

Mulamba Mvuluya. 1974. *Cultures obligatoires et colonisation dans l'ex-Congo Belge*. Brussels, CEDAF, no. 6–7

Mwabila Malela. 1979. *Travail et travailleurs au Zaire: Essai sur la conscience ouvrière du proletariat urbain de Lubumbashi*. Kinshasa, Presses Universitaires du Zaire

Ndaywel e Nziem. 1978. 'Les Archives du Zaire en question'. *Zaire Afrique* 124: 207–13

Newbury, Catharine M. 1984a. 'Ebutumwa Bw'Emiogo: the Tyranny of Cassava: a Women's Tax Revolt in Eastern Zaire'. *Canadian Journal of African Studies* 18, 1: 35–54

1984b. 'Dead and Buried or Just Underground? The Privatization of the State in Zaire'. *Canadian Journal of African Studies* 18, 1: 112–14

Nkongola Bakenda. 1975. 'Quelques aspects de l'urbanisation et du développement économique de la ville de Kisangani (1966–1974)'. Mémoire, UNAZA, Kisangani

Nsaman O. Lutu. 1983. 'Le Management face à la crise de l'administration publique zairoise'. *Zaire Afrique* 175: 271–80

Ntambwe Katshay. 193. 'Le Prêt usuraire: son histoire en général et sa pratique dans la société zairoise. A propos de la pratique dite "Banque Lambert"'. *Zaire Afrique* 175: 281–93

Nzinunu Mampuya. 1978. 'Les Femmes commerçantes de Kisangani et leur association AFCO'. Mémoire, UNAZA, Kisangani

Nzongola Georges. 1970. 'The Bourgeoisie and Revolution in the Congo'. *Journal of Modern African Studies* 8, 4: 511–30

1982. 'Class Struggle and National Liberation in Zaire'. *Contemporary Marxism* 6: 57–94

Obatela Rashidi. 1976. 'Carte de densité et de localisation de la population du Haut Zaire'. *Likondoli* (Lubumbashi), série B, 4 1: 57–64

Obbo, Christine. 1980. *African Women: their Struggle for Economic Independence.* London, Zed Press

Obserschall, Anthony. 1981. 'On. the Political Economy of Zaire'. Paper presented to the African Studies Association, Bloomington, Indiana

O'Brien, Philip J. 1975. 'A Critique of Latin American Theories of Dependency'. In Ivor Oxaal, Tony Barnett, David Booth, eds. *Beyond the Sociology of Development.* London, Routledge and Kegan Paul

Ollawa, Patrick E. 1983. 'The Political Economy of Development: a Theoretical Reconsideration of Some Unresolved Issues'. *African Studies Review* 26, 1: 125–55

Packard, Randall M. 1981. *Chiefship and Cosmology.* Bloomington, Indiana University Press

Parpart, Jane. 1986. 'Class and Gender on the Copperbelt: Women in the Northern Rhodesian Copper Mines 1926–64'. In Claire Robertson and Iris Berger, eds. *Women and Class in Africa*, pp. 141–60. New York, Holmes and Meier

Paul, James C. N. 1984. 'The World Bank's Agenda for the Crises in Agriculture and Rural Development in Africa: an Introduction to a Debate'. *African Studies Review* 27, 4: 1–8

Peemans, J. Ph. 1975a. 'Capital Accumulation in the Congo under Colonialism: the Role of the State'. In Peter Duignan and H. Gann *Colonialism in Africa* IV, pp. 165–212. Cambridge University Press

1975b. 'L'Etat fort et al croissance économique'. *Revue Nouvelle* (Brussels) Dec.: 515–27

1975c. 'The Social and Economic Development of Zaire since Independence: an Historical Outline'. *African Affairs* 74: 148–79

1980. 'Imperial Hangovers: Belgium, the Economics of Decolonization'. *Journal of Contemporary History* 15, 2: 257–86

1986. 'Accumulation and Underdevelopment in Zaire: General Aspects in Relation to the Evolution of the Agrarian Crisis'. In Nzongola-Ntalaja, ed. *The Crisis in Zaire: Myths and Realities*, pp. 67–83. Trenton, New Jersey: Africa World Press

Petras, James F. 1978. *Critical Perspectives on Imperialism and Social Class in the Third World.* New York: Monthly Review Press

Please, Stanley, and K.Y. Amoako. 1984. 'The World Bank's report on Accelerated Development in Sub-Saharan Africa: a Critique of some of the Criticism'. *African Studies Review* 27, 4: 47–58

Pons, Valdo G. 1969. *Stanleyville: an African Community under Belgian Administration.* London, Oxford University Press

Popelier, G.H. 1977. *Nature et évolution de l'agriculture zairoise (1958–1975).* Brussels, CEDAF, no. 6

Portes, Alejandro. 1976. 'On the Sociology of National Development: Theories and Issues'. *American Journal of Sociology* 82: 55–85

232

1983. 'The Informal Sector: Definition, Controversy, and Relation to National Development'. *Review* 7, 1: 151–74

Portes, Alejandro and John Walton. 1981. *Labour, Class and the International System*. New York, Academic Press

Prunier, G. 1983 'Le Magendo: essai sur quelques aspects marginaux des échanges commerciaux en Afrique Orientale'. *Politique Africaine* 9: 53–62

Rey, Pierre-Philippe. 1973. *Les Alliances des classes*. Paris, Maspero

Roberts, Bryan R. 1976. 'The Provincial Urban System and the Process of Dependency'. In Alejandro Portes and H. Browning, eds. *Current Perspectives in Latin American Urban Research*, pp. 100–31. Austin, Texas: Institute of Latin American Studies, University of Texas

Robertson, Claire. 1984. *Sharing the Same Bowl: a Socioeconomic History of Women and Class in Accra, Ghana*. Bloomington, Indiana Universitv Press

Roxborough, Ian. 1979. *Theories of Underdevelopment*. Atlantic Highlands, New Jersey, Humanities Press

Rymenam, Jean. 1977. Comment le régime Mobutu a sappé ses propres fondements'. *Le Monde Diplomatique* May: 8–9

1980. 'Classes sociale, pouvoir et économie au Zaire, ou comment le sous-développement enrichit les gouvernements'. *Génève-Afrique* 18: 41–54

Sahlins, Marshall. 1976. *Culture and Practical Reason*. University of Chicago Press

Sandbrook, Richard. 1972. 'Patrons, Clients and Factions: New Dimensions of Conflict Analysis in Africa'. *Canadian Journal of Political Science* 5, 1: 104–18

Schatz, Sayre. 1977. *Nigerian Capitalism*. University of California Press

1984. 'Pirate Capitalism and the Inert Economy of Nigeria'. *Journal of Modern African Studies* 22, 1:45–57

Schatzberg, Michael G. 1980a. *Politics and Class in Zaire: Bureaucracy, Business and Beer in Lisala*. New York: Africana

1980b. 'The State and the Economy: the "Radicalization" of the Revolution in Mobutu's Zaire'. *Canadian Journal of African Studies* 14, 2: 239–57

1982. 'Le Mal zairois: why policy fails in Zaire'. *African Affairs* 81: 324–48

Forthcoming. *The Dialectics of Oppression in Zaire*. Indiana University Press

Schmitz, Hubert. 1982. 'Growth Constraints on Small-Scale Manufacturing in Developing Countries: a Critical Review'. *World Development* 10, 6: 429–79

Schoepf, Brooke G., and Claude Schoepf. 1984. 'State Bureaucracy and Peasants in the Lufira Valley'. *Candian Journal of African Studies* 18, 189–93

Schumpeter, Joseph A. 1976. *Capitalism, Socialism and Democracy*. London, Allen and Unwin

Schuster, Ilsa M. Glazer. 1979. *New Women of Lusaka*. Palo Alto, Mayfield Publishing Company

1984. 'Constraints and Opportunities in Political Participation: the case of Zambian women'. *Génève Afrique* 22: 8–37

Schwartz, Alf. 1972. 'Illusion d'une émancipation et aliénation réelle de l'ouvrière zairoise'. *Canadian Journal of African Studies* 6, 2: 183–212

Sethuraman, S.V. 1976. 'The Urban Informal Sector: Concept, Measurement and Policy'. *International Labour Review* 114, 1: 69–81

Sherrill, Michael. 1973. *Unilever et l'Afrique*. Brussels, CEDAF

Shoumatoff, Alex. 1984. 'A Reporter at Large (Zaire): the Ituri Forest'. *The New Yorker*, Feb. 6

Sivirihauma Vukaragha. 1984. 'Problèmes de diffusion des innovations agricoles en milieu rural Nande (zones de Beni et Lubero)'. *Zaire Afrique* 184: 211–21

Sklar, Richard. 1979. 'The Nature of Class Domination in Africa'. *Journal of Modern African Studies* 17, 4: 531–52

Smith, M.G. 1983. 'The Role of Basic Needs and Provisions in Planning and Development'. *Canadian Journal of Native Studies* 3, 2: 341–60

# Bibliography

Société de Développment International Desjardins. 1981. 'Commercialisation des produits agricoles du nord-est du Zaire'. Vol. I. Lévis, Québec

Sosne, Elinor. 1979. 'Colonial Peasantization and Contemporary Underdevelopment: a View from a Kivu Village'. In Guy Gran, ed. *Zaire: the Political Economy of Underdevelopment*, pp. 189–210 New York, Praeger

Staniland, Martin. 1985. *What is Political Economy? A Study of Social Theory and Underdevelopment*. Newhaven, Yale University Press

Staudt, Kathleen A. 1982. 'Sex, Ethnic and Class Consciousness in Western Kenya'. *Comparative Politics* 1:149–67

Sudarkasa, Niara. 1973. *Where Women Work: a Study of Yoruba Women in the Marketplace and in the Home*. Anthropological Papers, Museum of Anthropology, University of Michigan, no. 53

Swainson, Nicola. 1977. 'The Rise of a National Bourgeoisie in Kenya'. *Review of African Political Economy* 8: 39–55

   1980. *The Development of Corporate Capitalism in Kenya 1918–1977*. University of California Press

Tanzi, Vito. 1982. *The Underground Economy in the US and Abroad*. New York: Lexington Books

Taylor, John G. 1979. *From Modernization to Modes of Production*. New York, MacMillan

Terray, Emmanuel. 1972. *Marxism and Primitive Societies*. New York, Monthly Review Press

Therborn, Goran. 1976. 'What Does the Ruling Class do When it Rules? Some Reflections on Different Approaches to the Study of Power in Society'. *The Insurgent Sociologist* 6, 3: 3–16

Tollens, Eric F. 1975. *An Economic Analysis of Cotton Production, Marketing and Processing in Northern Zaire*. Ph.D dissertation, Michigan State University

Tshibanda-Mbwebwe wa Tshibanda. 1974. 'Aux Origines de l'introduction des cultures de café et de thé en milieux indigènes du Kivu (1953–55)'. *Likondoli* (Lubumbashi). No. 2: 181–90

Tshund'Olela Epanyas. 1976. 'La Legislation sur le commerce ambulant au Congo (1896–1959)'. *Likondoli* (Lubumbashi) 2: 123–47

Vanderlinden, J. 1981. 'Les Hommes'. In ed., *Du Congo au Zaire 1960–1980*, pp. 57–107. Brussels, CRISP

Van der Steen, Daniel. 1978. *Elections et Reformes Politiques au Zaire en 1977. Analyse de la Composition des Organes Politiques*. Brussels, CEDAF, no. 2–3

Vansina, Jan. 'Mwasi's Trials'. *Daedalus* 111: 49–70

Vellut, J.L. 1979. 'Développement et sous-développement au Zaire'. *Génève-Afrique* 17, 1: 133–9

   1983. 'Mining in the Belgian Congo'. In David Birmingham and Phyllis Martin, eds. *History of Central Africa*, pp. 126–62. New York, Longman

Vercruijsse, Emile. 1984. *The Penetration of Capitalism: a West African Case Study*. London, Zed Books.

Verhaegen, Benoît. 1969. *Rébellions au Congo*. Vol. II. Brussels, CRISP

   ed. 1975. *Kisangani 1876–1976: histoire d'une ville*. Kinshasa, Presses Universitaires du Zaire

   1978. 'Impérialisme technologique et bourgeoisie nationale au Zaire'. In C. Coquery–Vidrovitch, ed. *Connaissance du tiers monde*, pp. 347–79, Paris, Union Générale d'Editions

   1979. 'Les Mouvements de libération en Afrique: le cas du Zaire en 1978'. *Génève-Afrique* 17, 1: 173–81

   1981. *Le Centre extra-coutumier de Stanleyville (1940–1945)*. Brussels, CEDAF

   1984. 'Paradoxes Zairois'. *Canadian Journal of African Studies* 18, 1:73–9

Verhaegen, Benoît and Kasongo Kisompoloke. 1979. *Emploi, salaire, prix et niveau de vie à Kisangani*. Les Cahiers du CRIDE (Kisangani), no. 37

Verhaegen, Benoît, B. Muamba Ngalula and Kisangani Endenda. 1984. 'La Marginalité, le mariage et l'instruction à Kisangani'. *Canadian Journal of African Studies* 18, 1: 131–37

Vwakyanakazi Mukohya. 1982. *African Traders in Butembo, Eastern Zaire (1960–1980): a Case Study of Informal Entrepreneurship in a Cultural Context of Central Africa.* Ph.D. dissertation, University of Wisconsin, Madison

Warren, Bill. 1973. 'Imperialism and Capitalist Industrialisation'. *New Left Review* 81: 2–44

Weeks, John, and Elizabeth Dore. 1979. 'International Exchange and the Causes of Backwardness'. *Latin American Perspectives* 21, 6, 2: 62–87

White, Luise. 1983. 'A Colonial State and an African Petty Bourgeoisie: Prostitution, Property and Class Struggle in Nairobi 1936–1940'. In Frederick Cooper, ed. *The Struggle for the City*, pp. 167–94. Beverly Hills, Sage

Willame, Jean-Claude. 1964. *Les Provinces du Congo. Structure et fonctionnement.* Cahiers Economiques et Sociaux, Kinshasa. Collection d'études politiques, no. 3

1972. *Patrimonialism and Political Change in the Congo.* Berkeley, Stanford University Press

1980. *Le Secteur mulinational au Zaire.* Brussels, CEDAF

1984. 'Zaire: système de survie et fiction d'état'. *Canadian Journal of African Studies* 18, 1: 83–8

Wipper, Audrey. 1975. 'The Maendeleo ya Wanawake Organization: the Co-optation of Leadership'. *African Studies Review* 18, 3: 99–120

Wolpe, Harold. 1972. 'Capitalism and Cheap Labour Power in South Africa: from Separation to Apartheid'. *Economy and Society* 1, 4: 229–52

1975. 'The Theory of Internal Colonialism: the South African Case'. In Ivor Oxaal, Tony Barnett, David Booth, eds. *Beyond the Sociology of Development*, pp. 229–52. London, Routledge and Kegan Paul

World Bank Country Study. 1980. *Zaire: Current Economic Situation and Constraints.* Washington, D.C.

Xydias Nelly. 1956. 'Labour: Conditions, Aptitude, Training'. In *Social Implications of Industrialisation and Urbanisation in Africa South of the Sahara*, pp. 275–367. UNESCO. Tensions and Technology Series. London: International African Institute

Yates, Barbara A. 1982. 'Colonialism, Education and Work: Social 'Differentiation in Colonial Zaire'. In Edna G. Bay, ed. *Women and Work in Africa*, pp. 127–52. Boulder, Colorado: Westview Press

Yoka Lye Mudaba. 1983 'Le Phénomène de la mode à Kinshasa'. *Zaire Afrique* 177: 25–30

Young, Crawford. 1965. *Politics in the Congo.* Princeton University Press

1970. 'Rebellion and the Congo'. In Robert Rotberg and Ali Mazrui, eds. *Protest and Power in Black Africa*, pp. 968–1011. Oxford University Press

1976. *The Politics of Cultural Pluralism.* Madison, University of Wisconsin Press

1982. 'Patterns of Social Conflict: State, Class and Ethnicity'. *Daedalus* 111, 2: 71–98

1983. 'Zaire: the Politics of Penury'. *School of Advanced International Studies Review* 3, 1: 115–30

1984. 'Zaire: is there a State?' *Canadian Journal of African Studies* 18, 1: 80–2

Young, Crawford, and Thomas Turner. 1985. *The Rise and Decline of the Zairian State.* Madison, University of Wisconsin Press

## Newspapers and trade journals

*Boyoma* daily newspaper, Kisangani

*Elima* daily newspaper, Kinshasa

*L'Entrepreneur.* Revue de l'Association Nationale des Entreprises du Zaire. Kinshasa

*Kasai* newspaper, Kananga and Mbuji Mayi

*Le Promoteur Zairois.* Bulletin d'Information du Centre de Commerce Internationale du Zaire. Kinshasa

*Salongo* daily newspaper Kinshasa

# Index

Abélès, M. 5, 6
AFCO 180–1, 182
Agriculture 34, 36, 37, 42, 43, 44, 45, 46, 47, 48, 49, 60, 62, 66, 69, 109, 120
Amin, S. 102
ANEZA 57, 152, 165, 208,219, 221; in Butembo 151
Anstey, R. 41
Arabs (*Arabisés*) 41, 60, 61, 84, 86
Army 50, 84, 91, 92; Force Publique 34
Articulation of modes of production 18–22, 25, 102–3, 160
Asians 64–6, 75–7, 105, 120, 153, 155, 160

Babua (sing. Mu-) 61, 84, 85
Bakumu 85, 124
Bskusu 84
Bambole 85, 124, 222
*Banque Lambert* 133
Barter 112, 127, 128, 129, 132–3, 152, 161; equivalences 132
Bates, R. 139 141, 164, 194, 195, 196, 200
Beans 98, 143, 144, 148, 151–2, 155, 161, 162, 169, 174, 222
Beckman, B. 17, 139, 217
Beer 116, 128, 131, 132, 162–3, 174, 190, 191
Belgian administration 31–2
Beni 143–4
Bergmans, L. 145, 150
Bernstein, H. 18, 21, 25–6, 216
Bernstein, H., and Campbell, B. 186
Berry, S. 2, 20, 27, 105
Beveridge, A.A., and Oberschall, A.A. 79, 101, 108
Bézy et al. 11, 33, 35, 36, 37, 38, 43, 44, 45, 47, 114, 115, 116, 122, 139, 189, 195, 197, 218, 221
Bianga, W. 113, 124, 129, 130, 146, 160, 196, 202
Bibeau, G. 65, 84
Bongele, Y. 85, 222

Bontinck, F. 41
*Boyoma* 8, 48, 61, 72, 97, 101, 114, 130–1, 163, 180, 189, 195, 218, 223
Bradby, B. 20
Brenner, R. 13, 14, 26
Bribery 112, 135; vocabulary for 137; *see* corruption
Bromley, R. and Gerry, C. 57–8
Buakasa, T. K. M. 207, 209
Buell, R. L. 33, 34, 35, 218
Bujra, J. 23, 170–1, 178, 183
Bulu-Bobina 201–2
Bumba, M. N. 199, 200
Butembo 143–4, 159

Callaghy, T. M. 15, 49, 50, 51, 52, 53, 136, 190, 203, 207, 211, 212, 213
Capitalism 15, 16, 26, 119; and dependency theory 13–14; African 16, 213; articulation with non-capitalist modes of production 18–22; and the second economy 23, 120; *see* peripheral capitalism
Caplan, P. 181
Chazan, N. 24, 139
Chiefs 35, 36, 40, 84, 127, 145; *see* traditional authorities
Church, Catholic 31, 32, 34; Protestant 158–9, 222
Clammer, J. 11
Class 14, 20–2, 29, 52–3, 54, 72, 118–22, 206–9; in dependency theory 13–14; Marxist model of 14; and ethnic groups 10, 28–9; *see* state-based class, political aristocracy, middle class
Class formation 22, 24, 27, 111, 202, 207; and ethnicity 81–6; among the Nande 149, 159–60, 164; and gender 168, 177; *see* middle class
Class relations 18, 53–4, 68, 75–81, 162–3
Class struggle 22, 23, 27, 111, 117, 164, 186, 202, 204–6, 210

237